Elgar Introduction to Organizational Stress Theories

ELGAR INTRODUCTIONS TO MANAGEMENT AND ORGANIZATION THEORY

Series Editors: Cary L. Cooper, *Alliance Manchester Business School, University of Manchester, UK* and Stewart R. Clegg, *School of Management, University of Technology Sydney, Australia*

Elgar Introductions to Management and Organization Theory are stimulating and thoughtful introductions to main theories in management, organizational behaviour and organization studies, expertly written by some of the world's leading scholars. Designed to be accessible yet rigorous, they offer concise and lucid surveys of the key theories in the field.

The aims of the series are twofold: to pinpoint essential history, and aspects of a particular theory or set of theories, and to offer insights that stimulate critical thinking. The volumes serve as accessible introductions for undergraduate and graduate students coming to the subject for the first time. Importantly, they also develop well-informed, nuanced critiques of the field that will challenge and extend the understanding of advanced students, scholars and policy-makers.

Titles in the series include:

Elgar Introduction to Organizational Discourse Analysis
Marco Berti

Elgar Introduction to Theories of Organizational Resilience
Luca Giustiniano, Stewart R. Clegg, Miguel Pina e Cunha and Arménio Rego

Theories of Social Innovation
Danielle Logue

Elgar Introduction to Theories of Human Resources and Employment Relations
Edited by Keith Townsend, Kenneth Cafferkey, Aoife M. McDermott and Tony Dundon

Organizational Project Management
Theory and Implementation
Ralf Müller, Nathalie Drouin and Shankar Sankaran

Elgar Introduction to Organizational Paradox Theory
Marco Berti, Ace Volkmann Simpson, Miguel Pina e Cunha and Stewart R. Clegg

Elgar Introduction to Organizational Improvisation Theory
António Cunha Meneses Abrantes, Miguel Pina e Cunha and Anne S. Miner

Elgar Introduction to Organizational Stress Theories
Kimberly E. O'Brien and Cary Cooper

Elgar Introduction to Organizational Stress Theories

Kimberly E. O'Brien

Department of Psychology, Central Michigan University, USA

Professor Sir Cary Cooper

Alliance Manchester Business School, University of Manchester, UK

ELGAR INTRODUCTIONS TO MANAGEMENT AND ORGANIZATION THEORY

Edward Elgar
PUBLISHING

Cheltenham, UK • Northampton, MA, USA

Published by
Edward Elgar Publishing Limited
The Lypiatts
15 Lansdown Road
Cheltenham
Glos GL50 2JA
UK

Edward Elgar Publishing, Inc.
William Pratt House
9 Dewey Court
Northampton
Massachusetts 01060
USA

Paperback edition 2023

A catalogue record for this book
is available from the British Library

Library of Congress Control Number: 2022937633

This book is available electronically in the **Elgar**online
Business subject collection
http://dx.doi.org/10.4337/9781789909838

ISBN 978 1 78990 982 1 (cased)
ISBN 978 1 78990 983 8 (eBook)
ISBN 978 1 0353 1688 5 (paperback)

Printed and bound by CPI Group (UK) Ltd, Croydon, CR0 4YY

Contents

List of figures   vi
Acknowledgments   vii

1   Foundations of job stress theory   1

2   Theories from behavioral health   12

3   Physiological stress theories   26

4   Theories of arousal and emotion   40

5   Theories of cognition and coping   54

6   Equity and exchange theories   67

7   Social information and evaluations   81

8   Theories about job demands and resources   95

9   Conservation of resources theory   109

10   Person-environment theories   123

11   Role-related stress theories   138

12   Sociocultural systems perspectives   153

13   Theories of motivation and self-regulation   167

14   Leadership and organizational support   182

15   Perspectives on job stress   197

Index   211

Figures

1.1   An illustrated count of job stress theories   9

2.1   1930s cigarette advertisement   13

3.1   The SAM and HPA responses to stress   30

6.1   Adams's (1965) equity theory   68

9.1   Buffering effect   112

10.1 Lewin's field theory   124

13.1 Job characteristics model   173

15.1 Integrated model of occupational stress   200

Acknowledgments

Thank you to reviewers who provided expert feedback and otherwise contributed to the finished product: Sarah Adams, Angeles Astorga, Rachel Pohlman, Terry Beehr, Skylar Duke, Tashia Evans, James Gerhart, Jeremy Henson, Yera Jeong, Maci Krites, Kyle Mann, Meisha-Ann Martin, Young-Kook Moon, Krystal Roach, Gina Rossitto, Nadia Schellenberg, Kristen Shockley, Shane Sizemore, and Mansik Yun. Thank you also to Terry Beehr, Alicia Grandey, and Paul Spector for your insights regarding job stress theories for the concluding section of this volume.

Acknowledgments

1. Foundations of job stress theory

THE IMPORTANCE OF JOB STRESS THEORY IN PSYCHOLOGICAL SCIENCE

Stress is common in the workplace, with 94 percent of American employees reporting job stress (Hansen, 2018) and 40 percent indicating that their jobs are very or extremely stressful (NIOSH, n.d.). Globally, 38 percent reported daily work stress in 2019 (Witters & Agrawal, 2021). Job stress has costs, both financial and humanistic. For example, the annual cost of lost productivity due to health-related absences is more than 84 billion USD (Witters & Liu, 2013). From a health perspective, 5–8 percent of healthcare costs are associated with workplace stressors, and sadly, job stress is believed to underlie 120,000 deaths each year (Goh, Pfeffer, & Zenios, 2016). Furthermore, job stress is related to performance and health outcomes, including lowered productivity, turnover, absenteeism, premature disability, accidents and injuries, and substance abuse (Murphy, 1996), as well as physical symptoms such as gastrointestinal problems and sleep disturbances (Nixon, Mazzola, Bauer, Krueger, & Spector, 2011). These organizational, societal, and individual costs of job stress have motivated research on understanding and mitigating job stressors and strains.

The purpose of this book is to provide an overview of job stress theory from a psychological perspective. Psychology is the scientific study of human behavior and is beholden to the scientific method in order to minimize bias and encourage replicable results. Psychology is recognized as a STEM (science, technology, engineering, and mathematics) field by the National Science Foundation, one of the most highly regarded scientific institutions. Occupational health psychology and industrial/organizational psychology are disciplines within the broader psychology area, and research in these fields relies on scientific methods and observations to inform practical suggestions for improving the health, satisfaction, and productivity of employees and other organizational constituents. In order to do this, psychologists research the ABCs of the human experience: Affect (emotions), Behavior (physical actions), and Cognitions (thoughts). Altogether, psychology has three successive goals: (1) *observe* the ABCs, in order to (2) *understand* the ABCs, in order to (3) *influence* the ABCs. Scientific *observations* of the ABCs can occur through the scientist's senses (e.g., hearing or seeing a workplace argument) or, more often, through measurement. In this way, anecdotes (e.g., stories, first-hand experiences) can become scientific evidence when subjected to scrutiny within the scientific method. The observations can, ideally, be organized into a theory.

What Is Theory?

A *theory* is a system of relationships that explains scientific observations. Theories organize and integrate many facts, and make predictions based on these. Frameworks and models are similar to theories, in that they give meaning to scientific observations and make predictions, but are often less comprehensive than theories and do not have an explanatory component. Within the English language, "theory" may colloquially refer to a "guess," sometimes leading nonexperts to dismiss scientific theories as tenuous and unproven. However, in science, we consider carefully validated theories to be of utmost value. To be validated, theory should be testable. Specifically, research should develop measures for relevant constructs, test the theory, identify moderators (e.g., boundary conditions), and ensure that findings replicate across a variety of situations. Theory is then used to provide context and meaning to observations that scientists have made. This allows researchers to establish future hypotheses and increase the rigor of scientific experimentation. When researchers are confident in the quality of their scientific findings, they can then apply the theory to a variety of practical solutions.

For example, if goal setting theory states that specific and measurable goals are most effective in a variety of settings, practitioners can feel confident recommending specific and measurable goals to college students as they prepare for midterms, dancers as they practice a choreography, and friends who are trying to eat healthier. Without reliable and valid observations, and without a framework to give meaning and context to these observations, we would need to test the effects of specific and measurable goals in relation to studying, dance, and health behaviors, across a variety of age ranges, separately. For example, a scientist might ask a dance instructor "what helped your dancers learn" and the dance instructor might say "I asked them to do it *one more time* until they could run it from beginning until end." The scientist, without a guiding framework, might suppose it is the social pressure, use of coercive power, or repetition that improved performance, instead of the specific and measurable goal (i.e., complete the choreography).

To summarize, carefully tested and derived theory is central to strong science, and may be relevant to practice. The scientist-practitioner model is the foundation for applied psychologies, such as industrial/organizational psychology, and describes how research findings and natural world applications are intertwined. The scientist-practitioner model is credited to social psychologist

Kurt Lewin and his action research model, which encourages collaboration between researchers and organizational stakeholders. Lewin argued that, ultimately, research findings are most useful when they can help solve practical organizational issues (Lewin, 1946).

What Is Stress?

Stress is a general term, used to refer to an emotional or physiological response to a potentially dangerous situation, or as an umbrella term covering causes of physiological stress and responses to these situations (or when the distinction between causes and effects is irrelevant). To this point, Meurs and Perrewé (2011, p. 1045) state, "It is a sign of confusion in stress research that our primary term (i.e., *stress*) has been conceptualized as the independent variable, the dependent variable, and the process itself." In other words, the term "stress" does not differentiate between the stimulus and the response. Current psychological research instead favors a distinction between the cause and effect, or stressor and strain. A *stressor* is any situation (positive or negative) that requires adaptation, such as job insecurity or planning for a wedding. In other words, it is the need to adapt, or the act of adapting, that leads to negative outcomes. On the other hand, *strain* refers to these negative outcomes of stressors, and can be manifested in physiological, psychological, or behavioral responses. Physiological strains reflect direct (e.g., increased blood pressure, DNA methylation) and indirect (e.g., vulnerability to H. Pylori, the bacteria that causes stomach ulcers) biological changes. Behavioral strains include, among others, decreased exercise, alcohol misuse, or reduced work performance. Psychological strains include emotions, such as guilt and anger, as well as cognitive errors, such as functional fixedness and rumination. Conversely, *eustress* reflects the effect of the stress response being channeled into positive and constructive outcomes (e.g., Selye, 1975) or positive aspects of the stress response itself (e.g., Nelson & Simmons, 2003). This could include developing skills, or in more serious situations, thriving and post-traumatic growth. For example, people who view their cancer diagnosis as a reason to make amends, practice self-forgiveness, or reorient their values may have less negative emotion and healthier behaviors than those who do not (e.g., Friedman et al., 2010). *Coping* is defined as the cognitive and behavioral effort required to manage the effects of stressors. The conceptualization of coping has evolved over time, starting perhaps as a Freudian-style defense mechanism, then considered as a stable personality trait (e.g., resilience), and later as cognitive and behavioral efforts (Lazarus & Folkman, 1987).

Although "stress" is used conversationally to refer to uncomfortable emotions or feelings regarding potential distress, "stress" is not an emotion. Unlike emotions, stress reactions (like fight or flight) cannot be completely inhibited.

The stress response can occur even when a person does not feel stressed or anxious. Consequently, stress is believed to be a reflex, not emotion. However, stress and emotion are linked (e.g., Lazarus, 1993). In fact, the American Psychological Association (n.d.) defines *anxiety* as "an emotion characterized by feelings of tension, worried thoughts, and physical changes like increased blood pressure." Ekman and early emotion theorists do not consider anxiety to be among the universal emotions, which include enjoyment, anger, surprise, disgust, fear, and sadness. However, Ekman (Paul Ekman Group, n.d.) states "persistent fear can sometimes be referred to as anxiety if we feel constantly worried without knowing why." To summarize, stress is not necessarily anxiety, and anxiety is not necessarily stress. A person can have stressors, strains, or physiological stress without anxiety (although it is unclear the extent to which the opposite is true).

That is to say, people can experience physiological stress without being "stressed out," and, without awareness, people are unlikely to prioritize managing their stress. Physiological stress is not always a pounding heart and flushing skin. Instead, physiological stress responses occur through two routes in the body that vary in speed. The faster route is the acute stress response through the sympathetic adrenomedullary axis, which occurs when the brain sends a signal through the spine to the adrenal medulla (inner part of the adrenal glands, which are small glands that sit atop the kidneys). Activation of this pathway is nearly instantaneous, preparing the body for fight or flight by freeing blood sugars and increasing oxygen, but can harm the body (e.g., dys-regulation of cytokines, inhibited wound healing) when exposure is repeated or prolonged. The hypothalamus-pituitary-adrenocortical axis, on the other hand, is associated with chronic stress (i.e., stress lasting longer than a week), as the effects take longer to initiate and can linger for days. In this process, the hypothalamus, pituitary gland, and adrenal cortex interact via hormones (chemical messengers in the blood), including adrenocorticotropic hormone (ACTH), and regulate reactions to stress through many related body processes. To elaborate, ACTH causes the release of cortisol (mostly), which has many systemic effects like slowing digestion, inappropriately triggering the immune response, and modulating energy storage and expenditure. Cortisol eventually suppresses ACTH production in the brain, unless prolonged stress (or some diseases) causes a resistance to cortisol. In summary, stress has pervasive effects across the body (e.g., digestive, cardiovascular, immune, and limbic systems), even when the person does not know they have stress.

Altogether, physiological stress does not completely overlap with feeling "stressed out." In this case, is strain dependent upon an objective characteristic of the work environment or bodily response, or more so the person's feeling or perception of this environment? This question is quite contentious and has been the subject of vociferous debate with no current resolution. For example, the cognitive theories of stress argue (or at least presuppose) that appraisal is more directly relevant to individual outcomes than the objective environment. Consequently, perception should be prioritized in job stress measurement and research (e.g., Perrewé & Zellars, 1999). However, the implication that perception is more important than objective experience is overtly disputed by those who believe that job stress research should be driven by practical concerns (e.g., Schaubroeck, 1999). If the process by which the stressor affects the strain doesn't matter, as it often doesn't in workplace interventions, then the mediator, perception, is largely irrelevant. From a measurement standpoint, the debate may be moot as self-report scales vary in terms of objectivity – rarely is a measure entirely objective or subjective. For example, asking "how many days did you work overtime this month" is more objective than asking a participant if they agree with the statement, "I am working too much." Even if the characteristics of the objective environment are irrelevant, and only perception matters, at least more objective measurement can help minimize common method variance.

A final consideration is that more objective measurement generally results in more actionable implications. Because job stress is an applied science, this is appealing to many researchers (e.g., Schaubroeck, 1999). However, there are many researchers who argue the opposite, particularly when appraisal is relevant to theoretical frameworks or justification imposed on the study (e.g., challenge hindrance stressors; Cavanaugh, Boswell, Roehling, & Boudreau, 2000). Taken together, objective environment and appraisal have separate but overlapping effects on strain. For example, we cannot know how much strain employees experience based only on the amount of red tape they encounter when *red tape* is operationalized as "number of forms to complete," an objective characteristic. However, we do know that more paperwork leads to more strain, there are between- and within-person variations on how much paperwork is "too much," and organizations should try to lessen the burden of paperwork-related strain (e.g., reduce paperwork or increase other resources). The overall consensus is that we need some research to study each (objective and subjective) and some to study both (e.g., mediational analysis).

A HISTORICAL PERSPECTIVE OF JOB STRESS THEORIES

Stress theories have evolved to incorporate the newest empirical research. Theories that were not readily testable or did not receive empirical support were adapted (e.g., the job demands-control model into the job demands-resource model) or discarded (e.g., allostasis). This was demonstrated by changes in the number of empirical studies on these topics over time. The earliest stress research takes a physiological approach and conceptualizes stress as a dependent variable, resulting from alarm, demands, or imbalances. Historical accounts typically credit the origins of stress research to Cannon (1915), who coined the phrase "fight or flight" to describe an organism's response to an external threat. Cannon and others adapt the term "stress" from the physical sciences, such that humans, much like a bridge, will bear physical pressure to some extent, after which strain will result. Researchers in the Cannon tradition, in fact, focused on temperature and seasonal changes as they relate to stress. Hans Selye also focused on physiological responses to stress, including changes to cortisol and glucose. After observing that cows responded to varied irritants with unvaried physiological changes, Selye (1975) defined *stress* as the nonspecific bodily response to any positive or negative demands.

Around the time that the fight or flight model was established, Laird became concerned with executive health, encouraging "every executive his own psychologist" (Laird, 1929, p. 13). However, in the early twentieth century, employment in many countries was characterized by mass production and assembly lines, with the rationalization of tasks and jobs (e.g., time and motion studies) continuing at least through the Second World War. Although job stress was not studied much at the time, employee feelings of dehumanization may have spurred large-scale strikes in the 1940s and 1950s. However, it was not until public health and preventive medicine contributed to a substantial increase in life expectancy that health promotion was consistently applied to organizational contexts, beginning with the science of occupational safety and ergonomics. In fact, until the 1970s, job stress research was deeply unpopular, with editors stating that the topic was unwanted within industrial/organizational psychology as "it smacks of clinical" (Beehr, 1998, p. 840). However, clinical psychology was unable to solve the problems of workplace stress, necessitating targeted research into this topic.

A few things probably contributed to the explosion of job stress research in the 1970s. Possibly, the Alameda County Study and Framingham Heart Study elicited understanding of the importance of behavioral health. Also, the civil rights movement gave voice to many, including employees who had been sacrificing their wellness for organizational profits. Within psychology, Holmes and Rahe (1967) conceptualized stress as the result of life changes and published a useful measure of live events. Adaptations of this scale are still commonly used. In the job stress context, Bhagat, McQuaid, Lindholm, and Segovis (1985) developed a similar checklist that included potentially stressful job and personal stressors, moving stress research directly into the workplace. Throughout the history of psychology, a validated measure predicted increased study of the topic (Bliese, Edwards, & Sonnentag, 2017).

Although intuitive, relationships with mental and physical symptoms were generally modest, prompting investigations into factors that might moderate these relationships, such as self-efficacy, social support, autonomy, and individual appraisal. Consequently, research into between-person differences in stressors and strains grew in richness in the 1980s and after. This added a layer of sophistication to our understanding of job stress and may have been facilitated by exhaustive reviews of job stress published in the 1970s. These painstakingly researched reviews predated internet databases but nonetheless assembled observations about job stress from a variety of related disciplines, leading to the earliest comprehensive job stress theories (e.g., facet theory, Beehr & Newman, 1978). These identified various job characteristics as chronic stressors. Prior to this point, the dominant operationalization of stressors was life change. These models also include individual differences that can act as buffers. Around this time, Karasek (1979) developed a model reflecting the effects of two key job characteristics, job demands and job decision latitude, on strain.

In the 1980s, the ripples of the cognitive revolution made their way into job stress research. Lazarus and Folkman defined *stress* in terms of the relationship (i.e., transaction) between the person and their environment, in which the person views their environment as taxing their resources and threatening their wellbeing. This interaction between stable and fleeting individual characteristics, as well as cues in the environment, was among the most sophisticated models to that point. Lazarus and Folkman's research on cognitive appraisal also emphasized coping, leading to efforts to study the form (e.g., problem- versus emotion-focused) and behaviors (e.g., seeking social support) that resulted from varying stressors. This emphasis on coping was probably related to societal changes at the time that affected organizational psychology more broadly (Jex & Britt, 2014). For example, improvements in technology led to new challenges like "bringing work home" and subsequent interest in the work–life interface. Similarly, women were entering the workforce in greater numbers and social justice improvements were resulting in legislation, ultimately leading to research on more organizational (rather than personnel) topics, such as group processes and fairness. Jobs in the service sector were increasing, leading to additional investigation on nonphysical stressors, such as emotional labor. All in all, the breadth of stressors and strains studied by job stress researchers increased during this time.

In some ways, research is coming to a full circle. A prime example is the conservation of resources theory (Hobfoll, 1989), which states that stress occurs when individual resources (objects, conditions, and personal characteristics that are valued in their own right or because they can help the individual achieve or protect other valued resources) are lost or threatened. Although Hobfoll acknowledged the importance of appraisal, he ignored "idiosyncratic" and "proximal" appraisals in favor of emphasis on the objective environment. He believes this to be more practical to measure than appraisal, more parsimonious, and more ethically applied to workplace settings. To elaborate, job stress interventions should focus on fixing stressful parts of the job, instead of training employees to reappraise unmitigated workplace stressors. In a similar turn of events, early stress measurement focused on physiological measures, but these became less common when validated measures of life change units and appraisal became available. However, there seems to be a return to physiological measures of stress on account of ease and affordability of such technology.

Previous research has determined that the most influential job stress theories are those that are specific to the workplace, can be readily measured and tested, and are relevant to white-collar and service-related populations (Bliese et al., 2017). These researchers also predict three trends that are particularly likely to stimulate the improvements to job stress theory: (a) access to physiological data due to technological advancement; (b) work-life-cycle models being tested via longitudinal databases focusing on work stressors, moderators, mediators, and strains to enhance our understanding of stress processes and the long-term effects of stressors; and (c) stress management intervention research to test these theories of stress that are fundamentally causal.

JOB STRESS THEORIES COVERED WITHIN THIS BOOK

Book Organization

For the most part, each chapter opens with a brief overview of the theories covered, what they have in common, and how they relate to job stress. Any relevant construct definitions or context needed to understand the theories (e.g., notable debates, frequent misconceptions) are delineated. After the opening, major theories are presented in a mostly orthogonal manner. Key tenets are defined and support for the theory is then presented. In many cases, research implications (e.g., recent findings, gaps in knowledge, methodological considerations) and organizational implications (e.g., practical suggestions for improving job stress) are presented next. Research and organizational suggestions often overlap, as researchers should test organizational suggestions before they are applied, and organizational agents should be aware of applications and gaps in understanding about the theory. When possible, suggestions for employees to reduce their stress are also included. Next, directly or indirectly relevant theories are summarized as theoretical extensions. These extensions are sometimes, but not inherently, weaker, smaller, newer, or adapted from the major theory. Nonetheless, they share sufficient description or prediction with the major theory as to warrant their inclusion (e.g., job demands-control theory and the job demands-control-support theory). In a few cases, theoretical integrations are described when the major theory has been explicitly synthesized with another relevant theory. The chapters generally end with concluding remarks about interpreting, applying, or improving these theories.

Content Coverage

For the purposes of this book, we will include theories, frameworks, and models that specifically describe the process by which people experience stressors or strains, as well as applicable stress theories (e.g., fight or flight; Cannon, 1915) and organizational theories (e.g., self-determination theory, Deci & Ryan, 2008) that do not specifically have a job stress focus, but either contributed to our current understanding of job stress or are readily transferable to future job stress applications. That said, inconsistency in definitions of stress complicated the process of identifying and categorizing stress- and job-relevant theories. For example, stress can be defined as an imbalance between situational demands and the resources available to manage the demands (e.g., Meurs & Perrewé, 2011). Or, the homeostatic definition of stress holds that stress is a condition in which expectations do not match the current or anticipated perceptions of the internal systems or external environment, and this discrepancy elicits a specific pattern of compensatory responses (Cannon, 1915). Furthermore, there is confusion regarding the

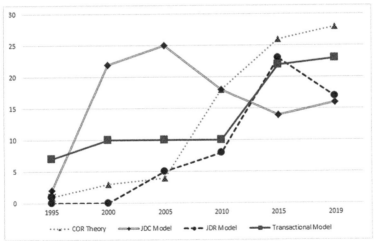

Notes: COR = conservation of resources; JDC = job demands-control; JDR = job demands-resources.
Source: From Moon's (2021) review of job stress theories published in three relevant journals across the past few decades.

Figure 1.1   *An illustrated count of job stress theories*

names of theories, with quasi-jingle and jangle fallacies (e.g., appraisal theory or transactional theory both refer to Lazarus & Folkman's 1987 cognitively mediated theory of stress). The largest difficulty, however, is the sheer number of theories. The quest to find something "interesting" has led to many theories but few tests of theories, in what can reasonably be considered theory proliferation. Altogether, the selection of theories required some judgment, and reviews of job stress theory provided a starting point (e.g., Bliese et al., 2017; see Figure 1.1).

Herein, scientifically validated (and a few popular press) job stress theories are evaluated and summarized. The goal is to favor breadth (number of theories covered), rather than depth (detailed analysis of each theory), covering only the most relevant and empirically validated theories at length. New and promising job stress theories that have not yet been validated are also emphasized, with notable gaps identified as targets for future research.

REFERENCES

American Psychological Association (n.d.). Anxiety. www.apa.org/topics/anxiety#
Beehr, T. A. (1998). Research on occupational stress: An unfinished enterprise. *Personnel Psychology*, *51*(4), 835–844.
Beehr, T. A., & Newman, J. E. (1978). Job stress, employee health, and organizational effectiveness: A facet analysis, model, and literature review. *Personnel Psychology*, *31*(4), 665–699.
Bhagat, R. S., McQuaid, S. J., Lindholm, H., & Segovis, J. (1985). Total life stress: A multimethod validation of the construct and its effects on organizationally valued outcomes and withdrawal behaviors. *Journal of Applied Psychology*, *70*(1), 202.
Bliese, P. D., Edwards, J. R., & Sonnentag, S. (2017). Stress and well-being at work: A century of empirical trends reflecting theoretical and societal influences. *Journal of Applied Psychology*, *102*(3), 389–402.
Cannon, W. B. (1915). *Bodily changes in pain, hunger, fear and rage*. Appleton & Company.
Cavanaugh, M. A., Boswell, W. R., Roehling, M. V., & Boudreau, J. W. (2000). An empirical examination of self-reported work stress among US managers. *Journal of Applied Psychology*, *85*(1), 65.
Deci, E. L., & Ryan, R. M. (2008). Self-determination theory: A macrotheory of human motivation, development, and health. *Canadian Psychology/Psychologie Canadienne*, *49*(3), 182–185.
Friedman, L. C., Barber, C. R., Chang, J., Tham, Y. L., Kalidas, M., Rimawi, M. F. ... & Elledge, R. (2010). Self-blame, self-forgiveness, and spirituality in breast cancer survivors in a public sector setting. *Journal of Cancer Education*, *25*(3), 343–348.
Goh, J., Pfeffer, J., & Zenios, S. A. (2016). The relationship between workplace stressors and mortality and health costs in the United States. *Management Science*, *62*(2), 608–628.
Hansen, B. (2018, September 6). Crash and burnout: Is workplace stress the new normal? Wrikes Institute. www.wrike.com/blog/stress-epidemic-report-announcement/
Hobfoll, S. E. (1989). Conservation of resources: A new attempt at conceptualizing stress. *American Psychologist*, *44*(3), 513.

Holmes, T. H., & Rahe, R. H. (1967). The social readjustment rating scale. *Journal of Psychosomatic Research, 11*(2), 213–218.

Jex, S. M., & Britt, T. W. (2014). *Organizational psychology: A scientist-practitioner approach* (3rd Ed.). John Wiley & Sons.

Karasek, Jr., R. A. (1979). Job demands, job decision latitude, and mental strain: Implications for job redesign. *Administrative Science Quarterly, 24*(2), 285–308.

Laird, D. A. (1929). *Psychology and profits*. Forbes.

Lazarus, R. S. (1993). Why we should think of stress as a subset of emotion. In L. Goldberger & S. Breznitz (Eds), *Handbook of stress: Theoretical and clinical aspects* (2nd Ed., pp. 21–39). Free Press.

Lazarus, R. S., & Folkman, S. (1987). Transactional theory and research on emotions and coping. *European Journal of Personality, 1*(3), 141–169.

Lewin, K. (1946). Action research and minority problems. *Journal of Social Issues, 2*(4), 34–46.

Meurs, J. A., & Perrewé, P. L. (2011). Cognitive activation theory of stress: An integrative theoretical approach to work stress. *Journal of Management, 37*(4), 1043–1068.

Moon, Y. K. (2021). A historical perspective of job stress theories. Unpublished manuscript.

Murphy, L. R. (1996). Stress management in work settings: A critical review of the health effects. *American Journal of Health Promotion, 11*(2), 112–135.

Nelson, D. L., & Simmons, B. L. (2003). Health psychology and work stress: A more positive approach. In J. C. Quick & L. E. Tetrick (Eds), *Handbook of occupational health psychology* (pp. 97–119). American Psychological Association.

NIOSH (National Institute for Occupational Safety and Health) (n.d.). Stress at work. Center for Disease Control and Prevention. www.cdc.gov/niosh/docs/99-101/

Nixon, A. E., Mazzola, J. J., Bauer, J., Krueger, J. R., & Spector, P. E. (2011). Can work make you sick? A meta-analysis of the relationships between job stressors and physical symptoms. *Work and Stress, 25*(1), 1–22.

Paul Ekman Group (n.d.). *Fear*. www.paulekman.com/universal-emotions/what-is-fear/

Perrewé, P. L., & Zellars, K. L. (1999). An examination of attributions and emotions in the transactional approach to the organizational stress process. *Journal of Organizational Behavior, 20*(5), 739–752.

Schaubroeck, J. (1999). Should the subjective be the objective? On studying mental processes, coping behavior, and actual exposures in organizational stress research. *Journal of Organizational Behavior, 20*(5), 753–760.

Selye, H. (1975). Confusion and controversy in the stress field. *Journal of Human Stress, 1*(2), 37–44.

Witters, D., & Agrawal, S. (2021, July 7). Americans' life ratings reach record high. Gallup. https://news.gallup.com/poll/351932/americans-life-ratings-reach-record-high.aspx

Witters, D., & Liu D. (2013, May 7). In U.S., poor health tied to big losses for all job types: Subpar health leads to elevated absenteeism across all 14 occupations examined. Gallup. https://news.gallup.com/poll/162344/poor-health-tied-big-losses-job-types.aspx

2. Theories from behavioral health

This chapter includes theories from psychoneuroimmunology, behavioral health, and health psychology. In general, these theories describe how our behaviors affect our wellbeing and vice versa. For example, psychoneuroimmunology is a field dedicated to studying the interaction between behavioral health and neuroendocrine activities, and how this interaction affects our immune function, in order to prevent the onset and progression of disease. Behavioral health is a field that studies how psychology (affect, behavior, and cognitions) affect health outcomes. These theories are relevant to job stress because they explain how job stress can manifest in poor health (a strain), and our health can affect our job stress. For example, illness might reduce the threshold for the perception of stressors or aggravate stressor–strain relationships. The stress-diathesis model and behavioral learning theories are very well supported and can explain how job stress results in poor health.

People must adhere to certain healthy behaviors in order to prevent stressors, mitigate the effect of stressors on strain, or recover from strain. Behavioral health theories can help explain when and how people choose to make healthy decisions or engage in healthy behaviors at work (e.g., participate in a stress management intervention, take rest breaks, use the stairs). These theories reflect adherence to stress-mitigating health behaviors and describe when people decide to seek professional healthcare, which health behaviors people choose to adopt, and how they incorporate these behaviors into their lives. Applied to the workplace, the health belief model, theory of planned behavior, and the transtheoretical model can guide the crafting of interventions by providing suggestions about how to design the training (e.g., should subjective norms be targeted, or attitudes about the health behavior) and which employees to target for inclusion in such programs. For example, the theories can help guide decisions like whether a rest break intervention should recruit employees who are *unaware* of the benefits of frequent rest breaks, or employees who are aware but perceive *barriers* to taking breaks.

CONTEXT: THE ORIGIN OF BEHAVIORAL HEALTH

From the 1930s until the 1950s, cigarettes were advertised as healthy (Gardner & Brandt, 2006; see Figure 2.1). Bed rest was recommended as a cure for ailments ranging from heart disease to back pain to emotional outbursts. Many of those guidelines we now know to be unhealthy. Our understanding of the behaviors that lead to good health (behavioral medicine) changed in the 1960s, following large epidemiological studies that challenged the prevailing wisdom at the time. The Framingham Heart Study (see Dawber, 1980) began in 1947, shortly after the Second World War, as cardiovascular disease began to replace infectious disease as a major source of mortality in the United States. Contrary to the prevailing belief of the time, these researchers found that cardiovascular disease (specifically, atherosclerosis) was not a normal and inherent part of the aging process and that the elderly did not tolerate hypertension better than younger adults. They ultimately provided early evidence regarding the role of inherited traits on cardiovascular disease. At about the same time, the Alameda County studies began to investigate social determinants of health and identified seven risk factors associated with mortality and poor physical health: excessive alcohol use, cigarette smoking, being obese, sleeping fewer or more than seven to eight hours per night, sedentary lifestyle, eating between meals, and skipping breakfast.

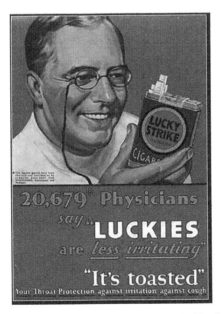

Note: In the 1930s, the health benefits of cigarettes were advertised by doctors and dentists.

Figure 2.1   *1930s cigarette advertisement*

Following these findings, a field of psychoneuroimmunology emerged in the 1970s, describing how stress and coping behaviors impact our central nervous system, and in turn, our immune function or other medical outcomes. Whereas medical models had previously emphasized the role of physiology in the stress reaction, a substantial portion of medical stress research now emphasized stress manifestation and management. For example, Selye (1956) discusses the role of inflammation as a mediator between stress-related (unhealthy) behaviors and immunological outcomes.

THE STRESS-DIATHESIS MODEL

This research contributed to development of the stress-diathesis model, which states that some people have a vulnerability (i.e., diathesis) to stress-related disease and psychological disorders. Diathesis factors can include genetics, childhood trauma, low socioeconomic status, hostility, or cardiovascular reactivity, among others. For these people, stressors are substantively more likely to result in outcomes such as substance use, cardiovascular disease, depression, and suicide risk. To illustrate, a meta-analysis of 17 studies shows that job stress, high demands, effort–reward imbalance, and work–family conflict are related to insomnia (Yang et al., 2018). The authors propose that sleep reactivity, or the tendency to exhibit pronounced sleep disturbance in response to a "sleep challenge" could be the mechanism for this effect. In fact, previous research has identified a relevant gene, which is specifically proposed to modify the effect of job stress on workers' sleep disorders (Huang et al., 2014).

Stress is also implicated in asthma, autoimmune disease, cardiovascular disease, HIV/AIDS management, and perhaps wound healing (e.g., Cohen, Janicki-Deverts, & Miller, 2007). However, the idea that stress can cause or exacerbate disease is still met with some skepticism within medicine because stress alone cannot directly cause disease (e.g., stomach ulcers typically result from the H. Pylori bacterium). Nonetheless, exposure is likewise insufficient to cause some disease. For example, in a study of 276 healthy adults (paid 800 USD each) who were placed into quarantine with a cold virus deposited into their nasal passages, severe chronic stress (1–6 months) was associated with double the risk of cold onset, compared with those with only routine stress (e.g., Cohen et al., 1998). Stress lasting more than two years was associated with a nearly four-fold risk relative to baseline. Specific types of stress were also associated with cold onset; interpersonal stressors doubled the risk of a cold and job stress was associated with 3.5 times the risk. This research demonstrates that stress can affect immune function, but more recent research has focused on immune modulation via conditioning.

BEHAVIORAL LEARNING THEORY

Although behavioral learning theory is a decidedly psychological approach, it seems to have been applied more within the context of behavioral medicine and psychoneuroimmunology than within work contexts. This seems like an omission, given strong evidence in support of classical and operant conditioning models. The classical conditioning model begins with identification of an unconditioned stimulus that results in an unconditioned response. For example, when receiving a puff of air to the eye (unconditioned stimulus), a person might blink (unconditioned responses). A neutral conditioned stimulus (e.g., bell) and the unconditioned stimulus are presented repeatedly in a specified order to elicit a conditioned response (e.g., blinking in response to a bell). Although some have argued that conditioning is unconscious, the balance of the evidence suggests humans who participate in these experiments are aware they are being conditioned, which is referred to as *contingency awareness* (see Lovibond & Shanks, 2002 for a review).[1]

Bandura (1971) argued that contingency awareness showed that people are not mechanically conditioned, and instead, people learn by actively seeking relevant information from the environment and choose appropriate responses based on this information. Within operant conditioning, *reinforcement* strengthens a behavior and *punishment* weakens a behavior. Additionally, *positive* refers to the addition of a stimulus, whereas *negative* marks the removal of a stimulus. For example, positive reinforcement is the addition of something to increase a behavior (e.g., a monetary reward for participating in a stress intervention) and negative reinforcement increases behavior through the removal of a stimulus (e.g., the behavior of taking pain medication is strengthened when it removes pain).

Principles of behaviorism can be applied to health behaviors (e.g., reward desirable behaviors to increase adherence) and stress (e.g., coercive power, or the ability to punish, is considered a stressor). Conditioning can also be applied to reactions that are not specifically behavioral. For example, the immune response can be conditioned. The immune system is modulated by hormones related to the HPA axis, such that exposure to stress can elicit immunomodulation. Repeated pairings of neutral features surrounding the stressful event can lead to a conditioned response. In other words, if a person experiences repeated trauma at work that results in immunomodulation, features of the work environment can potentially cause immunomodulation even when no stressful event is present. Although empirical research on this is pragmatically difficult, evidence from animal models suggests "reexposure to a symbolic stimulus previously associated with an immunomodulating agent or stressful life experiences – in biologically vulnerable individuals, immunocompromised hosts, or in the presence of a pathogen or a latent infection" can precipitate disease or reactivate underlying disease (Ader, 2003, p. 56). On the other hand, conditioning may be able to improve resistance to disease, or facilitate recovery from disease. The effect sizes are small but "there is no necessary relationship between the size of an effect and the biological importance of the effect" (Ader, 2003, p. 56).

Research and Practical Implications

The implications of conditioned immunomodulation in the workplace are massive, but testing must improve before organizational implications can be drawn. Instead, behavioral learning theories are currently implicated in job stress applications for other reasons. For one, it is worth noting that positive reinforcement is the most efficient and effective method of conditioning and has been applied successfully, albeit infrequently, to workplace behaviors (e.g., Wilson, Boni, & Hogg, 1997), but punishment has mixed results. Often, punishment does not direct people towards correct behaviors, and thus is ineffective. For example, a child punished for lying may associate punishment with being caught, and not the lie. Instead, rewards for being honest clearly indicate which behavior is desired. Several large meta-analytic reviews of the literature show that punishment also decreases trust between the person who applies the punishment and the person being punished (e.g., Gershoff, 2002). People who are punished learn to associate the punisher with negative outcomes through classical and operant conditioning, especially when aversive punishment (like pain or embarrassment) is applied (e.g., Gershoff, 2002). Not surprisingly, coercive power, which reflects the potential to discipline, punish, or withhold awards, is correlated with job stress at 0.72 (Erkutlu & Chafra, 2006). That said, carefully meted organizational sanctions are sometimes appropriate in the workplace. For example, observers trust supervisors who deliver justified sanctions over supervisors who don't (Wang & Murnighan, 2017). Overall, positive reinforcement is effective and is less likely to lead to job stress than punishment. In fact, workplace health promotions that enforce mandate participation through pay cuts or withholding bonuses are unpopular and incur legal liability (e.g., NPR, 2014).

HEALTH BELIEF MODEL

The health belief model is among the most widely used conceptual frameworks of health behavior and can be applied to behavior change and maintenance, thus guiding workplace wellness programs or stress mitigation interventions, for example. The health belief model was initially developed to explain the lack of participation in programs to prevent and detect disease (e.g.,

Hochbaum, 1958). In the health belief model, the expectancy that certain health behaviors can prevent or diagnose illness was explained in terms of the individual's beliefs about personal vulnerability and the likelihood that a health behavior will reduce that vulnerability. Specifically, the health belief model contains several characteristics that describe when people will seek and adhere to professional healthcare. The first is perceived *susceptibility*, which refers to beliefs about the likelihood of getting a disease or condition. This expectancy is often incorrect, sometimes due to *optimistic bias* (Gire & Shaahu, 2021). People exhibiting this bias believe that a disease is dangerous, but they will be spared the negative consequences of the disease for some reason. For example, an employee might correctly believe that stress can cause immune dysfunctions, however, they will not catch a cold because they exercise. Because this employee does not feel susceptible, they will be less likely to take measures to reduce their stress, illustrating the finding that optimistic bias precludes engaging in many health promotion behaviors. Second, beliefs regarding the *seriousness* of contracting an illness inform the decision of whether or not to engage in a health behavior. Seriousness can include both medical (e.g., worsening of the disorder) and social (e.g., embarrassment or isolation) consequences. Third, even if a person perceives *threat* (a combination of susceptibility and seriousness), the health behavior must still be seen as having a benefit in terms of reducing the harm of this disease. For example, someone might understand that they are susceptible to COVID-19 and that this is a serious disease, but not use masks because they do not perceive that masks inhibit the spread of the disease.

The model also describes factors that interfere with participation in health programs or behaviors. *Perceived barriers* interfere with undertaking health behaviors. This can include expectancies about the financial or social cost of the behavior, or lack of access to the health behavior. For example, a person who perceives threat from COVID-19 and understands that vaccines are safe and effective, but has no ride to the clinic or believes that they are not eligible for vaccination, might not attempt to get the vaccine. Furthermore, readiness to take action (perceived susceptibility and perceived benefits) can be thwarted due to a lack of *cues* to instigate action. For example, a person might want to take the stairs more often at work, but simply forget to do so.

Research and Practical Implications

In reviews of the literature, considerable support was found for this model across a variety of contexts, methodologies, and designs (e.g., Carpenter, 2010; Sulat, Prabandari, Sanusi, Hapsari, & Santoso, 2018). Across the reviews, it seems that perceived barriers were a substantial predictor with most health behaviors. Perceived susceptibility was found to influence preventative health behaviors, whereas perceived benefits were found to relate more strongly to behaviors related to treatment. Perceived severity was more mixed, as it seemed only to relate to treatment, and not diagnosis or prevention to the same degree. The effect of cues is less well documented than the other aspects of this model, but promising, and provides a useful avenue for future research. In the workplace, a quasi-experimental study showed that the health belief model for stress management education was effective in the reduction of nurses' stress levels and that perceived susceptibility, perceived severity, perceived benefits, cue to action, self-efficacy, and health behaviors showed a significant increase after training (Khazar, Jalili, & Nazary, 2019). Likewise, perceived barriers decreased in the intervention group compared to the control group.

This theory can be applied to workplace problems. For example, a frequent problem with stress management interventions is that the employees who most need a stress intervention are least likely to attend. The health belief model might address some factors that discourage employees from attending. Furthermore, the health belief model may provide guidance for identifying which beliefs may have the greatest impact on intentions to engage in stress management behaviors (e.g., attending a workshop, going for walks, taking work breaks). For example, strained employees may feel that they have too many barriers. In this case, management might be encouraged to reduce some other programs or commitments to allow workshop attendance. Conversely, employees might feel that they will not learn anything new (i.e., low perceived benefits) or cannot use any stress management skills (i.e., low self-efficacy). These employees might have already attended a number of such training programs. Clarifying unique benefits in the announcement or promotion of the program may help. Free donuts, for example, are likely popular but insufficient to outweigh the perceived cost of losing two hours of work when you already feel overwhelmed. Similarly, employees may be too busy to attend on Monday mornings and too depleted to attend on a Friday afternoon.

THEORY OF PLANNED BEHAVIOR

The study of attitudes and behavior became very popular in the 1960s. However, empirical studies showed only modest relationships between attitudes and behavior, leading some theorists to suggest eliminating attitude from behavioral models. In response, researchers demonstrated that attitude toward the behavior (for example, attitude toward vaccines) is a much better predictor of that behavior (getting vaccinated) than attitude toward the object the behavior is intended to affect (e.g., influenza; Ajzen & Fishbein, 1975). The theory of reasoned action and its successors were developed to describe the relationships between attitudes, intentions, and behaviors.

The theory of reasoned action asserts that the most important determinant of behavior is *behavioral intention*, which is informed by their *attitude* toward performing the behavior and any *subjective norms* associated with the behavior. *Perceived behavioral control* was added, resulting in what is known as the theory of planned behavior, in order to accommodate situations in which the person may not have complete choice over their actions. Perceived behavioral control is expected to precede behavioral intention and behavior (Ajzen, 1991), and more recently has been proposed to moderate the effect of intention on behavior (Ajzen, 2020). However, this newer interaction hypothesis has had little opportunity yet for empirical testing or support.

Subsequent research suggested further changes to the model. Specifically, the integrated behavioral model (e.g., Jaccard & Becker, 1985) holds that behavior is most likely to occur when (1) the person has a strong intention to perform the behavior, as well as the knowledge and skills to do so, (2) there are no environmental constraints, (3) the behavior is salient, and (4) the person has performed the behavior before.

Research and Practical Implications

Among the strengths of this model are that potential confounds (e.g., demographics) are part of the model, the purported causal relationships among constructs are clearly specified, measurements have been previously validated, and the computational methods are explicitly described (Ajzen & Fishbein, 1975). Specifically, Bayesian analysis or relative weights analysis can be used to calculate (respectively) the probable point value or unique contribution of each model component (i.e., attitudes, norms, perceived behavioral control). Other analytical methods can be used. For example, a review of the literature stated that most behaviors are under attitudinal control because attitudes significantly predict intentions in more datasets than subjective norms (Trafimow & Fishbein, 1995). That said, certain behaviors (i.e., volunteer work) seem to be under normative control (e.g., Warburton & Terry, 2000). This information provides guidance as to which constructs are most important to target in interventions. There is also guidance in terms of timing. The gap between intention measurement and behavioral enactment should be as small as possible. Ideally, measurement would occur directly prior to performance (Ajzen, 1991). Additionally, temporal stability and degree of intention formation (extent of thinking through the decision to act) have been demonstrated to be moderators of the intention behavior relationship.

The theory of planned behavior (and other theories in its lineage) has been applied to explain a variety of health behaviors, including exercise, diagnostic screening, and other forms of preventative health. In one study relevant to job stress, a comparison was made regarding the relative merits of the theories of reasoned action, planned behavior, and the integrative model. The data indicated that perceived behavioral (i.e., job) control predicted behavioral intentions more so for newer doctors than more senior doctors and that past behavior independently predicted intentions among more senior doctors (Bhattacherjee & Hikmet, 2007). This suggests that the integrative model represents more tenured doctors well, whereas the theory of planned behavior was a better fit for newer doctors.

An additional test of the theory of planned behavior shows that both individual cognitions (e.g., attitudes) and social-cognitive aspects (e.g., leadership) affect health promotion behaviors (Röttger et al., 2017). In this study, attitudes towards work health promotion and perceived behavioral control were the strongest predictors for work health promotion participation. Surprisingly, though, subjective norms had a negative effect on intention to participate in work health promotion activities, perhaps due to psychological reactance. Consequently, the implication is that leaders should devote more resources to enhancing behavioral control, rather than subjective norms, when recruiting for work health promotion programs.

Attitudes

Attitudes have received considerable attention within job stress research, and largely outside of the theory of reasoned action. *Attitudes* are defined in a variety of ways, including as a tendency to respond positively or negatively towards a person, situation, idea, or object and can include emotions, beliefs, and values (e.g., Thompson & Hunt, 1996). Attitudes are formed based on classical and operant conditioning, such that experiences or perceptions of the object inform attitudes. In that way, attitudes are difficult to change, as they potentially reflect years of conditioning. Early research considered attitudes to have a variety of functions, such as expressive (e.g., "this is an ethical brand") or utilitarian (e.g., "this is an effective brand"). It is difficult to manipulate attitudes, but persuasion seems to be more effective when messages match the attitude function. For example, marketing can be directed at utilitarian reasoning (e.g., "this is a safe car") or social status (e.g., "this is a luxury car").

Within the workplace, job attitudes such as job satisfaction and justice perceptions can be considered background stressors that predispose strain, or as strain resulting from other job stressors. Organizational development techniques like survey feedback can be used to improve the work environment. Survey feedback can be used to diagnose organizational characteristics, compare these to industry norms, present the findings to employees, and allow them to suggest changes. Organizations should follow through with these suggestions or lose any short-term improvements to job satisfaction.

TRANSTHEORETICAL MODEL

The transtheoretical model is an attempt to integrate the processes and principles of health behavior change across 300 models of psychotherapy, hence the name *transtheoretical* (Prochaska & DiClemente, 2005). Most central to the model are the stages of change, which improves upon previous research that represented change as a dichotomous event (e.g., smoker or nonsmoker). However, this model proposes that change happens in a nonlinear manner over six stages. In *precontemplation*, people do not intend to change within the near term (usually measured as six months), either because they are not aware of the consequences of their behavior (or lack thereof) or because they do not feel they can make the change. People in the *contemplation* phase know about the health risks and intend to change their behaviors. *Delay behavior* may occur in this stage, in which people put off the behavior change. In *preparation*, people intend to take action within a month. At this point, most people have already made progress towards the behavior (e.g., purchased a subscription to a relevant exercise program). Conversely, the *action* stage is marked by specific, overt modifications to their behavior (e.g., following the exercise program). In *maintenance*, people are working to prevent relapse, but tend not to apply change processes as frequently as people in the action phase. This phase lasts from six months to about five years. Finally, people in the *termination* stage have limited temptation and strong self-efficacy such that they are unlikely to return to their unhealthy behaviors even if they are stressed or otherwise vulnerable. However, this last stage has received little empirical testing.

When developing this theory, findings from hundreds of scientific papers were distilled into ten processes of change that were predictive of successful health behavior adherence (see Prochaska & DiClemente, 2005). *Processes of change* are the activities that people use to progress through stages and provide important guides for intervention programs, and each can be measured independently. Some of the processes most relevant to the workplace are as follows: (1) *consciousness raising* involves increased awareness about the causes, consequences, or treatments for a particular health behavior; (2) *self-re-evaluation* describes reappraisal of their self-image with and without an unhealthy behavior, such as their image as a workaholic; (3) *helping relationships* includes accepting and utilizing social support; and (4) *reinforcement management*, which refers to contingency contracts or other types of rewards.

Research and Practical Implications

The value of a stage theory is that messages can be targeted to people at various levels of the health adoption process, much like a needs analysis is used to identify the employees to target in an organizational training. In fact, research on the prevalence of the employee health readiness stage would allow for better practical suggestions. In other words, it would help stress management trainers to know the approximate stage distributions for relevant job stress behaviors, perhaps in specific jobs or organizations. In one example, data from 20,000 members of a health maintenance organization showed that only a small portion were ready for action across 15 health risk behaviors (Rossi, 1992). Consequently, targeting messages at employees in the precontemplation phase, such as a media campaign describing the benefits of the behavior change, would provide the best return on investment.

The transtheoretical model has been tested using randomized controlled trials regarding stress management and other worksite health promotion (Prochaska et al., 2018) as well as qualitative methods. In one such study, interviews about worksite physical activity identified barriers such as the low acceptability of physical activity in organizational norms, management disapproval, fear or reduced productivity, and organizational constraints (Planchard, Corrion, Lehmann, & d'Arripe-Longueville, 2018). Facilitators included improved physical fitness, weight loss, health, cognitive effectiveness, social self-esteem, and time and money savings. Furthermore, this theory has been directly extended to reflect organizational change, showing promising results (Prochaska, Prochaska, & Levesque, 2001).

However, there are limitations. For one, the large number of transtheoretical constructs makes it difficult to apply, but future research on the relative merits of each process of change would allow researchers to facilitate the efforts of intervention participants and practitioners. Another considerable limitation is that the transtheoretical model is not ideal for planning multiple behavioral changes (e.g., light physical activity and more frequent work breaks).

CONCLUDING REMARKS

Campaigns have emphasized the dangers of asbestos, glyphosate, and other exposures to worker health, calling for government regulation and organizational policies to protect employee wellness. However, only a few employees are exposed to these risk factors. Instead, nearly all employees are at risk of health problems due to job stressors (LaMontagne et al., 2014). In fact, much research on workplace stressors and strains comes from the same disciplines that study epidemiological risk factors and disease diatheses. For example, in the 1940s and 1950s, Rosenstock and Hochbaum (among others) began their famous studies on who chooses to get screened for tuberculosis, eventually culminating in the health belief model. These early researchers provided the groundwork for research into the complicated reasons that people may prefer to seek health advice from their parents or peers (or more recently, the internet) rather than from their doctors. To illustrate, only 48 percent of respondents believed that doctors make fair and accurate statements and advice all or most of the time, and 8 percent report that their doctors never or rarely do (NPR, 2019).

The long and extensive testing of these theories has allowed theoretical integration. In fact, a common direction in health behavior model testing is to determine its value when combined with other frameworks. However, much remains unknown. Regarding the theory of planned behavior, additional information on the behavior–intention gap would have implications for many work outcomes, including stress-related behaviors or job performance. One reason for the gap is presumed to be alternative behaviors (e.g., instead of attending the stress workshop, an employee might continue working on projects), but unlike other aspects of the model, these are hard to measure. Regardless, alternative behaviors reflect only a small amount of variance in the behavior–intention gap, such that there remains ample opportunity to make a contribution in this area.

Another gap in the literature reflects the finding that, despite their benefits, stage models tend to be inaccurate. Most step models cannot be tested using classical testing theory or Likert-style responses. Instead, forced choice or ipsative testing might be used. However, the categorization of variables leads to reduced power and overgeneralizations. Instead, a latent profile analysis, assigning people to "steps," might be more interpretable. That said, it is beneficial to target interventions at particular groups. Therefore, the stage models should not be dismissed.

A positive note is that we are beginning to see occupational health psychologists apply health psychology theories, such as the biopsychosocial model. This theory describes a person's health (often chronic pain; e.g., Byrne & Hochwarter, 2006) as a result of their physiology (the "bio" aspect), psychology (e.g., affect, behavior, cognitions), and social characteristics (e.g., socioeconomic status, culture, job stress). Continued efforts to integrate behavioral health theories with job stress will allow organizational psychologists to better understand the complex relationships between job stress and worker health.

NOTE

1. The *Big Bang Theory* episode in which Sheldon subverts Penny's autonomy by attempting to control her actions without her awareness via positive reinforcement is therefore not an accurate depiction of the conditioning process.

REFERENCES

Ader, R. (2003). Conditioned immunomodulation: Research needs and directions. *Brain, Behavior, and Immunity, 17*(1), 51–57.

Ajzen, I. (1991). The theory of planned behavior. *Organizational Behavior and Human Decision Processes, 50*(2), 179–211.

Ajzen, I. (2020). The theory of planned behavior: Frequently asked questions. *Human Behavior and Emerging Technologies, 2*(4), 314–324.

Ajzen, I., & Fishbein, M. (1975). A Bayesian analysis of attribution processes. *Psychological Bulletin, 82*(2), 261.

Bandura, A. (1971). *Social learning theory.* General Learning Press.

Bhattacherjee, A., & Hikmet, N. (2007). Physicians' resistance toward healthcare information technology: A theoretical model and empirical test. *European Journal of Information Systems, 16*(6), 725–737.

Byrne, Z. S., & Hochwarter, W. A. (2006). I get by with a little help from my friends: The interaction of chronic pain and organizational support on performance. *Journal of Occupational Health Psychology, 11*(3), 215–227.

Carpenter, C. J. (2010). A meta-analysis of the effectiveness of health belief model variables in predicting behavior. *Health Communication, 25*(8), 661–669.

Cohen, S., Frank, E., Doyle, W. J., Skoner, D. P., Rabin, B. S., & Gwaltney, Jr., J. M. (1998). Types of stressors that increase susceptibility to the common cold in healthy adults. *Health Psychology, 17*(3), 214.

Cohen, S., Janicki-Deverts, D., & Miller, G. E. (2007). Psychological stress and disease. *Journal of American Medical Association, 298*(14), 1685–1687.

Dawber, T. R. (1980). *The Framingham study: The epidemiology of atherosclerotic disease.* Harvard University Press.

Erkutlu, H. V., & Chafra, J. (2006). Relationship between leadership power bases and job stress of subordinates: Example from boutique hotels. *Management Research News, 5*, 285–297.

Gardner, M. N., & Brandt, A. M. (2006). "The doctors' choice is America's choice": The physician in U.S. cigarette advertisements, 1930–1953. *American Journal of Public Health, 96*(2), 222–232.

Gershoff, E. T. (2002). Corporal punishment by parents and associated child behaviors and experiences: A meta-analytic and theoretical review. *Psychological Bulletin, 128*(4), 539.

Gire, J. T., & Shaahu, A. I. (2021). Optimistic bias influences hazardous drinking among beer drinkers in Nigeria. *Journal of Substance Use, 26*(5), 517–523.

Hochbaum, G. M. (1958). *Public participation in medical screening programs: A socio-psychological study* (No. 572). US Department of Health, Education, and Welfare, Public Health Service, Bureau of State Services, Division of Special Health Services, Tuberculosis Program.

Huang, C., Li, J., Lu, L., Ren, X., Li, Y., Huang, Q., Lan, Y., & Wang, Y. (2014). Interaction between serotonin transporter gene-linked polymorphic region (5-HTTLPR) and job-related stress in insomnia: A cross-sectional study in Sichuan, China. *Sleep Medicine, 15*(10), 1269–1275.

Jaccard, J., & Becker, M. A. (1985). Attitudes and behavior: An information integration perspective. *Journal of Experimental Social Psychology, 21*(5), 440–465.

Khazar, N., Jalili, Z., & Nazary, L. (2019). The effect of educational intervention based on health belief model on nurses' stress management in intensive care units. *Iranian Journal of Health Education and Health Promotion, 7*(4), 300–311.

LaMontagne, A. D., Martin, A., Page, K. M., Reavley, N. J., Noblet, A. J., Milner, A. J. … & Smith, P. M. (2014). Workplace mental health: Developing an integrated intervention approach. *BMC Psychiatry, 14*(1), 1–11.

Lovibond, P. F., & Shanks, D. R. (2002). The role of awareness in Pavlovian conditioning: Empirical evidence and theoretical implications. *Journal of Experimental Psychology: Animal Behavior Processes, 28*(1), 3.

NPR (2014, December 11). Wellness at work often comes with string attached. www.npr.org/sections/health-shots/2014/12/09/369352885/wellness-at-work-often -comes-with-strings-attached

NPR (2019, August 2). Trust in science is rising, poll finds. www.npr.org/sections/ health-shots/2019/08/02/747561031/poll-finds-trust-in-science-is-rising

Planchard, J. H., Corrion, K., Lehmann, L., & d'Arripe-Longueville, F. (2018). Worksite physical activity barriers and facilitators: A qualitative study based on the transtheoretical model of change. *Frontiers in Public Health, 326.*

Prochaska, J. M., Prochaska, J. O., & Levesque, D. A. (2001). A transtheoretical approach to changing organizations. *Administration and Policy in Mental Health and Mental Health Services Research, 28*(4), 247–261.

Prochaska, J. O., Butterworth, S., Redding, C. A., Burden, V., Perrin, N., Leo, M., Planchard, J. H., Corrion, K., Lehmann, L., & d'Arripe-Longueville, F. (2018). Worksite physical activity barriers and facilitators: A qualitative study based on the transtheoretical model of change. *Frontiers in Public Health, 6,* article 326.

Prochaska, J. O., & DiClemente, C. C. (2005). The transtheoretical approach. *Handbook of Psychotherapy Integration, 2,* 147–171.

Rossi, J. S. (1992). Stages of change for 15 health risk behaviors in an HMO population. Paper Presentation at 13th Meeting of the Society for Behavioral Medicine, New York.

Röttger, S., Maier, J., Krex-Brinkmann, L., Kowalski, J. T., Krick, A., Felfe, J., & Stein, M. (2017). Social cognitive aspects of the participation in workplace health promotion as revealed by the theory of planned behavior. *Preventive Medicine, 105,* 104–108.

Selye, H. (1956). *The stress of life.* McGraw-Hill.

Sulat, J. S., Prabandari, Y. S., Sanusi, R., Hapsari, E. D., & Santoso, B. (2018). The validity of health belief model variables in predicting behavioral change: A scoping review. *Health Education, 118*(6), 499–512.

Thompson, R. C., & Hunt, J. G. (1996). Inside the black box of alpha, beta, and gamma change: Using a cognitive-processing model to assess attitude structure. *Academy of Management Review, 21*(3), 655–690.

Trafimow, D., & Fishbein, M. (1995). Do people really distinguish between behavioural and normative beliefs? *British Journal of Social Psychology, 34*(3), 257–266.

Wang, L., & Murnighan, J. K. (2017). The dynamics of punishment and trust. *Journal of Applied Psychology, 102*(10), 1385.

Warburton, J., & Terry, D. J. (2000). Volunteer decision making by older people: A test of a revised theory of planned behavior. *Basic and Applied Social Psychology, 22*(3), 245–257.

Wilson, C., Boni, N., & Hogg, A. (1997). The effectiveness of task clarification, positive reinforcement and corrective feedback in changing courtesy among police staff. *Journal of Organizational Behavior Management, 17*(1), 65–99.

Yang, B., Wang, Y., Cui, F., Huang, T., Sheng, P., Shi, T., … & Huang, Y. N. (2018). Association between insomnia and job stress: A meta-analysis. *Sleep and Breathing, 22*(4), 1221–1231.

3. Physiological stress theories

Before *job stress* theories, there were *stress* theories. These early stress theories were physiological in nature and conceptualized stress as an automatic and adaptive response. In particular, these theories describe both acute (i.e., fight or flight) and chronic (e.g., general adaptation syndrome) stress responses. In some of these theories, stress is conceptualized as allostasis, which is the act of maintaining homeostasis. Allostasis benefits the body by allowing our important physiological systems to stay within a certain limit (e.g., maintaining a set body temperature despite the room temperature), but too much change can cause allostatic load. The stressor-strain model similarly assumes that strain is an automatic, reflexive reaction to stressors. The kindling hypothesis describes a specific neurological mechanism through which stressors of descending intensity over time can result in a strain response (e.g., panic attack). Finally, ergonomic theories, such as the multiple resource theory, consider basic human anatomical and physiological processes (e.g., sensation), are more directly applicable to the workplace. However, all of these theories describe stressor-strain reactions on and off the job. Increased attention to these processes, perhaps facilitated by more convenient and inexpensive physiological measures (e.g., heart rate monitor), may help to advance our understanding of these processes within the workplace.

HOMEOSTASIS AND THE NEGATIVE FEEDBACK LOOP

The study of stress as the outcome of physiological processes to maintain homeostasis has a long and nonlinear history, likely starting with Bernard and his investigations into the *milieu intérieur*, or the idea that various mechanisms within the body communicate with each other, provide feedback, and regulate physiological systems through equilibrium processes (see Cooper, 2008 for a historical account). Bernard was among the first to write about dynamic internal systems that maintain a specific internal state, as well as the importance of studying these continually compensating processes in live organisms. However, vivisection was largely considered unethical even at that time, interfering with his ability to test many of his postulates.[1] Other weaknesses with his ideas were later improved upon. For example, Cannon (1932) refined Bernard's idea of the milieu intérieur by suggesting that instead of specific set points, there would be some variability within acceptable ranges, leading to Cannon's intentional choice of the term *homeostasis*, rather than *homostasis* (as "homeo" means "similar"). Later, Selye (1951) considered the outcomes of failing to maintain homeostasis in his general adaptation syndrome model.

In another revision, Weiner (a genius who earned his PhD from Harvard at age 18) incorporated the role of the *negative feedback loop*, or signals that dampen a response, into the concept of homeostasis. This negative feedback loop helped to explain some previously confusing observations about homeostasis, such as how the bodily processes return to a previous state. For example, within the hypothalamic-pituitary-adrenal (HPA) axis, corticotropin-releasing hormone (CRH) is secreted by the hypothalamus, which stimulates the anterior pituitary to release adrenocorticotropic hormone (ACTH). ACTH acts upon its target organ, the adrenal cortex, to release cortisol. This process does not simply peter out. Instead, in a negative feedback loop, cortisol acts upon the hypothalamus and pituitary to block the production of CRH and ACTH. Thus, the HPA axis has inherent characteristics that switch off activation. Weiner's negative feedback loop was applied in many disciplines, perhaps due to his role as a generalist studying engineering, philosophy, politics, and psychology, and as a mathematics professor at MIT (see Hellman, 1982 for a comprehensive account of Weiner and his achievements). Later, he proposed cybernetic theory, which is also applicable in a variety of sciences (e.g., in physics this is often referred to as equilibrium theory).

THE FIGHT OR FLIGHT RESPONSE

Cannon is widely considered a pioneering figure in stress research. His enormous contributions to the field include (1) the fight or flight response, (2) homeostasis, and (3) the Cannon–Bard theory of emotion. Although his specific propositions are hard to test or did not receive strong empirical support, these propositions underlie many of our current beliefs about stress. For example, Cannon's (1932) fight or flight is generally regarded as the standard human response to acute stress. Physiologically, this state is characterized by sympathetic nervous system activation that triggers the adrenal medulla and produces a hormonal cascade (e.g., norepinephrine, epinephrine) into the bloodstream. This acute stress response is believed to underlie responses to any kind of stressor, ranging from attacks by predators to social embarrassment (at least among primates). In other words, the human body cannot distinguish between adaptive and disadvantageous triggering of the fight or flight response. If the acute stress response occurs too often, this would drain bodily resources.

Beyond Fight or Flight

Researchers have suggested that aggressing or fleeing may be somewhat adaptive for males, but likely counterproductive for those involved with maternal investment in offspring (Taylor et al., 2000). Attacking a predator or fleeing by the mother could leave offspring vulnerable. Instead, it would be more adaptive for females to respond to stress with behaviors that involve quieting their children, removing them from a dangerous situation, or otherwise protecting them from further threat. To this point, for men, there appears to be a link between sympathetic activation and hostility, whereas women's hostility is not consistently linked to sympathetic arousal (Girdler, Jamner, & Shapiro, 1997). These observations led researchers to investigate the role of oxytocin in the stress response of females, as well as how stress responses may lead to a drive for belonging and nurturing (entitled the *tend and befriend* response).

Other researchers found that osteocalcin, a bone hormone, was more closely related to the acute stress response than epinephrine (e.g., Berger et al., 2019). Mice without osteocalcin had no stress response, whereas mice without adrenaline, but that had osteocalcin, exhibited the acute stress response. Because osteocalcin can increase insulin secretion and sensitivity (at least in animal models), this finding has implications for obesity and diabetes. This research is new and the relationship between osteocalcin, stress, and diabetes is not yet clear, but future research on osteocalcin might help explain the complex relationship between stress and diabetes.

Research and Practical Implications

The organizational applications of fight or flight from a physiological standpoint are intuitive. Specifically, when possible, organizations should minimize conditions that cause an acute stress response. This may not be avoidable for certain professions, such as military or police work. This can be resolved through differential stress responses. That is to say, even though humans share a neuroendocrine response, we might react differently to the response. For example, arousal theory might suggest that people who prefer higher levels of arousal may be better suited for those jobs.

Another key implication is the importance of maintaining heterogeneous research samples. Prior to 1995, only 17 percent of participants in laboratory studies of physiological stress responses were women. Although meta-analytic studies comparing men and women show only small and inconsistent differences in strain (e.g., Purvanova & Muros, 2010), the neglect of women in research samples contributed to earlier limitations in the understanding of the acute stress response.

SELYE'S GENERAL ADAPTATION SYNDROME

Selye built upon Bernard's milieu intérieur and Cannon's concept of homeo-stasis. When forces (e.g., seasonal changes) disrupt a system beyond its "range of stability," the person (or other animal) must act (i.e., cope) to restore its optimal state. The stress response work of Selye (1951) argued that stress is the nonspecific response of the body to a demand, regardless of whether the demand resulted in pleasant or unpleasant conditions. Subsequent research demonstrated that organisms exhibit a broad range of behavioral and phys-iological responses to stressors, and sometimes adapt to new set points of physiological systems.

Selye is (in)famous for his nondiscriminating perspective on stress. Although it is widely accepted that different stressors, perceptions, situations, coping abilities, and personality characteristics can alter the stressor-strain response, Selye emphasized the nonspecific outcomes and determinants. Certainly, there is benefit to a more nuanced study of stressors and strains, but viewing the stress response from a systemic perspective led to a vast amount of generalizable knowledge. For example, Selye noticed while in medical school that patients often had numerous complaints in common, regardless of their diagnosis. He further observed that one of his instructors would make the correct diagnosis based on the patients' presenting history and physical findings. These instructors, however, ignored the generic and common complaints, including fatigue, reduced appetite, involuntary weight loss, and depressed mood. Selye described these nonspecific symptoms as "syndrome of just being sick," and began his own research on the effects of illness itself on patient wellness. Although medicine is carefully devoted to specific diagnoses of illness, Selye focused on people's universal reactions to illness, without differentiating between the diagnoses. For example, when injecting cows with a variety of noxious agents, all cows (regardless of toxin) developed the same problems. He attributed these to stress and through careful experimentation identified the HPA axis as central to the stress response.

Selye (1951) articulated the stress experience as a process of adaptation, arguing for what he called the *general adaptation syndrome*. According to Selye, the stages of the stress process progress from an *alarm* reaction to the situation, to *resistance* to the stressor, and *exhaustion* when the body does not return to the range of stability. This is fundamentally different from Cannon's fight or flight, which emphasizes an immediate stress reaction. These differ-ences contributed to their unique findings – Cannon's study of the role of the sympathetic-adreno-medullar (SAM) axis in the acute stress response versus Selye's study of the HPA axis in chronic stress (see Figure 3.1).

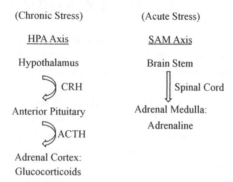

Note: The acute and chronic stress responses correspond to the SAM and HPA routes, respectively.

Figure 3.1   The SAM and HPA responses to stress

Selye viewed stress as a valuable, unavoidable part of life. He argued that, ultimately, stress is not always an experience to be avoided (Selye, 1975). In fact, some stressful experiences (i.e., eustress) are associated with positive feelings and wellbeing. However, the most prominent occupational stress theories developed since that time focus predominantly on the negative consequences of stressors (Meurs & Perrewé, 2011).

ALLOSTATIC LOAD

What Selye called alarm, later researchers conceptualized as allostasis (McEwen, 2005). *Allostasis* is the process of maintaining homeostasis, referred to as *stability through change*, and includes the adjustment of various bodily systems (cardiovascular, neuroendocrine, and others) to cope with threats to homeostasis. In other words, allostasis is the mechanism and homeostasis is the end result. Allostatic processes operate around certain set points, although set points may adapt to chronic demands that push them beyond their range of stability. Although the HPA axis is one allostatic process, allostasis revolves around the central nervous system as the main regulating mechanism for physiological reactions, either directly in response to stressors or when anticipating the need for adaptation. Consequently, allostasis has a cognitive appraisal component, as organisms must actively perceive and anticipate demands or stressors.

Allostatic load is the wear and tear on the bodily systems due to the chronic overactivity or inactivity of physiological systems of allostasis, and this concept is frequently attributed to McEwen (1998). Allostasis involves maintaining stability (homeostasis) through change in both environmental stimuli and physiological mechanisms. Environmental changes (e.g., storms, seasonal changes) and life history changes (e.g., pregnancy) increase the difficulty of maintaining the stability of these physiological parameters. Although most physiological parameters (e.g., blood oxygen, temperature) are maintained within a narrow range, allostatic systems that maintain these parameters (e.g., cardiovascular and immune systems) all show large variabilities in activity (e.g., blood pressure or pulse).

When allostatic systems are not deactivated as needed, they put load on the body, draining resources from other systems and inhibiting the normal protection afforded by these systems. This can occur in three ways (McEwen, 1998). Type 1 load describes frequent stress, which causes increased blood pressure and down the line can potentially cause myocardial infarction. Type 2 load occurs when allostatic processes do not shut down as required. This can cause elevated glucocorticoids and, eventually, metabolic disorders. Type 3 load refers to inadequate response by allostatic processes. This is believed to contribute towards autoimmune diseases and inflammation.

Research and Practical Implications

Although the implications of allostatic load to the workplace are indirect, there are a few takeaways here. For one, stress has profound, nebulous, and systemic effects on the body. Consequently, after periods of extended activation, active attempts to rest and recover are required. It is not sustainable to consistently overwork oneself.

Another takeaway is that we have no good physiological measures of stress. Instead, we have several measures that are each deficient. In other words, stress reaction can cause changes in blood pressure, interleukins, cytokines, cortisol, CRH, skin conductance, and an array of other indicators, but no single indicator is very interpretable. Furthermore, when stress is elevated for some time, the set points can change or the allostatic processes can become depleted. Depleted systems do not function even when there is a stressor. Cortisol, for example, is measured as a within-person variable. Cortisol (change) is low among those with low stress and higher among those with moderate amounts of stress. However, when the person experiences chronic, severe stress, the cortisol response will become stable (either depleted and no longer functioning or constantly overactive), resulting in low cortisol (change) readings among people with the most stress. In other words, a low amount of cortisol could mean either low or high stress, and is therefore uninterpretable. Instead, allostatic load is typically measured with an index or composite of multiple allostatic markers, including blood pressure, cholesterol, glucose, and inflammation (e.g., c-reactive protein). Job stress, in particular, has been shown to be related to increased blood cholesterol, lipids, and sugars, as well as obesity and metabolic disorders (e.g., Steptoe, Owen, Kunz-Ebrecht, & Mohamed-Ali, 2002). In particular, high job demands and low job control were associated with increased glycolipid allostatic load. Specifically, job demands were related to physiological markers in the blood, and decision latitude with secondary health outcomes (e.g., obesity). Furthermore, interpersonal conflict at work is related to an increase in certain interleukins (a type of pro-inflammatory chemical messenger; Girardi et al., 2015).

THE STRESSOR-STRAIN MODEL

The stressor-strain model is a basic cause-and-effect reaction with a straight-forward interpretation: when exposed to a stressor, people will exhibit strain. This model is similar to the previous physiological models in its parsimony, but differs in that it separates the cause of stress (the stressor) from the response (strain). The acute and chronic stress responses can be interpreted within this framework. To illustrate, the fight or flight response describes alarm (stressor) precipitating an acute stress response (strain), or chronic stress occurs when an internal discrepancy between the actual and preferred state (stressor) causes allostatic load (strain). The distinction between stressor and strain is very useful, though, as it has led to increasingly sophisticated measurement, testing, and understanding of the underlying contributions to stress, as well as a more comprehensive understanding of stress responses.

The stressor-strain response has been considered the definition of occupa-tional stress (Beehr, 1998) or the core of most occupational models of stress (Stetz, Stetz, & Bliese, 2006). Within this framework, cognitive mediation may or may not occur, and if it does happen, can reflect conscious (e.g., via cognitive appraisal) or unconscious (e.g., in the "black box") processes. Frequently studied stressors include organizational constraints, quantitative and qualitative job demands, interpersonal conflict, role ambiguity or conflict, and the physical environment. Strains typically studied include emotional responses (e.g., anxiety, burnout), physiological reactions (e.g., often meas-ured as physical symptoms), or work behaviors (e.g., organizational citizen-ship behavior, counterproductive work behavior).

Meta-analytic evidence shows that stressful work situations can be stable (measured as between-level variability) or, less frequently, episodic (measured as within-level variability; Pindek, Howard, Krajcevska, & Spector, 2019). However, there are stronger episodic (rather than stable) relationships between stressors and emotional strains, but because behavioral and physical strains take longer to manifest, these are better modeled as a stable or between-person effect. Finally, this meta-analysis also showed that emotional reactions mediate the relationship between stressors and more distal strains, such that stressors and emotions are most meaningfully investigated as a within-person variable. This observation is consistent with affective events theory (see Ashkanasy, Humphrey, & Huy, 2017).

THE KINDLING HYPOTHESIS

The kindling hypothesis describes a situation in which stressors play a large role in the initial occurrence of affective mood episodes (i.e., strain), but after repeated exposures, neural sensitization occurs and gradually lesser amounts of the stressor become necessary to cause an episode (Post, 1992). In other words, it describes a sensitization that leads to exacerbated stressor-strain responses over time. It is believed that, at some point, the episode might even spontaneously manifest. This hypothesis developed from observations of seizure activity in mice after applying an electrical stimulation to part of the brain. Initially, a stronger electrical current was required, but the threshold for the strength of the current needed to elicit a seizure diminished each time. In other words, electrical currents that initially did not induce a seizure became capable of initiating seizures after repeated exposures. After some time, an electrical current is no longer required and spontaneous epilepsy develops. This is believed to occur via functional and structural changes to neural activity that lead to sensitization. Kindling is applied to the understanding of epilepsy, bipolar disorder, post-traumatic stress disorder (PTSD), and others. However, it is worth noting that in cases of less intense stressors, the opposite of kindling – habituation – can occur (see Chapter 11, this volume).

Research and Practical Implications

This is quite concerning. This model implies that the threshold required to elicit strain becomes lower over time, but has not been studied within job stress. The methodologies used in job stress research are generally unable to address whether kindling may occur. Three applications in which this might be applicable include jobs that are associated with risk of PTSD or secondary trauma (e.g., military, social work), ostracism, and prejudice/discrimination. Empirical research already provides evidence for a kindling effect within PTSD. This may contribute to the high rates of burnout among the jobs most likely to be associated with secondary trauma (e.g., emergency medical technicians, child protective services). After an initial traumatic event (e.g., seeing an injured person), an employee might have a panic attack, vomit, get dizzy, withdraw, or perhaps even develop PTSD. After this initial event, stressors of lesser intensity (e.g., hearing about an injured person) might elicit similar responses, and perhaps in rare cases, eventually cause the person to burn out and leave the profession.

There may not be as much straightforward evidence for kindling within social stressors, but it seems likely. *Ostracism* (i.e., being ignored and excluded) activates the same parts of the brain as physical pain, which aligns with subjective statements of people reporting that pain hurts (see Williams, 2009). Ostracism has a high priority within attentional organization (i.e., it redirects attention to the ostracism and is difficult to ignore) and is believed to alert the victim to environmental information and resolve the cause of the pain. However, ostracism precludes the ability for a person to meet four fundamental needs: belonging, self-esteem, control, and meaning. Specifically, repeated or persistent ostracism depletes resources that could be invested in needs fulfillment and eventually leads to helplessness and depression. This could likely be exacerbated by kindling – initial acts of ostracism likely need to be stronger at first, but over time, even smaller or ambiguous acts could cause feelings of helplessness or depressive mood episodes. Because the ostracism detection systems are sensitive to begin with (i.e., favoring overdetection in the presence of ambiguous cues), kindling effects seem more likely than habituation.

This process is not unlike what might happen with prejudice and discrimination, and has been theoretically linked to racism (Waller, 2003). Although overt racism is often culturally proscribed, modern racism can manifest through color-blind attitudes (which deny historic contributions to systematic differences that exist today) and covert discrimination, such as housing segregation, overpolicing, disenfranchisement, wage inequalities, and health disparities. Traumatic events like being pulled over by police likely have a large *impact* (to borrow a term from arousal theory), and over time, events with lesser impact (e.g., microaggressions) may be likely to elicit the same strain outcomes. Although this threshold lowering could occur for various reasons other than neurological sensitization (e.g., learning and conditioning), the threshold modification effect alone could provide necessary information about understanding the outcomes of repeated exposure to discrimination on the human experience.

ERGONOMICS

Ergonomics, also called *human factors*, refers to a scientific discipline dedicated to the understanding of interactions between humans and elements of a system (broadly defined) in order to reduce human error and improve human wellbeing, human performance, and system performance. Ergonomics is more broad than the aforementioned physiological stress models and includes physical (e.g., physiology, anatomical), workplace (e.g., job design, safety), and cognitive (e.g., human–computer interaction, decision-making) domains. This research leans heavily into both basic (e.g., human mechanics) and applied (e.g., redesign) functions. Within this field, researchers consider how people sense and perceive the world around them, and they use this information to optimize systems (e.g., computer software, work station design, office chairs, grocery store layouts) to suit human competencies or provide training to optimize humans towards their systems (e.g., typing classes).

To illustrate, consider an anecdote[2] about American B17 bomber aircraft during the Second World War. Aircraft have many levers, buttons, and dials for the pilot to interpret and manage, while flying in high-stress combat situations with divided attention, no less. The landing gear and wing flaps were both operated by levers that were nearly identical in size, shape, and location. When attempting to land on navy aircraft carriers, human error was experienced when the levers were confused, leading to injury and death (and, of course, expensive repair costs). Pilots were retrained and disciplined, but the problem was not resolved until the interface was redesigned and the shape of the handles changed – one to a disc and one to a square (Chapanis, 1953). That is to say, some human error likely cannot be managed away, but must be redesigned away.

Sensation and perception are two closely related but separate processes that are relevant to ergonomics. *Sensation* is physiological and refers to input about the objective world obtained by sensory receptors (e.g., optical, olfactory), whereas *perception* is psychological and describes the process by which the brain ascribes meaning to these inputs. The popular social media white dress/blue dress debate (Winkler, Spillmann, Werner, & Webster, 2015) illustrates the difference between these systems. Even though each person's visual receptors are approximately equal (barring color blindness), many people confidently perceived the dress as either white or blue due to differences in perception, which can result from a variety of circumstances (e.g., conditioning, past experience, context of inputs surrounding the focal object).

Wickens's (2002) multiple resource theory within the field of ergonomics holds that people perceive and interpret sensory information in *stages* (perceptual and cognitive/working memory versus selection and execution of tasks) and that the *coding* (e.g., spatial, verbal) of processing varies. Each sensory *modality* (e.g., auditory, visual) is also distinct. Different cognitive resources are needed within and across each dimension (stage, code, modality). Some resources can (and some cannot) be used at the same time without a detriment to performance. It follows that tasks requiring the use of different resources can often be effectively performed together and that interference results when information competes for the same cognitive resources.

Research and Practical Implications

Consistent with multiple resource theory, several meta-analyses have confirmed that people are able to handle more information when it is conveyed in different ways (e.g., Prewett, Elliott, Walvoord, & Coovert, 2012). For example, military equipment including a helmet-mounted display (visual) accompanied by an earpiece (auditory) and torso-mounted vibrotactors (e.g., a vibrating vest; tactile) can simultaneously transmit information about the person's location via a map on the display and allow communication via the earpiece. Alerts and directions (e.g., move left or right) can be effectively conveyed via the vibrating vest. That said, visual displays are generally the easiest to interpret, allow a broad range of incoming information, and often have priority in an information search.

This has implications for a variety of information-processing situations, including military equipment, driving, video games, consumer product design, public safety, and of course the workplace. For example, while using a smart phone, you might receive auditory (e.g., the phone rings), visual (e.g., the caller's phone number appears), and tactile information (e.g., the phone vibrates to confirm that you accepted the call). Attempts to convey all of this information via one method of encoding (e.g., verbal, like reading a recipe while listening to a podcast) or modality (e.g., listening to a podcast while listening for the doorbell to ring) could result in overload. Information-processing demands such as these can lead to poor decision making, slower response times, and perceived stress, but ergonomics attempts to minimize load (e.g., overload, distractions) and maximize comprehension.

Sensory overload can lead to cognitive depletion via overload and distraction. This can lead to strains like delayed information searches, poor cognitive performance, and faulty decision making. However, this theory has not been investigated within the job stress literature with any regularity. Future research on workload and demands for attention management could be very useful to reduce strain via job redesign or user training. There may even be individual differences. For example, a person receiving a great deal of information may feel overwhelmed. However, a person who feels confident that they can cope with this amount of information (e.g., self-efficacy) may not incur added arousal due to anxiety. This is certainly an area in which increased research attention could allow important implications for both organizations (e.g., job design) and employees who are attempting to multitask.

Organizational design efforts to incorporate ergonomics have been perfunctory in many cases (e.g., standing desks). There is a wealth of information that can contribute to worker productivity and wellbeing that is not being utilized. For example, future research on cognitive load can be used to develop software notifications, or organizational policies surrounding them, that work with human processing. For example, a notification system that only activates at user-determined time points, instead of a constant and distracting barrage of emails that must be cognitively triaged while attending to other work activities, would improve productivity and decrease stress for many office workers. Note, the "user-determined" aspect is pivotal. A key finding within this research has been that users are much more satisfied with changes to the system when they have the autonomy to modify (or deactivate) them. Adapting to change is inherently taxing, and even when changes are expected to reduce workload, the initial resource investment to learn the changes will have short-term costs. If employees can choose when to incur these costs, this also reduces stress.

CONCLUDING REMARKS

The research on physiological stress began well over a hundred years ago, leading to important discoveries about the effects of stress on health. However, fundamental relationships between stress and health remain unclear. One such disputed relationship is the link between stress, obesity, and diabetes. Although all three seem to co-occur, the causal order of these variables required further explication. Aside from obfuscated physiological indicators, there have been other limitations of the research on allostatic load. For example, McEwen and Wingfield (2003) acknowledged that their model was deficient due to an overly narrow emphasis on glucocorticoids, which many researchers incorrectly believed to be a direct and comprehensive measure of energy expenditure. Instead, future research on allostatic markers, as well as osteocalcin, may be fruitful for further study. Identification of finer measures of physiological stress and load may be the key to understanding the complex and dynamic processes among the body systems.

There are many stress theories outside of job stress that are well supported and have wide-ranging outcomes. These theories are even being applied to workplace contexts, but they are not typically appearing in job stress journals. This is an unwelcome gap because these studies are not reaching organizational stakeholders or informing the ongoing dialogue occurring in these journals. Even proof of concept (e.g., a lab study in which people's criteria for perceiving ostracism may decrease over repeated exposures per the kindling hypothesis) would be valuable. Note that in this example, a decreased threshold for ostracism perception could occur from neural sensitivity (i.e., kindling), but also conditioning or learning. The methods used to differentiate processes such as these are outside of the repertoire of organizational researchers, but interdisciplinary teams could combine complementary knowledge to advance our understanding of job stress.

NOTES

1.   Bernard advocated for vivisection despite the protests of many, including his own family. According to Mary Midgley's (1983) *Animals and why they matter*, a domestic incident led to his entire family leaving him. His ex-wife, Marie

Francoise Martin, became a vocal opponent of vivisection and is believed to have created the first anti-vivisection society in Europe.
2. Out of respect, I want to acknowledge that this anecdote was relayed to me by Dr. Herbert Meyer (1917–2006), who was, among other roles, a Second World War flight instructor and renowned industrial psychologist.

REFERENCES

Ashkanasy, N. M., Humphrey, R. H., & Huy, Q. N. (2017). Integrating emotions and affect in theories of management. *Academy of Management Review, 42*(2), 175–189.
Beehr, T. (1998). An organizational psychology meta-model of occupational stress. In C. L. Cooper (Ed.), *Theories of Organizational Stress* (pp. 6–27). Oxford University Press.
Berger, J. M., Singh, P., Khrimian, L., Morgan, D. A., Chowdhury, S., Arteaga-Solis, E., Horvath, T. L., Domingos, A. I., Marsland, A. L., Yadav, V. K., Rahmouni, K, Gao, X., & Karsenty, G. (2019). Mediation of the acute stress response by the skeleton. *Cell Metabolism, 30*(5), 890–902.
Cannon, W. B. (1932). Homeostasis. In *The wisdom of the body*. W. W. Norton.
Chapanis, A. (1953). Psychology and the instrument panel. *Scientific American, 188*(4), 74–82.
Cooper, S. J. (2008). From Claude Bernard to Walter Cannon: Emergence of the concept of homeostasis. *Appetite, 51*, 419–427.
Girardi, D., Falco, A., De Carlo, A., Benevene, P., Comar, M., Tongiorgi, E., & Bartolucci, G. B. (2015). The mediating role of interpersonal conflict at work in the relationship between negative affectivity and biomarkers of stress. *Journal of Behavioral Medicine, 38*(6), 922–931.
Girdler, S. S., Jamner, L. D., & Shapiro, D. (1997). Hostility, testosterone, and vascular reactivity to stress: Effects of sex. *International Journal of Behavioral Medicine, 4*(3), 242–263.
Hellman, W. D. (1982). *Norbert Wiener and the growth of negative feedback in scientific explanation; with a proposed research program of "cybernetic analysis."* Dissertation, Oregon State University.
McEwen, B. S. (1998). Stress, adaptation, and disease: Allostasis and allostatic load. *Annals of the New York Academy of Sciences, 840*(1), 33–44.
McEwen, B. S. (2005). Stressed or stressed out: What is the difference? *Journal of Psychiatry and Neuroscience, 30*(5), 315.
McEwen, B. S., & Wingfield, J. C. (2003). The concept of allostasis in biology and biomedicine, *Hormones and Behavior, 43*(1), 2–15.
Meurs, J. A., & Perrewé, P. L. (2011). Cognitive activation theory of stress: An integrative theoretical approach to work stress. *Journal of Management, 37*(4), 1043–1068.
Midgley, M. (1983). *Animals and why they matter*. University of Georgia Press.
Pindek, S., Howard, D. J., Krajcevska, A., & Spector, P. E. (2019). Organizational constraints and performance: An indirect effects model. *Journal of Managerial Psychology, 34*(2), 79–95.
Post, R. M. (1992). Transduction of psychosocial stress into the neurobiology of recurrent affective disorder. *American Journal of Psychiatry, 149*, 999–1010.
Prewett, M. S., Elliott, L. R., Walvoord, A. G., & Coovert, M. (2012). A meta-analysis of vibrotactile and visual information displays for improving task performance.

IEEE Transactions on Systems, Man, and Cybernetics, Part C (Applications and Reviews), *42*(1), 123–132.

Purvanova, R. K., & Muros, J. P. (2010). Gender differences in burnout: A meta-analysis. *Journal of Vocational Behavior*, *77*(2), 168–185.

Selye, H. (1951). The general-adaptation-syndrome. *Annual Review of Medicine*, *2*(1), 327–342.

Selye, H. (1975). Confusion and controversy in the stress field. *Journal of Human Stress*, *1*(2), 37–44.

Steptoe, A., Owen, N., Kunz-Ebrecht, S., & Mohamed-Ali, V. (2002). Inflammatory cytokines, socioeconomic status, and acute stress responsivity. *Brain, Behavior, and Immunity*, *16*(6), 774–784.

Stetz, T. A., Stetz, M. C., & Bliese, P. D. (2006). The importance of self-efficacy in the moderating effects of social support on stressor–strain relationships. *Work and Stress*, *20*(1), 49–59.

Taylor, S. E., Klein, L. C., Lewis, B. P., Gruenewald, T. L., Gurung, R. A., & Updegraff, J. A. (2000). Biobehavioral responses to stress in females: Tend-and-befriend, not fight-or-flight. *Psychological Review*, *107*(3), 411–415.

Waller, R. J. (2003). Application of the kindling hypothesis to the long-term effects of racism. *Social Work in Mental Health*, *1*(3), 81–89.

Wickens, C. (2002). Multiple resources and performance prediction. *Theoretical Issues in Ergonomics Science*, *3*(2), 159–177.

Williams, K. D. (2009). Ostracism: A temporal need-threat model. *Advances in Experimental Social Psychology*, *41*, 275–314.

Winkler, A. D., Spillmann, L., Werner, J. S., & Webster, M. A. (2015). Asymmetries in blue-yellow color perception and in the color of "the dress." *Current Biology*, *25*(13), 547–548.

4.   Theories of arousal and emotion

Emotion and cognitive-emotional theories of stress emerged at about the same time as physiological stress theories, and early research was dedicated to defining and identifying emotions within a purely physiological (i.e., arousal) and evolutionary framework. Early emotion models, such as the James–Lange and Cannon–Bard theories, specifically postulate about whether emotion was a reaction to, or co-occurred with, physiological arousal. However, after Darwin's postulates about discrete emotion in *The Expression of Emotions in Man and Animals*, more researchers began to study cognitive and cultural components of motivation. In particular, this work inspired Ekman, a renowned leader in emotion research, to state "*Expression* is the first pioneering study of emotion and in my view should be considered the book that began the science of psychology" (Ekman, 2009, p. 3449). Ekman, Friesen, and Ellsworth (1982) wrote that the basic emotions are happiness, sadness, fear (or anxiety), anger, and disgust. One important criterion for a basic emotion is that the facial expression associated with it should be recognized pan-culturally.

Emotion theories are, at times, broad, nebulous, and indistinct. Furthermore, early cognitive emotion theories are particularly obtuse because of nonstandardized, narrative writing styles, as well as inconsistent terminology and limited empirical testing. Research does not consistently indicate whether emotions are discrete or indistinct, stable or fleeting, or reactive versus anticipatory (Ashton-James & Ashkanasy, 2005). Vivisection was among the more sophisticated research methods at the time (it is worth noting that Darwin was strongly against it), which is not conducive to studying emotion. So, it is no surprise that emotion theory has improved over time with more appropriate testing.

Triplett's (1898) study of bicyclists was among the first arousal theories, beginning a stream of research that studied optimal and characteristic levels of arousal as a curvilinear effect. This was followed by other arousal and activation theories (e.g., Lindsley's research on the reticular activation system (RAS), Zajonc's drive theory of social facilitation), and eventually personality theory. Another direction of emotion theory was to define and categorize the discrete emotions (e.g., Russell's circumplex model, negative affectivity), although there was still overlap with arousal research. Broaden and build theory, still nested within the evolutionary study of emotions, is unique in its emphasis on positive emotions. Affective events theory (AET) did not start as a job stress theory, but is among the emotion theories most often applied directly to the workplace. However, these theories are relevant as hyperarousal is stressful (it has been argued less successfully that hypoarousal is stressful as well), and stressors can cause emotional strain (e.g., the stressor-emotion model). Arousal and emotion theories are likely to continue to be applied to the workplace, as the technology to peer inside the black box becomes more comfortable to the participant, and more affordable to the researchers.

AROUSAL THEORY

Arousal theory, also called the Yerkes Dodson Law (1908), states that performance is maximized at a moderate level of arousal. *Arousal*, in this context, represents a state of being *physiologically* alert. The optimal amount of arousal varies depending on the complexity of the task, such that simpler (i.e., inherently low-arousal) tasks require more arousal than complex tasks. When arousal is too low, motivation is low or boredom occurs, leading to low performance. When arousal is too high, the individual can experience anxiety and an acute stress reaction (i.e., fight or flight response). Although arousal theory is not explicitly about emotions, many emotion theories (such as the circumplex model) are adapted from the observations of human arousal.

Research and Practical Implications

Despite the age of this theory, it is still being researched and supported. For example, researchers found that noise (generally considered to be a stressor) possibly reduces the boredom and monotony of low-complexity jobs. As such, exposure to reasonable noise levels may offset the understimulation via optimal arousal in these simple jobs (Melamed et al., 1999). Another study found that people low in negative affectivity become more comfortable with increased accountability (Hall, Hochwater, Perrewé, & Ferris, 2003). The authors postulated that some level of stress or arousal associated with accountability increased the motivating potential. However, high levels of accountability seemed to lead to fear and helplessness.

Many arousal researchers also discourage teaching or learning something new under pressure. Because performing a behavior while hyperaroused leads to poor performance, learning a new behavior while hyperaroused is likely to lead to learning poor performance (e.g., Eysenck, 1976). Although intuitive, specific tests of this proposition are rare.

An important limitation to arousal theory is lack of support for hypoarousal as being detrimental to performance. Instead, research has generally shown that hyperarousal is more harmful than hypoarousal. These findings changed the direction of future research on arousal theory, which was mostly adapted into drive theory (see below). Altogether, the findings on this theory suggest that training should not be undertaken in an acutely hyperaroused state. When the risk of slower learning or picking up bad habits is low, then hyperarousal matters less. Some arousal researchers suggest that training be undertaken alone, when possible.

Theoretical Extension: Drive Theories

The effects of arousal on performance have been well documented. For example, Triplett was a bicyclist who observed that people cycle faster in a race than individually. In 1898, he attributed this performance to enhanced motivation, at least part of which comes from the mere presence of others. This finding (called "co-action") contributed to drive theory, arousal theory, and Zajonc's (1965) drive theory of social facilitation, which holds that performance on easy or familiar tasks is better when arousal is higher as the result of social facilitation. However, performance on difficult or new tasks is better when there are fewer people around, due to social inhibition. The drive theory of social facilitation also distinguished between performance and learning, showing that learning was more often negatively affected by "the presence of conspecific organisms" (as drive theories were often tested in cockroaches, rats, and other nonhuman animals; Zajonc, 1965).

Hull's (1943) drive reduction theory was among the original attempts to frame the motivation behind all human behavior. Hull believed that behavior was one of the ways that an organism maintains homeostasis. Within drive reduction theory, *drive* refers to arousal and an intrinsic motivation to maintain homeostasis, although later applications include drives that reflect motivation to meet a specific goal. There are two types of drives – primary drives are directly related to survival (e.g., food and water) and secondary drives are acquired through conditioning (e.g., money, social status), although later research moved away from this distinction. People experience arousal when there is a discrepancy between the amount of the resource they need or want, relative to the amount they have. To reduce this arousal, people are driven to obtain the missing resource. Combining arousal theory and drive reduction theory, the implication is that we may seek behaviors or activities that allow us to maintain our optimal level of arousal (e.g., cortical activity, glucocorticoid level). Many motivation theories, particularly need theories, are directly or indirectly adapted from early drive theories.

Maslow's hierarchy of needs (which states that people have needs that must be met in order, starting from deficiency needs like food and water and moving towards safety/security then love/belonging) is one such motivational theory. It is not well supported empirically, largely because it is difficult to test. Nonetheless, this is not infrequently applied within organizational interventions (e.g., Chron Contributor, 2020; Wilson, n.d.) and even precipitated McGregor's (1960) writings on Theory X and Theory Y in management.

ACTIVATION THEORY

Although some researchers use the terms arousal and activation interchange-ably, arousal pertains to an alert and energized bodily state, whereas activation manifests as task-directed energy. The core tenet of activation theory is that humans have a characteristic level of activation. That is, each individual has a preferred pattern of activation that they maintain through their behaviors, which allows the central nervous system (especially the cerebral cortex) to function most efficiently (Lindsley, 1956). *Activation* is defined as the state of neural excitation in the RAS of the central nervous system that facilitates goal-directed behavior. A major function of the RAS is to maintain an optimal level of activation by magnifying or filtering sensory information, but the RAS is also implicated in habituation. Over time, nonvarying stimuli cause declining receptor activity (adaptation) and activation level (habituation). This, in turn, results in enhanced behavioral (e.g., reaction time) and cerebral (i.e., information-processing) performance. In other words, it becomes easier to do tasks that are overlearned.

Despite conceptual differences between arousal and activation, attempts to study activation have been hampered by overlap with arousal. For example, it is unclear whether high arousal levels cause high activation levels and/or are a result of high activation levels. Part of the reason for the confusion is that direct measurement of activation level is difficult. Electrodes must be placed in the brainstem, where the RAS is located, for electrical activity to be recorded. As reported by Gardner and Cummings (1988), "humans are averse to having such measures made upon them, only indirect measures of activation level are usually obtained in research on humans." Instead, testing is done in nonhuman animals or via indirect measures (e.g., electroencephalograms). Furthermore, the typical measures of arousal (e.g., blood pressure, skin conductance due to sweating) are deficient and do not capture the multifarious physical manifesta-tions (Gardner & Cummings, 1988).

Research and Practical Implications

Organizational research on arousal theory has considered the effects of impact on strain. *Impact* describes the degree to which a situation increases the person's activation level. Consistent with this theory, individuals engage in activation-increasing behaviors in low situation impact (e.g., calm) envi-ronments, and activation-decreasing behaviors when in high situation impact (e.g., stressful) environments (Thompson, 1981). In a theoretical application of the model to the workplace, job stressors were conceptualized as conditions that cause an individual's activation level to deviate from their characteristic level and coping strategies as impact-modifying behaviors (e.g., job crafting) to return activation to its characteristic level (Gardner & Cummings, 1988). Furthermore, vulnerability to job stressors may reflect sensitivity to non-characteristic activation levels. Job and task characteristics such as intensity, complexity, cognitive difficulty, novelty, and variation in stimuli are expected to cause divergence from characteristic activation levels, and an index of these characteristics could be used to measure impact. An implication of this model is that jobs with low information-processing requirements are associated with success across a wider range of activation levels. Instead, for high-impact jobs, only a low and narrow range of activation levels would result in success. This is a promising idea for future research, but job stress researchers have moved away from studying activation theory. Instead, they have more recently favored a theoretical extension – the cognitive activation theory of stress.

Theoretical Extension: Cognitive Activation Theory of Stress

According to the cognitive activation theory of stress, the stress response is an essential and adaptive physiological response to *alarm*, which is defined as a discrepancy between physiological set points and actual levels (Ursin & Eriksen, 2004). Sustained discrepancies may lead to allostatic load and decreased physical and mental wellbeing. To prevent this, the alarm initiates specific behaviors to cope with the situation depending on what seems most likely to elicit a positive outcome, considering both the stressor and resources available for coping (Meurs & Perrewé, 2011). The anticipated positive outcome is framed as an expectancy, consistent with previous work in behaviorism.

Specifically, *coping* is considered a learned or conditioned expectancy that most responses lead to a positive outcome (i.e., a positive response expectancy). In other words, coping is inherently successful in this framework, and coping is measured as positive results (not, for example, number of attempts to cope or type of coping; Meurs & Perrewé, 2011). Coping, therefore, leads to a reduced arousal level. This theory was developed from arousal and activation theory (stating that arousal results in activation) mostly to explain the low arousal level of test animals (e.g., rats) in what seemed like poor conditions (Ursin & Eriksen, 2004). This low arousal is attributed to helplessness and hopelessness. Specifically, in addition to a positive expectancy (coping), there is also a null expectancy (helplessness) and a negative expectancy (hopelessness). *Helplessness* is the acquired expectancy that there is no relationship between response and outcomes. In other words, no behavior can change the outcomes, and events are beyond the organism's control. Finally, *hopelessness* is the opposite of coping, defined as the acquired expectancy that most or all responses lead to a negative result.

Theoretical Extension: Arousal-Activation Theory of Personality

Eysenck's (1967) personality theory is based upon biological differences between individuals (see Brocke & Battmann, 1992 for an overview of changes to the model since its inception). He posits that *extraversion* is a function of individual differences in RAS sensory thresholds. Extraversion is proposed to be characterized by stimulation-seeking behaviors, whereas introversion is associated with stimulation-avoidant behaviors, to achieve optimal levels of stimulation (Eysenck, 1967). These propositions are well supported, but Eysenck's theory is limited in that it does not explain stimulation-neutral trait behaviors or describe other personality traits as well.

Instead, the "big five factor" personality model has superseded all other personality models, with researchers debating its merits as a grand unified theory of personality (e.g., Digman, 1990). This model is the most reliable and well validated across many cultures, and regardless of the method of testing (e.g., content analysis of personal description, sorting dictionary terms, factor analysis of empirical items), five factors routinely emerge. These are agreeableness, conscientiousness, emotional stability/neuroticism, extraversion, and intellectualism/openness to experience (e.g., McCrae et al., 2005). *Neuroticism* is most relevant to job stress, as it is defined as the extent to which a person experiences negative feelings, is emotionally reactive, and is prone to distress. Research on neuroticism generally overlaps with negative affectivity (see below), as "trait [positive affectivity] and [negative affectivity] roughly correspond to the dominant personality factors of extraversion and anxiety/ neuroticism, respectively" (Watson, Clark, & Tellegen, 1988, p. 1063). Not surprisingly, neuroticism meta-analytically correlates with emotional exhaustion at 0.44 (0.52 disattentuated; Swider & Zimmerman, 2010).

COGNITIVE THEORY OF EMOTIONS

After arousal theory, researchers became more interested in defining and describing discrete emotions, as well as the purpose of these emotions from an evolutionary standpoint. The cognitive theory of emotions (Oatley & Johnson-Laird, 1987) provides helpful content for considering the role of emotion in job stress. In this theory, emotions are presumed to have important cognitive functions. Although the researchers use the term "cognitive," they state "we do not claim that all emotions derive from thinking. Some do and some do not." Instead, Oatley and Johnson-Laird (1987) emphasize that emotions are based on communications (termed *emotion signals*) that physiologically orient the body towards a particular "mode" or elicit an "action tendency" (i.e., likelihood to engage in a specific action, like how sadness may facilitate withdrawal behaviors). These signals include happiness, sadness, fear, anger, and disgust. These signals are used to communicate externally to others and within the self in order to bypass complex cognitive processing. Initially, researchers proposed that (within humans) these modes can be modified by the propositional (i.e., meaningful) content of the cognitive evaluation that initiated the emotion signal, or be experienced as emotions that have occurred for no apparent reason (e.g., Oatley & Johnson-Laird, 1987). However, more recent postulating assumes that emotion must have a precipitating cause (e.g., Frijda, 1993). The concept of specific modes and action tendencies is well accepted within the evolutionary-based emotions literature, as they explain how and why emotions evoke bodily changes. In fact, there is some overlap between the energizing and motivating properties of emotions in ways that look like motivational drives. Overall, emotions likely drive (or reward/ punish) specific action urges that helped human ancestors survive.

Theoretical Extension: Circumplex Model

In response to the earlier theories of discrete emotions (e.g., Oatley & Johnson-Laird, 1987), the circumplex model (Russell, 1980) proposes that affective states arise from two fundamental neurophysiological systems, one related to a pleasure–displeasure continuum and the other to arousal/activation. Each discrete emotion can be understood as a combination of varying degrees of pleasure and activation. For example, high-pleasure arousal is associated with excitement, and low-pleasure arousal with contentment. On the displeasurable side, high arousal is associated with distress, and low arousal with depression. These and other specific emotions arise out of patterns of activation within these two neurophysiological systems, together with interpretations and labeling of these emotional experiences.

This model has applications within the work domain. For example, consistent with the model, a review of the literature shows that optimal job performance is most likely when subjective wellbeing reflects a combination of high activation and high pleasure (Bakker & Oerlemans, 2011). This review also clarifies why job satisfaction is not an emotion. Specifically, job satisfaction reflects only low to average levels of activation (and high pleasure) and refers to a more cognitive evaluation of the job. Cognitions are not sufficient to enhance proximal performance. Instead, work engagement and the emotion of happiness at work are more likely to immediately predict job performance. However, research in this area is limited, as the most appropriate methods to assess these states include dynamic measures like daily diaries and daily reconstruction methods (Bakker & Oerlemans, 2011).

Warr's (2007) four quadrant model of affective wellbeing was adapted from the circumplex model of affect. The quadrants include work engagement, workaholism, burnout, and job satisfaction. *Work engagement*, characterized by both high activation and high pleasure, is defined as a positive, fulfilling, work-related state of mind. On the other hand, *workaholism* refers to a compulsive drive to work excessively hard and is marked by high activation and displeasure. *Burnout* is at the opposite pole from work engagement, describing a state of deactivation and displeasure, and characterized as a persistent, work-related state of ill-being that reflects emotional exhaustion, cynicism, and reduced professional efficacy. *Job satisfaction*, as the opposite of workaholism, is characterized by deactivation and pleasure, and is typically defined as the employee's global positive feeling about their job.

NEGATIVE AFFECTIVITY

Negative affectivity refers to a disposition experiencing negative emotional states across situations and time, and is frequently equated with the dimension of neuroticism or the inverse of emotional stability from the five-factor model of personality (Watson & Clark, 1984). Negative affectivity is defined as a higher-order, unidimensional personality variable reflecting the extent to which an individual experiences high levels of distressing emotions such as anger, hostility, fear, and anxiety. According to the authors, negative affectivity also includes affective states such as disgust, guilt, scorn, self-dissatisfaction, and social rejection. Although they propose and discuss positive affectivity, negative affectivity has received much more attention.

Research and Practical Implications

Although negative affectivity *theory* (i.e., a hierarchical model of emotion) is not relevant within job stress, a large amount of research has investigated negative affectivity in the organizational context. In particular, negative affectivity seems to be an important moderator of the stressor-strain response, or perhaps a predictor of the stressor-strain response. Burke, Brief, and George (1993) go so far as to say that negative affectivity should be controlled in all job stress research, as the preponderance of evidence suggests that negative affectivity consistently biases study of the stressor–strain relationship. Spector, Zapf, Chen, and Frese (2000) disagree and delineate five reasons why negative affectivity is likely related to job stress in a meaningful and substantive way (although a sixth reason does account for potential bias). For example, negative affectivity may predispose a person towards negative treatment (the causal explanation) or lower the threshold required to perceive stress (the stress perception explanation). Either way, the inclusion of negative affectivity within job stress research allows better testing of these possible relationships.

BROADEN-AND-BUILD THEORY

Quite unlike negative affectivity, broaden-and-build theory emphasizes positive emotion. Specifically, it was developed to identify the purpose of positive emotions, as negative emotions (e.g., sadness, anger) have clear action tendencies, but positive emotions (e.g., joy, contentment) do not. The original hypothesis (in which positive emotions reflected the "undoing" of negative emotions) was not well received, garnering scorn from a colleague at a professional conference. Of the criticism, Fredrickson (2013, p. 14) writes, "Both his words and intonation hit me hard, and I left the podium with less confidence and more doubts than I had had when I approached it." The experience motivated her to hone her logic and eventually propose broaden-and-build theory. After diligent study of evolutionary theory, she carefully explored the circumstances in which positive emotions occur in order to deduce their adaptive purpose. She observed that positive emotions likely build an individual's resources for survival over longer time points by encouraging the development of knowledge, skills, and social support. Thus, in an appropriate example, she states "the broaden-and-build theory was itself evoked by pointed criticism and my own initial negative emotional responses to it. Yet my wish to be open to that criticism and learn from it coaxed me to expand the scope of my thinking about positive emotions, which allowed me to discover more of their unsung value" (Fredrickson, 2013, pp. 16–17). In other words, Fredrickson's emotional response to criticism encouraged her to broaden her approach to the problem, gaining new insights and building experiences that contributed towards her growth and development at a later time.

Research and Practical Implications

In a study of positive emotion at work, gratitude is proposed to encourage employees to broaden and build (Scandura & Sharif, 2016). Although Herzberg's (1968) two-factor theory posited that *hygiene*, like pay, has only a demotivating component and no motivating component, pay may lead to gratitude. Gratitude, then, would result in positive outcomes consistent with the broaden-and-build theory. Herzberg's two-factor theory did not withstand empirical scrutiny, as both hygiene and motivators contributed to motivation, so the confounding role of gratitude may explain the indistinctive (perhaps, broadened) influences. The practical implication is that leaders should express gratitude for pay and other job characteristics so that employees might also recognize the benefits and evoke feelings of gratitude.

AFFECTIVE EVENTS THEORY

AET explains the relationship between employees' internal experiences (e.g., cognitions, emotions, mental states) and their reactions (e.g., performance, organizational commitment, job satisfaction) to incidents that occur in their work environment (Weiss & Cropanzano, 1996). Specifically, *affective events* arise from emotion-eliciting intra-organizational environments, although more recent research has also included extra-organizational events (Ashton-James & Ashkanasy, 2005). Extra-organizational affective events include organizational change and societal events, among others. Intra-organizational affective events include the physical environment (e.g., noise, temperature), social characteristics, and leader–member exchanges. These affective events include positive (e.g., uplifts) and negative (e.g., hassles) emotional incidents at work and result in lasting affective reactions that manifest as job attitudes (e.g., job satisfaction, organizational commitment) and job performance (Ashton-James & Ashkanasy, 2005). The central tenet of the theory is that affective *states* mediate the effects of the affective *events* on attitudes and behavior.

Weiss and Cropanzano (1996) describe how emotional reactions precede performance and interrupt ongoing behavior to redirect behavior toward the affective event. Specifically, emotions cause people to be preoccupied with the emotion and persistently direct behavior towards the affective state. This concept is similar to the action tendencies described in past literature. Emotional reactions are therefore likely to interfere with job performance, unless the affective event was particularly relevant to task activities (Weiss & Cropanzano, 1996). Specifically, emotional reactions are likely to produce responses incompatible with job demands or can drain the cognitive resources needed for job performance. This is true as both positive and negative emotions are likely to interfere by redirecting resources from task performance. However, the performance decrements of negative emotions are generally larger than those of positive emotions because negative emotions are more salient, due to their purpose of signaling a threat. It is also possible, although unlikely, that affective events facilitate job performance by increasing arousal levels or activation of performance-compatible behaviors, or have no effect on job performance (see Weiss & Cropanzano, 1996).

In addition to affect-driven behavior, AET also describes an alternative judgment-driven pathway between an event and work behavior (Weiss & Cropanzano, 1996). In this pathway, events cause an affective reaction, but the event is reappraised in a cognitive process via attitudes (e.g., job satisfaction), which direct judgment-driven behaviors. This pathway takes longer, but sometimes still takes just a few seconds.

Research and Practical Implications

A key objective of AET was to encourage researchers to think about proximal causes of affect and behavior, as the majority of the organizational research is oriented towards more stable between-person comparisons (Weiss & Cropanzano, 1996). Unfortunately, there is still little research that does this, likely due to difficulty in measuring within-person changes. A few notable exceptions have mostly upheld AET. For example, AET predicts employee decisions to engage in counterproductive work behavior (CWB) following observations of supervisor CWB (Reynolds Kueny, Francka, Shoss, Headrick, & Erb, 2020). These studies typically use experience sampling methodology or daily diaries, but an interview method has also been used. In one such example, researchers found that team dispersion (an abusive supervision tactic) incurs negative emotions towards the supervisor, causing even positive events to be viewed suspiciously (Nguyen, Ashkanasy, Parker, & Li, 2019). Altogether, empirical research has been spotty and it is difficult to identify specific trends (although a few of the studies seem to focus on interpersonal stressors) or gaps in need of specific attention. In general, it seems that negative emotions have stronger action tendencies, and consequently, AET is more amenable to testing with negative workplace events.

Theoretical Extension: Stressor-Emotion Model

The stressor-emotion model is a bit more specific than AET and states that stressors experienced in the work environment may induce negative emotions in some individuals. These emotions, in turn, may lead them to engage in aggressive behavior towards others (Hauge, Skogstad, & Einarsen, 2009). Processes leading up to aggressive behavior are further related both to individual characteristics and to whether the individual perceives him or herself to be in control of the situation inducing the experience of stress and negative emotions. This theory was extended into the stressor-emotion model of CWB, developed from the frustration-aggression hypothesis, and suggests that perceived stressors in the workplace leading to the arousal of negative emotions increase the likelihood of CWB (Spector & Fox, 2005).

CONCLUDING REMARKS

At first, arousal and drive theories were used to explain human behavior. Much research needs to take place to differentiate arousal and activation. Or, the opposite approach should take place, such that activation and arousal theories are integrated. If research should move forward with differentiating arousal and activation, certain methodologies and measurements (see Gardner

& Cummings, 1988) should be used. For example, self-reporting measures of arousal seem to reflect activation better than arousal. Additionally, because simple jobs can be performed successfully across a wider range of activation levels, the hypothesis that optimal activation leads to better performance is less accurate for jobs with low information processing. In other words, there may be a suppressor effect and job complexity should be controlled. Further, researchers note that experimental within-subject designs offer more information about activation and arousal than between-subject designs (e.g., operationalized as extraversion). Finally, Gardner and Cummings (1988) suggest that feedback about performance may act as a confound, as knowledge of failure can increase arousal and activation.

Aside from arousal, valence is important within emotion research. Across the literature, we see a model emerge in which negative emotions are likely discrete and positive emotions are not. Ekman, for example, only identifies one positive emotion (Ekman et al., 1982). Perhaps this is because negative emotions, more so than positive emotions, prompt distinct action tendencies (Fredrickson, 2013). To illustrate, negative feedback (a stressor) may cause sadness or anger, which would have potentially differential effects than another stressor like work overload, which may instead lead to fear or guilt. The circumplex model might suggest that guilt and anger are not so different, such that arousal (rather than the discrete emotion) may be more relevant to the outcome. For example, guilt and sadness, both low-arousal, negative emotions, may relate to withdrawal, whereas anger might relate to aggression or CWB. The control precedence of action tendencies from negative emotions are likely more relevant to the workplace than the broadening and building associated with positive emotions, as reflected in the large number of studies on negative affect, compared to those on positive affect. The very meaning of *stress* implies distress, not eustress.

REFERENCES

Ashton-James, C. E., & Ashkanasy, N. M. (2005). What lies beneath? A process analysis of affective events theory. In *The effect of affect in organizational settings*. Emerald Group Publishing.

Bakker, A. B., & Oerlemans, W. (2011). Subjective well-being in organizations. In K. Cameron & G. Spreitzer (Eds), *The Oxford handbook of positive organizational scholarship* (Vol. 49, pp. 178–189). Oxford University Press.

Brocke, B., & Battmann, W. (1992). The arousal-activation theory of extraversion and neuroticism: A systematic analysis and principal conclusions. *Advances in Behaviour Research and Therapy, 14*(4), 211–246.

Burke, M. J., Brief, A. P., & George, J. M. (1993). The role of negative affectivity in understanding relations between self-reports of stressors and strains: A comment on the applied psychology literature. *Journal of Applied Psychology, 78*(3), 402–412.

Chron Contributor (2020). The hierarchy of needs for employees. https://smallbusiness
.chron.com/hierarchy-needs-employees-20121.html

Digman, J. M. (1990). Personality structure: Emergence of the five-factor model. *Annual Review of Psychology, 41*, 417–444.

Ekman, P. (2009). Darwin's contributions to our understanding of emotional expressions. *Philosophical Transactions of the Royal Society B: Biological Sciences, 364*(1535), 3449–3451.

Ekman, P., Friesen, W. V., & Ellsworth, P. (1982). What are the similarities and differences in facial behavior across cultures. *Emotion in the Human Face, 2*, 128–144.

Eysenck, H. J. (1967). *The biological basis of personality*. Thomas.

Eysenck, M. W. (1976). Arousal, learning, and memory. *Psychological Bulletin, 83*(3), 389.

Fredrickson, B. L. (2013). Positive emotions broaden and build. In M. Zanna (Ed.), *Advances in experimental social psychology* (Vol. 47, pp. 1–53). Academic Press.

Frijda, N. H. (1993). Moods, emotion episodes, and emotions. In M. Lewis, J. Haviland-Jones, & L. Feldman Barrett (Eds), *Handbook of Emotions* (3rd Ed., pp. 381–403). Guilford Press.

Gardner, D. G., & Cummings, L. L. (1988). Activation theory and job design: Review and reconceptualization. *Research in Organizational Behavior, 10*, 81–122.

Hall, A. T., Hochwater, W. A., Perrewé, P. L., & Ferris, G. R. (2003, November). Job autonomy as an antidote to the dysfunctional effects of accountability as a stressor: Implications for job satisfaction and emotional exhaustion. In *Southern Management Association 2003 Meeting*, 557.

Hauge, L. J., Skogstad, A., & Einarsen, S. (2009). Individual and situational predictors of workplace bullying: Why do perpetrators engage in the bullying of others? *Work and Stress, 23*(4), 349–358.

Herzberg, F. (1968). One more time: How do you motivate employees. *Harvard Business Review, 65*.

Hull, C. L. (1943). *Principles of behavior: An introduction to behavior theory*. Appleton-Century.

Lindsley, D. B. (1956). Physiological psychology. *Annual Review of Psychology, 7*(1), 323–348.

McCrae, R. R., Terracciano, A. et al. (2005). Universal features of personality traits from the observer's perspective: Data from 50 cultures. *Journal of Personality and Social Psychology, 88*(3), 547–561.

McGregor, D. (1960). Theory X and theory Y. *Organization Theory, 358*(374), 5–7.

Melamed, S., Ugarten, U., Shirom, A., Kahana, L., Lerman, Y., & Froom, P. (1999). Chronic burnout, somatic arousal and elevated salivary cortisol levels. *Journal of Psychosomatic Research, 46*(6), 591–598.

Meurs, J. A., & Perrewé, P. L. (2011). Cognitive activation theory of stress: An integrative theoretical approach to work stress. *Journal of Management, 37*(4), 1043–1068.

Nguyen, H., Ashkanasy, N. M., Parker, S. L., & Li, Y. (2019, July). Abusive supervision dispersion: An affective events theory perspective. *Academy of Management Proceedings, 1*, 12330.

Oatley, K., & Johnson-Laird, P. N. (1987). Towards a cognitive theory of emotions. *Cognition and Emotion, 1*(1), 29–50.

Reynolds Kueny, C. A., Francka, E., Shoss, M. K., Headrick, L., & Erb, K. (2020). Ripple effects of supervisor counterproductive work behavior directed at the organization: Using affective events theory to predict subordinates' decisions to enact CWB. *Human Performance, 33*(5), 355–377.

Russell, J. A. (1980). A circumplex model of affect. *Journal of Personality and Social Psychology, 39*(6), 1161.

Scandura, T. A., & Sharif, M. M. (2016). Gratitude as a broaden-and-build emotion at work. In D. L. Stone & J. H. Dulebohn (Eds), *Human resource management theory and research on new employment relationships: Research in human resource management* (pp. 75–108). Information Age.

Spector, P. E., & Fox, S. (2005). The stressor-emotion model of counterproductive work behavior. In S. Fox & P. E. Spector (Eds), *Counterproductive work behavior: Investigations of actors and targets* (pp. 151–174). American Psychological Association.

Spector, P. E., Zapf, D., Chen, P. Y., & Frese, M. (2000). Why negative affectivity should not be controlled in job stress research: Don't throw out the baby with the bath water. *Journal of Organizational Behavior, 21*(1), 79–95.

Swider, B. W., & Zimmerman, R. D. (2010). Born to burnout: A meta-analytic path model of personality, job burnout, and work outcomes. *Journal of Vocational Behavior, 76*(3), 487–506.

Thompson, S. C. (1981). Will it hurt less if I can control it? A complex answer to a simple question. *Psychological Bulletin, 90*(1), 89–101.

Triplett, N. (1898). The dynamogenic factors in pacemaking and competition. *American Journal of Psychology, 9*(4), 507–533.

Ursin, H., & Eriksen, H. R. (2004). The cognitive activation theory of stress. *Psychoneuroendocrinology, 29*(5), 567–592.

Warr, P. (2007). Searching for happiness at work. *The Psychologist, 20*(12), 726–729.

Watson, D., & Clark, L. A. (1984). Negative affectivity: The disposition to experience aversive emotional states. *Psychological Bulletin, 96*(3), 465–490.

Watson, D., Clark, L. A., & Tellegen, A. (1988). Development and validation of brief measures of positive and negative affect: The PANAS scales. *Journal of Personality and Social Psychology, 54*(6), 1063–1070.

Weiss, H. M., & Cropanzano, R. (1996). Affective events theory. *Research in Organizational Behavior, 18*(1), 1–74.

Wilson, G. (n.d.). Maslow's theory of motivation: Driving your teams to success. Successfactory. www.thesuccessfactory.co.uk/blog/maslows-theory-of-motivation -driving-your-teams-to-success

Yerkes, R. M., & Dodson, J. D. (1908). The relation of strength of stimulus to rapidity of habit-formation. In E. Boe & R. Church (Eds), *Punishment: Issues and experiments* (pp. 27–41). Ardent Media.

Zajonc, R. B. (1965). Social facilitation. *Science, 149*(3681), 269–274.

5. Theories of cognition and coping

Cognition involves both deliberate and automatic ways of knowing. Cognition is generally considered to be separate from emotion, but they are often intertwined. For example, emotions can direct attention and influence cognitive judgments (e.g., motivated reasoning) or memories (e.g., cue dependent recall). Some models of emotion indicate that a cognition (e.g., appraisal, label) must precede an emotion (e.g., Lazarus, 1991). The cognitively mediated theories of stress often include coping and emotion regulation. *Coping* describes constantly changing cognitive and behavioral efforts to manage the internal and external demands of transactions that tax or exceed a person's resources (Lazarus & Folkman, 1984). *Emotional regulation* refers to both automatic and controlled attempts by an individual to influence which emotions they experience and how they express their feelings. Ultimately, these theories are more sophisticated than their predecessors because they consider how and when people positively or negatively react to stressors.

The cognitive theories of stress evolved from emotion theories. For example, Lazarus's (1991) cognitively mediated emotion model and transactional model of stress differed from earlier emotion and stress theories, which largely presumed that human behaviors and feelings were reflexive and either evolutionarily adaptive or conditioned. However, Lazarus recognized that event perception is inherent in human experience, as humans are cognitively aware of when they have been conditioned (*contingency awareness*; e.g., Weidemann, Satkunarajah, & Lovibond, 2016).

TRANSACTIONAL THEORY

The primary tenet of the transactional model is that the interaction (i.e., transaction) between the person and environment leads to stress (Lazarus & Folkman, 1984). Specifically, *stress* is therefore defined as "a particular relationship between the person and the environment that is appraised by the person as taxing or exceeding his or her resources and endangering his or her well-being" (Lazarus & Folkman, 1984, p. 19). Because of the emphasis placed on cognitive appraisal, rather than the environment itself, this model is also called the cognitively mediated or appraisal model of stress. Appraisals can be deliberate, but are often automatic. The two appraisals most central to this theory of stress are *primary appraisals*, which reflect whether the situation is relevant to the individual, and *secondary appraisals*, which reflect whether the perceiver believes they can cope with their demands. Primary appraisal includes three categories: (1) *irrelevant* encounters with no personal significance; (2) *benign-positive* encounters that may be desirable; and (3) *threatening* encounters that are potentially harmful or challenging. For example, if a person hears a dog barking, they might think the dog is barking at a squirrel (irrelevant appraisal), the dog is seeking attention (benign-positive appraisal), or the dog is chasing off an aggressor (threat appraisal).

If, via primary appraisal, individuals determine that they have a stake in the encounter, they will engage in a secondary appraisal. This is used to determine if the individual can satisfactorily manage (i.e., cope with) the perceived harm, threat, or challenge. Coping is generally considered to take two forms: *problem-focused coping*, which is oriented towards changing the stressor, and *emotion-focused coping*, which is intended to modulate the resultant negative emotions (Lazarus & Folkman, 1984). Other forms of coping have also been proposed (e.g., seeking social support, taking control) and are generally considered to be nested within the two broader categories of problem- and emotion-focused coping. Although there are many variables that direct the choice of coping response, perceptions of personal control over the situation have a large contribution to "coping" decisions. *Personal control* refers to an individual's belief in their ability to create a desired change in the situation. This is associated with choosing problem-focused coping. Coping is often followed by the third cognitive appraisal, entitled *reappraisal*, which incorporates changes in both primary and secondary appraisals. In the above example with the barking dog, if a person determines there is no aggressor, they might continue to surveille the environment.

Research and Practical Implications

Transactional theory is almost unilaterally supported over a huge number of contexts, including when applied to job stress, and is still quite popular (e.g., Kriz, Jolly, & Shoss, 2021; McCarthy, Lambert, Mosley, Fitchett, & Dillard, 2021; Zhang, Zhang, Ng, & Lam, 2019). Specifically, although stressors may have some unconscious manifestations (e.g., denial; Lazarus, 1991) or physiological reflexes, the majority of stressors seem to be appraised or at least cognitively labeled. Research generally supports that appraisals and coping influence psychological stress outcomes. However, more research is needed to determine how people choose a coping method (e.g., problem- or emotion-focused coping) beyond personal control. In particular, the cost of the coping choice has received some attention. This is to say, people likely consider the costs (e.g., efforts, vulnerability in front of others) of a particular coping method to determine if it is worthwhile. Problem-focused coping may have a higher initial cost than emotion-focused coping, but in the long run, may prevent or mitigate strain better. Consistent with this idea, emotion-focused coping is likely to drain resources over time.

Because coping is based on context, there is no best way to cope. Successful coping in one context may be counterproductive in another context (Lazarus, 1993). Nonetheless, people use both coping strategies in 98 percent of coping episodes (although one tends to dominate; Folkman & Lazarus, 1980). There is a folk belief that emotion-focused coping is ineffective, but this might confound the coping style with the cause of stress (or characteristics thereof). For example, a person might not choose problem-focused coping if they have no control over the situation. Situations with low personal control generally have worse outcomes, so the choice of emotion-focused coping may obfuscate the generally poor starting position of the person coping. This disdain for emotion-focused coping may be perpetuated by actor–observer bias, in which the observer believes that the people who are using emotion-focused coping are whiny or lazy, but fails to understand the situational constraints surrounding the coping event. Emotion-focused coping is far better than no coping, and inappropriate attempts to problem solve may approximate superstition (e.g., audience rituals that are sincerely believed to influence the outcome of a sporting event). In other words, both types of coping are valuable and necessary.

Even escape/avoidance coping (e.g., distancing oneself from the source of stress and the emotions that arise as a result of the stress process) is necessary and beneficial sometimes. For example, stressor detachment is important for mitigating allostatic load. However, escape conditioning can perpetuate some stress responses. If an individual consistently escapes/avoids a stressor, they might not learn (in the conditioning sense) that exposure is nonthreatening, leading to continued strain. In fact, it is possible for people to confuse escape/ avoidance of the stressor with problem-focused coping. For example, let's say an employee is afraid of elevators but was asked to move into an office on a higher floor. The employee might feel as though requesting an office on the ground floor (or quitting their job) feels like active problem solving, whereas accepting the anxiety of being in an elevator sounds passive, lazy, or unambitious. However, avoiding the elevator is better described as escape and subverts effective coping. Instead, the employee could meet with a therapist provided by an *employee assistance program* (i.e., programs that aim to provide various resources to improve employee wellbeing) to be encouraged to safely feel uncomfortable (e.g., acceptance and commitment therapy) or participate in exposure therapy (i.e., gradual exposure to a stressor in an attempt to pair the stressful stimuli with a more calm response). Both of these should help employees reorient their appraisals.

Theoretical Integration: Transactional Attributional Model of Stress

Attributions are different from appraisals in that they reflect a person's beliefs about the causes of events. Specifically, Heider (1958, p. 82) proposed that "the result of an action is felt to depend on two sets of conditions, namely, factors within the person and factors within the environment." Building off this research, Weiner (1985) proposed causal attribution theory, a theory of motivation and emotion in which three causal attributions play a key role: *locus* of causality (whether the cause is related to the perceiver's ability or effort, or external, such as due to the task or luck), *stability* (will the cause continue over time), and *controllability* (is the cause under someone's volitional control). The process of ascribing attributions is called the *attributional search*.

This theory is well tested and some observations have been made about the distinctive appraisals (see Perrewé & Zellars, 1999 for an overview). Findings indicate that the locus of causality and controllability dimensions have the highest priority in an attributional search and predict interpersonal emotions and behaviors. At the construct level, there have been complaints that the causality and controllability attributions are not orthogonal. Specifically, empirical support for a distinct locus of causality dimension is strong, but less consistent support has been found for a separate controllability dimension. Evidence indicates that the controllability dimension is distinct from the locus of causality dimension in only some situations. This controllability dimension appears to be analogous to situational perceptions of control in transactional theory (Lazarus & Folkman, 1984).

Due to this overlap, a model integrating transactional theory and attribution theory was proposed (Perrewé & Zellars, 1999). In this model, primary appraisal includes motivation incongruence, which occurs when demands exceed perceived capabilities. Motivational incongruence is similar to Lazarus's appraisal, and these inform primary appraisal of stress or anxiety. Anxiety then leads to a search for the causes of the stress, including internal or external causes. Internal causes might reflect controllable causes (e.g., lack of effort) or uncontrollable causes (e.g., ability). External causes may also reflect controllable and uncontrollable causes, but stemming from the organization. These appraisals predict the emotions of guilt, shame, anger, and frustration. The discrete emotions are associated with different responses. For example, guilt inspires problem solving, including increased effort. On the other hand, shame, anger, and frustration induce emotion-focused coping, such as withdrawal or cognitive reappraisal (e.g., positive thinking). After coping behaviors are enacted, the employee may engage in reappraisal, restarting the cycle. Altogether, this model integrates research from various areas of job stress and has the potential to be well validated. In fact, this model has been cited nearly 500 times, however, it has not been directly tested. In particular, additional research on the role of discrete emotions in coping would help to validate this model.

Theoretical Extension: Cognitive-Emotion Theory of Organizational Change

This model describes a planned organizational change in which employees are expected to go through a cognitive-emotional process as described within Lazarus (1991). This process facilitates sense making (i.e., understanding the change), emotion regulation, and appropriate performance. According to this model, the change process often entails four sequential but distinguishable stages of an emotional reaction (Liu & Perrewé, 2005). Incorporating transactional theory, the first three stages reflect primary appraisal (e.g., goal relevance and congruence), secondary appraisal (e.g., potential of success, social implications), and a coping stage (e.g., proactive or passive), respectively. The last phase reflects the outcomes of the change. The model also includes factors that may influence the emotion process, specifically, the communication of information and individual attributions. Emotions of excitement or fear mediate the three stages, and type of information communication moderates various processes. The individual outcome of planned change and related emotions are subjected to an attributional search, and may result in discrete emotions (e.g., pride, guilt, anger), in turn influencing subsequent behaviors and attitudes (e.g., exit, voice, loyalty). Like the Perrewé and Zellars (1999) transactional attributional model of job stress, this theory has also been cited frequently but not subjected to empirical scrutiny.

A HOLISTIC MODEL OF STRESS

Another theory that incorporates appraisal and coping is the holistic model of stress. Herein, Nelson and Simmons (2003) clarify the stressor-strain model by incorporating Selye's research on eustress, however, they define eustress as positive *aspects* of the stress response (compared to Selye's perspective of the positive *effects* of the stress response). In their model, work stressors (including role stressors, interpersonal demands, physical demands such as noise, workplace policies like promotion and discrimination, and job conditions such as wages) lead to eustress and distress (separately), as moderated by individual differences in resilience. Eustress and distress lead to stress outcomes including physical and mental health, work performance, and social relationships. When this occurs, eustress can be savored (perhaps analogous to Fredrickson's (2001) concept of broadening; see Chapter 4, this volume), whereas distress is managed with coping cognitions (e.g., self-talk) and behaviors. Both savoring and coping lead to reappraisal of the stressor and can moderate stress outcomes. A contribution of this study is their emphasis on coping as a behavior or cognition, which is more amenable to change than stable traits. In what seems to be an ongoing theme, this model has not been empirically tested.

THE EMOTION REGULATION MODEL

Emotion regulation refers to the (mainly) cognitive processes by which people manipulate how they experience and express emotions. These processes can be automatic or deliberate and under conscious awareness or not (Thompson, 1990). There are many ways to operationalize emotion regulation, including behavioral observation, self-reported emotional experience, or physiological responses (e.g., Webb, Miles, & Sheeran, 2012). In Gross's (2015) emotion regulation model, various strategies were described. For one, *cognitive distraction* entails redirecting focus from an affective event to more pleasant situations, providing short-term emotional relief. This strategy is expected to be inefficient in the long term, but meta-analytic findings indicate that distraction was an effective means of emotion regulation (using behavioral, experiential, and physiological measures) at least in laboratory experiments ($d = 0.27$; Webb et al., 2012). Another presumably ineffective strategy is *expressive suppression*, defined as the avoidance of outward expressions of emotions, and is used to regulate interpersonal impressions (e.g., pretending not to be disappointed by an unwanted gift). This strategy also mitigated short-term emotional outcomes ($d = 0.32$; Webb et al., 2012). A third strategy that is frequently studied is *reappraisal*, which is proposed to be more effective. This entails cognitively reinterpreting (e.g., positive self-talk) a stressful situation in order to alter its emotional impact. This strategy has moderate cognitive costs, but is a good investment in that there is less use of cognitive resources later on. Reappraising the emotional stimulus ($d = 0.36$) was somewhat more effective than reappraising the emotional response in these laboratory studies ($d = 0.23$; Webb et al., 2012).

Emotion regulation research is somewhat predicated on the job stress and coping tradition. Emotion regulation and coping have similarities and some researchers use the terms interchangeably (Gross, 2015). For example, coping and emotion regulation are both forms of regulation, and both involve controlled, purposeful efforts (Compas & Bettis, 2019). In fact, coping can be interpreted as emotion regulation under stress. However, there is a major difference in that coping refers to a variety of responses to stress, whereas emotion regulation only involves emotions but over a broader range of situations. For example, stifling the expression of positive affect after winning a game is emotion regulation but not coping.

The research on emotion regulation perhaps got its start in the psychoanalytic tradition. To set the stage, the psychodynamic tradition assumes there are three components of the psyche. The *id* is an irrational child, hedonistic and concerned only with pleasure, which is opposed by the equally irrational super-ego. The *super-ego* represents all of the unreasonable and contradictory internalized societal pressures. The *ego* manages these two desires – one to be selfish and the other to be selfless. The psychodynamic study of coping states that anxiety coping arises from (1) situational demands that overwhelm the ego and (2) strong id and super-ego impulses competing for expression. This process is thought to be outside of conscious awareness (in fact, the term *unconscious* traditionally refers to this specific process in which the ego controls internal processes, and some researchers avoid the term for this reason). In the Freudian perspective, an *ego threat* arises when the ego perceives that it might be unable to constrain the id's impulses in a reasonable and realistic way that is satisfactory to the super-ego. *Ego defense* is the general term given to processes that regulate these two types of anxiety and their resultant strains. Note that ego defense should not be confused with ego depletion, which is more relevant to motivation and self-regulation. Although emotion regulation originated from the psychoanalytic tradition, it is distinguished by the inclusion of adaptive, conscious coping processes.

Theoretical Extension: Emotional Labor

Emotional labor is considered to be the process of regulating emotions at work in accordance with *display rules* (i.e., expectations for appropriate emotional expression; Grandey, 2015), or in exchange for payment such that employees are commodifying their emotional expressions (e.g., Hochschild, 1983). Emotional labor borrows from emotion regulation theory, describing how employees, particularly service workers, regulate their emotion using mostly cognitive processes. For example, employees might engage in attentional deployment to think of past experiences that elicited emotions like those they are required to display. This is considered a form of *deep acting*, which occurs when employees change their internal emotional state to match display rules and allow the genuine expression of felt emotions. Another form of deep acting is reappraisal (e.g., looking on the bright side). On the other hand, *surface acting* involves only changing the emotional expression, which requires continuous effort via response modulation. This tactic engenders more strain, and the superficial modulation of emotions is associated with increased arousal and, eventually, decreased wellbeing (e.g., cancer, coronary heart disease; Gross, 1998). Overall, these components are described in a process model in which situation cues (e.g., interaction expectations and emotional events) lead to emotional labor (both surface and deep acting). The type of emotional labor is affected by individual differences and organizational factors (e.g., autonomy). Emotional labor then leads to long-term individual and organizational wellbeing consequences.

Grandey (2000, 2015) delineates some deficiencies in the testing of emotional labor/regulation theory, which affords useful suggestions for future research. For one, insufficient attention has been allotted to the potentially confounding role of payment for emotional labor. This is a large oversight because money is quite important and can override many other motivations and compensate for a variety of slights (e.g., social distress and physical pain; Zhou, Vohs, & Baumeister, 2009). Another gap in the emotional labor literature is the lack of experimental designs. This can be remedied through better integration with the emotional regulation literature, which has perhaps overemphasized experimental research. That is to say, the strengths of the emotional labor and emotion regulation literatures complement one another. Furthermore, the surface and deep acting categorization of emotional labor may be overly restrictive, and future research more closely tied to emotion regulation theory may allow new insights. Specifically, emotional labor may be better described via antecedent-focused and response-focused regulation strategies, which are analogous to deep acting and surface acting. For example, cognitive reappraisal is generally considered a form of deep acting but can reflect an antecedent-focused strategy due to the emphasis on modulating internal states by re-evaluating the situation (i.e., antecedents of the emotional response). On the other hand, emotional suppression, a form of surface acting, may be categorized as a response-focused strategy by modifying only the emotional response (i.e., expressed emotions).

IMPLICATIONS OF COGNITIVE ABILITY IN JOB STRESS

As stated by Kim and Glomb (2010), there would be no area of organizational psychology unrelated to general mental ability, as "cognitive ability is to psychology as carbon is to chemistry" (Brand, 1987, p. 257). These researchers found that people with high intelligence reported being victimized more ($r = 0.18$, $p < 0.05$), although inspection of their correlation tables shows that intelligence was not correlated with job stress ($r = 0.03$). Other job stress research considered the issue of person–job fit between a person's cognitive job requirements and intelligence. One such study found that high job complexity was associated with increased alcohol, tobacco, and marijuana (but not cocaine) use when the employee's cognitive ability was low (e.g., Oldham & Gordon, 1999). Despite a lack of zero-order correlations indicating clear benefits of intelligence on job stress, theoretical writings frequently discuss the merits of intelligence as a cognitive resource, buffering the effects of job demands and contributing towards resource building (e.g., Hobfoll, 2001).

It is, in fact, surprising that there is a segment of organizational outcomes unabetted by intelligence. Instead, perhaps certain confounds (e.g., cognitive complexity) need to be controlled. Alternatively, it may be the case that narrow cognitive functions (e.g., attention) are better predictors of stress-related outcomes than general mental ability.

Use of media technology or information communications technology is damaging to the cognitive control system (Badre, 2020). Although controversial and of heterogeneous quality, these studies align with other research in organizational psychology. Specifically, interruptions, distractions, multitasking, and surprises can interrupt flow and tax our ability to control attention (see Leroy, Schmidt, & Madjar, 2020). This problem is likely exacerbated during COVID-19, as working from home is more often (relative to pre-pandemic) associated with having nonwork demands (e.g., children interrupting, other people at home making distracting noises; Leroy et al., 2020). Office workers can be interrupted every 3–11 minutes even while in the office. Consequently, cognitive control is extremely important to maintain and develop in order to cope with frequent workplace interruption. Instead, media technology inhibits our ability to dismiss competing demands and this amplifies existing difficulties with focusing on task behaviors. This may occur because multitasking is a state of attending to one activity and then another, which sensitizes our signal detection system to extra-task cues and feedback (Badre, 2020). One study shows that people who typically use multiple types of media simultaneously (e.g., various computer applications, print media, and mobile phone at the same time) had difficulty ignoring distractions during working memory tasks and were slower performing task switching (Ophir, Nass, & Wagner, 2009). When attempting to balance two goal-directed tasks, the signal detection systems may become vigilant to any alarm outside of the active task. To illustrate, consider an employee who is very focused on preparing a report. They may have on noise-canceling headphones or otherwise direct attention only to that task. Then, consider an employee who is working on a report while waiting for a package to arrive. They may check their phone for updates, get distracted by email notifications, or startle each time they hear a car door close outside. Empirical research on the topic is scant, and with mixed findings, but evidence is pointing in the direction that media multitasking is associated with worse cognitive performance (Uncapher & Wagner, 2018).

Regulation of media technology use and multitasking is deeply unpopular, which is surprising given the likely decrements to cognitive resources (Wang & Tchernev, 2012). However, the cognitive decrements probably happen slowly and can be attributed to other causes (e.g., inadequate sleep, dehydration), so that the consequences of media use are not salient. Furthermore, multitasking and media interruptions may seem adaptive and rewarding, like a welcome break. Uses and gratification theory states that media technology that facilitates multitasking (e.g., smart phones) has improved access and control over media consumption (Katz, Blumler, & Gurevitch, 1973). If a person becomes bored while reading and has an interjecting thought to search for funny cat videos, access to such a distraction is often only an arm's length away. After repeated distractions with positive reinforcement (e.g., enhanced mood), the neurological systems may become conditioned to search for distractions and entertain cognitive interjections. However, this research is controversial, with limited and methodologically questionable studies being leveraged as evidence. The lack of investigation into this area within the job stress domain, and organizational psychology more generally, is nonetheless surprising.

In a process that is not entirely dissimilar, web content is associated with reading for satisficing, which describes reading until incremental gains in knowledge are no longer rewarding (Duggan & Payne, 2009). Eye-tracking research shows that people tend to seek information from web content in an F-shaped pattern (e.g., Buscher, Cutrell, & Morris, 2009), emphasizing only parts of the content available. This act of skimming, which identifies and retains only the very most valuable words, is common when reading (or at least, searching for information) within web content. Therefore, casual internet reading may inhibit verbal ability or word search ability, if language systems become trained for efficiency and not depth.

Overall, it seems that media use (especially when multitasking) may inhibit important cognitive functions, including language production and flow. *Flow*, defined as an optimal, intrinsically motivated, internal state, characterized by intense concentration and enjoyment (Csikszentmihalyi, 1990), is empirically linked ($r = 0.68$, Rivkin, Diestel, & Schmidt, 2018) and nearly synonymous with *engagement* (a positive, fulfilling, work-related state of mind; Bakker & Demerouti, 2008). Consequently, interruptions to flow are associated with (at least) the job strains of reduced engagement and increased frustration. Further investigation of methods to buffer or counteract these strains (e.g., an intervention limiting employees to one type of media at a time) may provide insight to inform job stress theory (perhaps by integrating flow theory), as well as organizational policy. Until then, the balance of the evidence suggests that concerned individuals should attempt to minimize multitasking. This is especially true for those who believe they are good at multitasking,[1] because strong empirical evidence indicates that self-efficacy for multitasking is negatively related to multitasking performance. In other words, the people who think they are the best at multitasking are the worst at it (Badre, 2020, p. 135).

CONCLUDING REMARKS

Cognitive theories include cognitive ability models (e.g., general mental ability, selective attention), but regarding job stress, cognitive appraisal is the most immediately relevant. The cognitive theories of stress typically involve a cognitive evaluation as the mediator between a stressor-strain response. These theories also frequently include emotion. For example, Lazarus (1991) argues that an emotion is the response to some cognitive activity that generates meaning for an individual. Happiness, for example, was the realization of progress towards a specific goal. Thus, the role of appraisals in the generation of meaning is pivotal to understanding, and in some cases, regulating emotions. Emotion regulation is a form of coping, and can take the form of cognitive (e.g., reappraisal, new strategies) and behavioral (problem-solving) attempts. Some research distinguishes between control coping and avoidance/escape coping. Control strategies are proactive, such as making a plan or thinking about your positive traits (e.g., fluid compensation). Escape and avoidance coping include avoiding the situation or not thinking about it (much like escape and avoidance conditioning). Some avoidance is necessary, as it allows you to detach from the stressor. See Latack and Havlovic (1992) for a comprehensive overview on coping measurement and categorizations.

Because of this emphasis on emotion and appraisal, the transactional model might be integrated with affective events theory (Weiss & Cropanzano, 1996) to better predict proximal affective predictors of workplace strain. Similarly, Fredrickson's (2013) broaden and build theory has some commonalities with savoring in the holistic model of stress (Nelson & Simmons, 2003). In this model, the focus is on coping behaviors or processes rather than a stable coping style or personality trait, which is valuable. Because coping is not a trait, it is more amenable to behavioral or structural intervention. This definition also distinguishes coping from coping effectiveness.

NOTE

1.　Badre (2020) describes how you can test this for yourself. Time yourself saying the alphabet then counting to 26. It might take 10–15 seconds or so. Then, time yourself multitasking by alternating as in A1, B2, C3. It is quite likely to take more than 15 seconds.

REFERENCES

Badre, D. (2020). The Tao of multitasking. In *On Task* (pp. 130–156). Princeton University Press.

Bakker, A. B., & Demerouti, E. (2008). Towards a model of work engagement. *Career Development International, 13*(3), 209–223.

Brand, C. (1987). The importance of general intelligence. In S. Modgil & C. Modgil (Eds), *Arthur Jensen: Consensus and controversy* (pp. 251–265). New York: Falmer.

Buscher, G., Cutrell, E., & Morris, M. R. (2009, April). What do you see when you're surfing? Using eye tracking to predict salient regions of web pages. In *Proceedings of the SIGCHI Conference on Human Factors in Computing Systems*, 21–30.

Compas, B. E., & Bettis, A. H. (2019). Coping and emotion regulation. In M. J. Prinstein, E. A. Youngstrom, E. J. Mash, & R. A. Barkley (Eds), *Treatment of disorders in childhood and adolescence* (4th Ed., pp. 539–559). Guilford Press.

Csikszentmihalyi, M. (1990). Flow: The psychology of optimal experience (Vol. 1990). Harper and Row.

Duggan, G. B., & Payne, S. J. (2009). Text skimming: The process and effectiveness of foraging through text under time pressure. *Journal of Experimental Psychology: Applied*, *15*(3), 228–242.

Folkman, S., & Lazarus, R. S. (1980). An analysis of coping in a middle-aged community sample. *Journal of Health and Social Behavior*, *21*(3), 219–239.

Fredrickson, B. L. (2001). The role of positive emotions in positive psychology: The broaden-and-build theory of positive emotions. *American Psychologist*, *56*(3), 218–226.

Fredrickson, B. L. (2013). Positive emotions broaden and build. *Advances in Experimental Social Psychology*, *47*, 1–53.

Grandey, A. A. (2000). Emotional regulation in the workplace: A new way to conceptualize emotional labor. *Journal of Occupational Health Psychology*, *5*(1), 95–110.

Grandey, A. A. (2015). Smiling for a wage: What emotional labor teaches us about emotion regulation. *Psychological Inquiry*, *26*(1), 54–60.

Gross, J. J. (1998). Antecedent-and response-focused emotion regulation: Divergent consequences for experience, expression, and physiology. *Journal of Personality and Social Psychology*, *74*(1), 224–237.

Gross, J. J. (2015). Emotion regulation: Current status and future prospects. *Psychological Inquiry*, *26*(1), 1–26.

Heider, F. (1958). *The psychology of interpersonal relations*. John Wiley & Sons.

Hobfoll, S. E. (2001). The influence of culture, community, and the nested-self in the stress process: Advancing conservation of resources theory. *Applied Psychology*, *50*(3), 337–421.

Hochschild, A. (1983). Comment on Kemper's "social constructionist and positivist approaches to the sociology of emotions." *American Journal of Sociology*, *89*(2), 432–434.

Katz, E., Blumler, J. G., & Gurevitch, M. (1973). Uses and gratifications research. *Public Opinion Quarterly*, *37*(4), 509–523.

Kim, E., & Glomb, T. M. (2010). Get smarty pants: Cognitive ability, personality, and victimization. *Journal of Applied Psychology*, *95*(5), 889–901.

Kriz, T. D., Jolly, P. M., & Shoss, M. K. (2021). Coping with organizational layoffs: Managers' increased active listening reduces job insecurity via perceived situational control. *Journal of Occupational Health Psychology*, *26*(5), 448–458.

Latack, J. C., & Havlovic, S. J. (1992). Coping with job stress: A conceptual evaluation framework for coping measures. *Journal of Organizational Behavior*, *13*(5), 479–508.

Lazarus, R. S. (1991). Progress on a cognitive-motivational-relational theory of emotion. *American Psychologist*, *46*(8), 819–834.

Lazarus, R. S. (1993). Coping theory and research: Past, present, and future. *Psychosomatic Medicine*, *55*(3), 234–247.

Lazarus, R. S., & Folkman, S. (1984). *Stress, appraisal, and coping*. Springer Publishing.

Leroy, S., Schmidt, A. M., & Madjar, N. (2020). Interruptions and task transitions: Understanding their characteristics, processes, and consequences. *Academy of Management Annals*, *14*(2), 661–694.

Liu, Y., & Perrewé, P. L. (2005). Another look at the role of emotion in the organizational change: A process model. *Human Resource Management Review, 15*(4), 263–280.

McCarthy, C. J., Lambert, R. G., Mosley, K. C., Fitchett, P. G., & Dillard, J. B. (2021). Teacher appraisals of demand–resource imbalances in racially concentrated schools: An extension of transactional theory with Black, Hispanic, and White US teachers. *International Journal of Stress Management, 28*(1), 24–31.

Nelson, D. L., & Simmons, B. L. (2003). Health psychology and work stress: A more positive approach. In J. C. Quick & L. E. Tetrick (Eds), *Handbook of occupational health psychology* (pp. 97–119). American Psychological Association.

Oldham, G. R., & Gordon, B. I. (1999). Job complexity and employee substance use: The moderating effects of cognitive ability. *Journal of Health and Social Behavior, 40*(3), 290–306.

Ophir, E., Nass, C., & Wagner, A. D. (2009). Cognitive control in media multitaskers. *Proceedings of the National Academy of Sciences, 106*(37), 15583–15587.

Perrewé, P. L., & Zellars, K. L. (1999). An examination of attributions and emotions in the transactional approach to the organizational stress process. *Journal of Organizational Behavior, 20*(5), 739–752.

Rivkin, W., Diestel, S., & Schmidt, K. H. (2018). Which daily experiences can foster well-being at work? A diary study on the interplay between flow experiences, affective commitment, and self-control demands. *Journal of Occupational Health Psychology, 23*(1), 99–111.

Thompson, R. A. (1990). Emotion and self-regulation. In R. A. Thompson (Ed.), *Nebraska Symposium on Motivation, 1988: Socioemotional development* (pp. 367–467). University of Nebraska Press.

Uncapher, M. R., & Wagner, A. D. (2018). Media multitasking, mind, and brain. *Proceedings of the National Academy of Sciences, 115*(40), 9889–9896.

Wang, Z., & Tchernev, J. M. (2012). The "myth" of media multitasking: Reciprocal dynamics of media multitasking, personal needs, and gratifications. *Journal of Communication, 62*(3), 493–513.

Webb, T. L., Miles, E., & Sheeran, P. (2012). Dealing with feeling: A meta-analysis of the effectiveness of strategies derived from the process model of emotion regulation. *Psychological Bulletin, 138*(4), 775–808.

Weidemann, G., Satkunarajah, M., & Lovibond, P. F. (2016). I think, therefore eyeblink: The importance of contingency awareness in conditioning. *Psychological Science, 27*(4), 467–475.

Weiner, B. (1985). An attributional theory of achievement motivation and emotion. *Psychological Review, 92*(4), 548–573.

Weiss, H. M., & Cropanzano, R. (1996). Affective events theory: A theoretical discussion of the structure, causes and consequences of affective experiences at work. In B. M. Staw & L. L. Cummings (Eds), *Research in organizational behavior: An annual series of analytical essays and critical reviews* (Vol. 18, pp. 1–74). Elsevier Science/JAI Press.

Zhang, Y., Zhang, Y., Ng, T. W. H., & Lam, S. S. K. (2019). Promotion- and prevention-focused coping: A meta-analytic examination of regulatory strategies in the work stress process. *Journal of Applied Psychology, 104*(10), 1296–1323.

Zhou, X., Vohs, K. D., & Baumeister, R. F. (2009). The symbolic power of money: Reminders of money alter social distress and physical pain. *Psychological Science, 20*(6), 700–706.

6. Equity and exchange theories

Justice can be conceptualized in various ways within the job stress research, and most of these involve cognitive evaluations of a discrepancy between what was needed, promised, or deserved, and what was received. Initial research perhaps comes from anthropology (e.g., Malinowski, 1932) and refers exclusively to economic exchanges. Homans (1958), whose expertise reflected behavioral sociology and no formal training (he believed that training was only for dogs), extended the work on material exchange by including the concept of symbolic value (e.g., recognition, status). Blau (1964) further contended that a successful series of economic exchanges (typically short-term, quid pro quo arrangements involving tangible resources with economic value) can evolve into a social exchange. Compared to economic exchanges, social exchanges have longer time spans, are more likely to involve symbolic resources, and typically exclude line by line "score keeping" in favor of more global assessments. For illustration, this is the difference between requesting separate checks for each diner at a restaurant, versus evenly splitting a single check among all diners.

The connection between justice and job stress is multidirectional and strong, both conceptually and empirically. To illustrate, justice perceptions sometimes reflect a stressor, a type of stress appraisal, a mediator or moderator in the stressor–strain relationship, or even overlapping constructs (Vermunt & Steensma, 2005). In fact, negative responses to inequitable rewards have been labeled "psychological distress" (Adams, 1963) and unfair exchanges are said to be met with attempts to cope (e.g., Greenberg, 1984). In other words, justice theories are job stress theories.

CONTEXT: JINGLE, JANGLE, JUSTICE

Justice theories are intuitive and well supported, but inconsistencies in testing, conceptual overlap, loose application of theory, and simultaneous derivation of similar models by different researchers have led to both jingle and jangle fallacies. *Jingle fallacies* describe an erroneous association between two dissimilar ideas that have the same name. Conversely, a *jangle fallacy* occurs when two identical ideas are perceived as different because they are labeled inconsistently. For example, a jingle fallacy can occur between Adams's (1965) social exchange theory and Homans's. Although both theories pertain to social exchange, Adams explains a mathematical ratio of efforts and rewards, whereas Homans describes the economic transactions within a social relationship. Thus, the label "social exchange theory" is accurate, in that both theories involve social exchanges, but the title should not be applied so wantonly as to disregard the wide differences between the two. Adams's (1965) social exchange theory can also be used to exemplify the jangle fallacy. Adams's (1965) social exchange theory and Adams's (1965) equity theory both refer to the same theory (although reference to Adams's theory as a social exchange theory is less common; Cropanzano & Mitchell, 2005). In the original article, the theory was termed the theory of inequity (Adams, 1965), adding to the inconsistencies.

EQUITY THEORY (ADAMS, 1965)

The earliest theory of justice can be attributed to Aristotle, who writes that distributive justice reflects "an equality of ratios." Some time later, Adams (1965) developed the equity theory of distributive justice by explicating how individuals judge the fairness of their exchanges at work (Figure 6.1). These evaluations are based on a mathematical comparison of the inputs they contribute and the outcomes (i.e., outputs) they receive to the input–outcome balances of their reference groups. When individuals perceive that their own input–outcome ratio is comparable to that of the reference group, they perceive the workplace as equitable. Dissimilar ratios, conversely, lead to perceptions of inequity.

$$\frac{\text{Personal Input}}{\text{Personal Output}} - \frac{\text{Referent Input}}{\text{Referent Output}} = \text{Equity}$$

Note: Equity is the equality of ratios, and people can alter their inputs or outputs to even the balance.

Figure 6.1   Adams's (1965) equity theory

Theoretical Extensions

This theory has inspired a number of theoretical extensions. The justice judgment model (Leventhal, 1976), for example, describes under what conditions people should use specific justice norms, which include *equality* (e.g., even, same), *equity* (e.g., merit-based), and *need*. To illustrate, imagine two room-mates are negotiating how they will pay for their electric bill. They could agree to split the bill in half (equality), proportionally based on use (equity), or proportionally based on income (need). Ultimately, the appropriate justice norm for this situation is dependent on the roommates' desired outcome. In this example, equity allocation might encourage more conservative electricity use, whereas equal allocation would lead to greater group cohesion.

Another theoretical extension emphasizes the role of individual differences. Specifically, equity sensitivity refers to a continuum ranging from benev-olent to entitled. *Benevolence* is characterized as having greater tolerance for under-reward, whereas *entitlement* indicates having greater tolerance for over-reward. However, the middle state of *equity sensitivity* best fits early con-ceptualization of equity reactions, as this describes discomfort with inequities in either direction (e.g., Adams, 1965).

A complement to distributive justice within equity theory is *procedural justice*, which refers to fairness in the allocation process, rather than the alloca-tion outcome. The procedural justice theory posits that justice is of fundamen-tal value to individuals and the broader society, such that chronic perceived unfairness can lead to strain. Just exchanges are guided by procedures that minimize bias, create consistent allocations, rely on accurate information, are correctable, represent the concerns of all recipients, and are based on prevail-ing moral and ethical standards (Leventhal, 1976).

Finally, the organizational justice model (Colquitt, 2001) also describes the balance between effort and workplace rewards. This theory posits that perceived inequity in the effort–reward ratio is related to negative health outcomes. This relationship results from individuals' attempts to address the distress caused by workplace inequity, perhaps by reducing efforts or request-ing additional compensation. If these attempts to remedy the situation fail, employee turnover may increase as workers pursue employment under more equitable conditions.

Research and Practical Implications

Although equity theory established a valuable foundation for evaluating workplace exchanges, testing was initially limited by confounds (e.g., attempts to study injustice were intertwined with threats to employee self-esteem or job security). However, recent testing methods have allowed researchers to isolate the equity of ratios more effectively and have still shown good empir-ical support. For example, justice is shown to pre-empt counterproductive work behaviors much like other stressors (Fox, Spector, & Miles, 2001). A meta-analysis indicates that the relative risk of coronary heart disease resulting from organizational injustice is 1.62 (Kivimäki et al., 2006). In other words, injustice can result in serious organizational and personal outcomes.

One area that was not supported comes from early overpayment research, in which equity theory posited that individuals would reduce inequity by adjusting inputs and outcomes. However, for workers with fixed outcomes (e.g., pay rate for hourly workers), overpayment did not lead to increased productivity, and may in fact lead to decreases in quality of work over time, such that any benefit from the overpayment effect is short-lived (Lawler, 1968). Furthermore, monetary incentives can increase unethical behavior when there is the opportunity for financial gain (Bellé & Cantarelli, 2019). Thus, money as an incentive can be effective, but it has its limitations and may only be effective under certain conditions. Further research on alternative compensation formats, informed by the equity research, would inform practical implications.

Aside from overpayment, justice theory is fairly well validated. Nonetheless, some gaps still remain. For example, monetary rewards may be interesting to study to correct imbalances resulting from a variety of injustices. Money elicits positive attitudes (e.g., self-confidence) and mitigates negative affect among individuals (e.g., physical and psychological distress; Zhou, Vohs, & Baumeister, 2009). However, there are times when money may not be the most effective nor appropriate incentive. For example, a monetary penalty may not be strong enough to encourage workers to engage in behavior that they perceive as an impediment to their primary goal (Wu & Paluck, 2021). Furthermore, beliefs about money differ across cultures, such that money can be perceived as a symbol of evil or success (Tang, Furnham, & Davis, 2002).

Justice research also demonstrates that researchers should probably reconsider including interactional justice as a unique subfacet. Procedural justice was once thought to include two subfactors: *fair formal procedures* (e.g., participative policies, minimizing bias) and *interactional justice* (fairness of the treatment an employee receives in the enactment of formal procedures or in the explanation of those procedures). More recently, though, researchers have treated interactional justice as auxiliary to procedural justice. Interactional justice now reflects how people generally treat each other (e.g., avoiding rude remarks). In this sense, interactional justice is not justice, as there are no ratios, but may instead reflect an actual–preferred discrepancy. To illustrate, consider that items on the interactional justice scale include statements such as "Your supervisor treats you in a polite manner." Imagine that a supervisor was not polite to an employee. Would the employee say "That was not fair" or would they say "That was not nice"? Consequently, other constructs (e.g., incivility, abusive supervision) capture interpersonal relationship quality better than justice, which has a specific comparative evaluation.

This might be moot because research shows that distributive justice and procedural justice both inform an overall sense of justice, which in turn is associated with outcomes (e.g., Ambrose & Schminke, 2009). In other words, the distinction between distributive and procedural justice may not matter in many contexts and should be combined unless there is a genuine theoretical justification for separating them. A good rule of thumb is that if the hypotheses do not make substantively different predictions for the discrete justice perceptions (e.g., distributive and procedural are both expected to have a positive linear relationship with a criterion variable) then the global (additive) justice construct is the more appropriate choice. It seems that the global perception is most relevant on average, as meta-analytic research shows a rho = 0.64 between distributive and procedural justice, indicating substantial overlap (Hauenstein, McGonigle, & Flinder, 2001).

However, there is an alternative explanation – overall justice perceptions may cyclically interact with the discrete justice perceptions (Jones & Skarlicki, 2013). In other words, distributive and procedural justice may cause overall justice perceptions, which may later inform distributive and procedural justice, and so on. This would give the impression of indistinctiveness among distributive, procedural, and global justice perceptions. This hypothesis has not been tested, but an experiment in which global (or discrete) justice is manipulated, and then unrelated discrete (or global) perceptions measured, may be a good way to approach this question.

FAIRNESS THEORY

Shifting away from equity, fairness theory (Folger & Cropanzano, 2001) asserts that individuals engage in counterfactual thinking to determine the fairness of a decision-making event and whether authorities should be blamed for that event. More specifically, individuals are expected to react to a decision-making event by first evaluating whether they were harmed or threatened (i.e., *would* evaluation). If an individual determines that an injury has occurred, they next appraise whether the authority can be blamed (i.e., *could* evaluation). Finally, the authority figure will only be blamed if the individual believes that an ethical principle regarding social conduct has been violated (i.e., *should* evaluation).

Research and Practical Implications

This theory is infrequently tested, but empirical results have been consistent with this model. For example, one study shows that *could* evaluations had less of an impact on justice perceptions and other outcomes (e.g., emotional, behavioral) than other evaluations (Farthing, 2011). Another study shows that justice mediates the relationship between hindrance stressors and job performance (Zhang, LePine, Buckman, & Wei, 2014). The mechanism proposed for this invokes counterfactual thinking, such that "an imagined alternative situation with lower levels of hindrance stressors will be perceived as being preferable, and thus more fair, because in the imagined alternative, the organization has not violated the norms of reciprocity" (Zhang et al., 2014, p. 678). It is worth noting that this specific mechanism was not tested in this study.

FAIRNESS HEURISTIC THEORY

Despite the similarities in the name, fairness heuristic theory is unrelated to fairness theory. This theory posits that individuals in organizations are faced with a social dilemma, such that cooperating with organizational agents can lead to benefits, but leaves the employee vulnerable to exploitation (e.g., Lind, Kray, & Thompson, 2001). Consequently, people use *fairness heuristics* as a psychological shortcut to decide whether to cooperate with authorities. The fairness heuristic (typically operationalized as trust) is derived from fairness perceptions or cognitive evaluations of fairness, which are based on observable behaviors (e.g., met expectations; Blau, 1964). The fairness heuristic theory has three sequential, cyclical stages: the judgmental phase, use phase, and the phase-shifting event. The fairness heuristic is formed quickly during a *judgmental phase* based on a first impression by using whatever fairness information is available, however limited. Once formed, people will rely on the heuristic during the *use phase*, which can influence future interactions and perpetuate the fairness heuristic. People remain in the use phase until a *phase-shifting event* occurs (e.g., an organizational change), which causes the individual to reconsider fairness levels and return to the judgmental phase. Fairness heuristic theory was later adapted into uncertainty management theory, which accounts for additional aspects of life that may contain uncertainty (Lind & van den Bos, 2002).

Research and Practical Implications

This theory is infrequently tested, but experiments have shown support for the effects of early fairness experiences on fairness judgments and acceptance of authority (Lind et al., 2001). This first impression effect may be important to various workplace applications, including interpersonal prejudice and discrimination. For example, if the supervisor is from an untrusted group (e.g., not a member of the dominant religion) or violates norms associated with trustworthiness (e.g., heavily tattooed), the supervisor may not be trusted. This can result in noncompliance with supervisory requests or demanding of a tit-for-tat exchange relationship. This type of suspicion and distrust may especially harm minority group supervisors, who may already be hypervisible or overly monitored due to their group status.

SOCIAL EXCHANGE THEORY (BLAU, 1964)

Social exchange involves a series of interpersonal interactions that generate obligation. The interactions are reciprocal and dependent upon the actions (or expected actions) of the other person, and repeated interactions over time can comprise a relationship. Social exchange theories describe one or more of the following components: a series of interdependent transactions (i.e., outcomes are based on mutual activities of group members); a folk belief (i.e., cultural expectation) regarding reciprocity; a moral norm (i.e., cultural mandate); or exchanges as types of relationships between two or more people (see Cropanzano & Mitchell, 2005, for a review).

A principal tenet of Blau's (1964) social exchange theory is that interactions among two or more interdependent people may evolve into trusting, loyal, and reciprocal commitments over time if group members adhere to certain *exchange rules* (i.e., "a normative definition of the situation that forms among or is adopted by the participants in an exchange relation"; Emerson, 1976, p. 351). *Reciprocity* is one such rule of exchange and reflects the folk belief that people get what they deserve and exchanges eventually even out (Gouldner, 1960). Related *just world beliefs* describe faith in the idea that individuals are rewarded or punished based on their (un)fulfillment of obligations. Some researchers consider just world beliefs to be a type of cognitive error, as this model is not supported by empirical observation or theoretical mechanisms. Although inaccurate, this belief is associated with at least one positive effect. Specifically, belief in karma mitigates the desire for revenge (Bies & Tripp, 1996).

Other types of relationships (as well as relationship expectations and norms) exist beyond reciprocity, including *negotiation*. Negotiated interactions are marked by explicit, often quid pro quo, agreements, leading to a better understanding of obligations. However, reciprocity manifests in better work relationships than negotiations because reciprocity encourages trust, and in turn commitment, to one another (Molm, Takahashi, & Peterson, 2000). Reciprocity and negotiated agreements are the most studied exchange rules, although others are more visible outside of psychology and management (see Fiske, 1992). For example, *altruism* describes when people help others at a personal cost and without remuneration.

Research and Practical Implications

Social exchange has been applied to workplace phenomena. For example, consider that organizational citizenship behavior (OCB) is defined as behavior not formally rewarded by an organization. Nonetheless, employees who report high distributive justice are more likely to engage in OCB even though OCB will not be rewarded. In line with social exchange theory, Organ (1990) states that employees often conflate economic exchanges with social exchanges, such that an employee might enact OCB based on their positive relationship with the organization, not because the contract requires it.

Despite the value of the social exchange framework and enormous amount of empirical research generated, more questions remain. Due to a lack of operational definitions, unaddressed confounds, lack of understanding of relevant cognitive processes, and an inability to predict inaction (i.e., failure to reciprocate positive treatment), the overall applications and tests of the model are incomplete and fractured. Some studies, for example, conflate the reciprocity rule with social exchange norms altogether. Future research testing the integrated theoretical models proposed in the literature (see Cropanzano, Anthony, Daniels, & Hall, 2017) would provide much needed clarification.

Theoretical Extension: Resource Theory

Like the previous theories, Foa and Foa's (1974) resource theory pertains to the exchange of resources between two interdependent parties. However, they are unique in their articulation of the resources exchanged. These six categories of resources (i.e., love, status, information, money, goods, and services) can be described in terms of their particularism and concreteness. *Particularism* refers to whether the value of a resource is affected by who provides it. For example, feedback might be more valuable from the supervisor than from a customer, whereas money is equally valued whether it comes from a supervisor's bonus or a customer's gratuity. The second dimension refers to the resource's *concreteness*, meaning how tangible or specific the resource is. Receiving a gratuity, for example, has both tangible (e.g., monetary) and symbolic (e.g., gratitude) qualities. This theory is well validated outside of job stress, but theory testing within the workplace context following the recommendations of Mitchell, Cropanzano, and Quisenberry (2012) would help inform organizational practices regarding the types of resources recommended in workplace exchange relationships.

EFFORT–REWARD IMBALANCE

The effort–reward imbalance model was initially offered as a complement to job control-demands theory, but emphasizing the work contract, rather than characteristics of the job task (Siegrist, 2016). This originates from within physiological stress research, social exchange theory, and identity theory in order to explain psychological contributions to cardiovascular disease (see van Vegchel et al., 2005). Specifically, lack of reciprocity or fairness between effort and reward can cause emotional distress, which in turn leads to adverse health outcomes (e.g., cardiovascular disease, depression; Siegrist, 2016). According to this model, the work role fulfills individual self-regulation needs, in that work offers opportunities for acquiring self-efficacy (e.g., successful performance), self-esteem (e.g., recognition), and self-integration (e.g., belonging to a significant group). Based on the norm of reciprocity, the employee expects rewards in exchange for any efforts. When high effort and low reward cause imbalance, self-regulation is thwarted.

There are three key components to this model. *Effort* is expended in exchange for rewards from the organization and society overall. *Rewards* can include money (or compensatory rewards), esteem, and career opportunities/ job security. *Overcommitment* refers to attitudes, behaviors, and emotions that reflect excessive effort and a strong desire for approval and esteem. Excessive efforts are believed to be caused by perceptual distortion (such as an underestimation of challenges and an overestimation of resources), which is motivated by a recurrent need for approval and esteem (Siegrist, 1996). In other words, overcommitment distorts the perception of both high efforts and low reward, and therefore influences employee health indirectly. An *imbalance* between effort and rewards can lead to strain via negative emotions, which in turn activate physiological stress. Sustained or repeated activation of the autonomic nervous system may contribute to the development of cardiovascular disease directly or through health-adverse behavior (Siegrist, 2016).

The model has changed over time. For example, the model has been extended to other psychological and behavioral outcomes (e.g., turnover, counterproductive work behavior; Siegrist, 2016), and vital exhaustion was added as the mediator in the imbalance–cardiovascular disease relationship (Appels, 1997). The three major tenets have remained more or less the same, though. They are: (1) a high effort–low reward imbalance increases the risk of poor health; (2) a high level of overcommitment may independently increase the risk of poor health, even when there is no imbalance; and (3) an effort–reward imbalance, combined with a high level of overcommitment, leads to the highest risk of poor health.

In order to remedy a high effort–low reward imbalance, people might reduce their effort or cognitively reappraise their own contributions as less. In these cases, imbalance might not influence health in the long term. However, there are some specific circumstances in which people maintain an imbalance, including when they have few alternatives (e.g., high unemployment rates), expected long-term gains (e.g., an imbalance now in hope of a promotion), or high levels of trait overcommitment. The view of overcommitment as an individual difference is fairly well supported, as overcommitted people experience perceptual distortions that cause them to inappropriately overestimate their demands and coping resources more often than their less involved colleagues

(Siegrist, 2012). However, there is within-person variation as interventions are able to modify overcommitment.

Research and Practical Implications

Within the workplace, most effort–reward imbalance studies showed that imbalance is related to worse wellbeing and heightened emotional exhaustion (van Vegchel, De Jonge, Bosma, & Schaufeli, 2005). Furthermore, high trait overcommitment was related to less job satisfaction and more burnout. Research on the moderating effect of overcommitment on the relationship between effort–reward imbalance and job-related wellbeing were inconsistent across five studies (van Vegchel et al., 2005). The few intervention studies based on the effort–reward imbalance model have mostly attempted to modulate overcommitment. In a randomized controlled trial, 54 male bus drivers were divided into two groups, one of which was informed of the adverse effects induced by the imbalance (the control group), and the other was encouraged to develop suggestions for structural changes to overcome the imbalance (the intervention group; Aust, Peter, & Siegrist, 1997). The mean level of overcommitment was reduced in the intervention group for at least three months. Using a different approach, Irie, Tsutsumi, Shioji, and Kobayashi (2004) administered an effort-reward questionnaire to 441 employees as part of a survey feedback intervention. When Type A behaviors were individually modified, reports of overcommitment, self-reported sleepiness, dullness, and burnout symptoms were reduced. However, there was no random assignment and no evidence of a decrease in imbalance.

There are straightforward organizational applications of the effort–reward imbalance model (see Tsutsumi & Kawakami, 2004). For example, this model states the benefits of both monetary and compensatory rewards, which include (among others) benefits, flextime, and recognition. That said, the self-esteem dimension may be the most responsive type of reward and should be prioritized (Tsutsumi & Kawakami, 2004). Furthermore, the "job opportunities" reward can be provided through mentoring, clarification of the steps for promotion, or vocational training. These activities can also increase self-esteem and reduce perceptions of job insecurity. Overall, creating a supportive environment itself not only raises employee self-esteem but also mitigates harm from existing imbalance.

However, important questions remain unanswered. In one concerning finding, the deleterious health effects of imbalance are greater among lower-status and lower-paying jobs (Kuper, Singh-Manoux, Siegrist, & Marmot, 2002). This may reflect a larger problem, perhaps contributing to disparities in cardiovascular disease. Research should continue to assess the extent of this problem, as little is understood about the multifarious factors that contribute to health disparities. Even less is known about resolving them. On one hand, it seems belittling and superficial to suggest that "other" rewards can mitigate imbalances, but this is an empirical question that may provide at least some direction for addressing health disparities. That said, it is clear that paying people more, especially those in low-status and low-paying jobs, would help correct health disparities. Sometimes, we are too creative in trying to solve the problem when the answer is to pay people better. Some sacrifices would have to be made, but interventions may be less effective than giving people money so they can participate in their preferred stress-reduction activities (e.g., fishing, reading). Future research should investigate where the tradeoff occurs (e.g., is a stress intervention that costs 10 USD per person more effective than giving people 5, 10, or 20 USD each?) and what moderators are important (e.g., base pay).

CONCLUDING REMARKS

In summary, the theories of social exchange accurately describe interpersonal exchanges, monetary and otherwise. Although there is ambiguity within and overlap between the theories, the overall tenets (e.g., unequal exchanges lead to strain) are intuitive and empirically supported. Future research must carefully justify, operationalize, and measure the constructs in order to contribute positively to the existing knowledge. In particular, additional inquiry into the processes of social exchange and competing models posed in Cropanzano et al. (2017) would address gaps within the justice literature.

Another takeaway is that reciprocation is almost ubiquitously valuable. As an organizational agent, it is important to reciprocate positive treatment without turning business relationships into symbolic exchanges. A small shop owner befriending their customers, or a local dance teacher providing a service to people with similar interests, may begin to feel uncomfortable with receiving money from those with whom they now have a social exchange. Unless this transition from economic exchange to social relationship is consistent with the context and expectancies (e.g., farmers market), it would be risky to move away from the norms of economic exchange. However, showing trust in the customer to return payment at a later date may be reciprocated in symbolic acts (e.g., positive reviews, loyalty).

Research efforts that could improve our understanding of justice would include concerted attempts to integrate the interactional injustice literature with similar literatures and might quickly and efficiently expand the knowledge base. For example, the tit-for-tat or spiral theory of incivility (e.g., Andersson & Pearson, 1999) explains how subtle mistreatment can spiral into more aggressive treatment, consistent with the norm of reciprocity. This might be particularly useful to bridge with justice research, and particularly interactional justice research, as the processes of incivility are more clearly delineated than within justice theories. Similarly, a direction for future research on the effort–reward imbalance model involves the potentially cyclical nature of burnout and justice. If an employee is physically or emotionally fatigued, then job demands will be more effortful, modifying the ratio of efforts and rewards. Recovery experiences like detachment and relaxation (Chapter 8, this volume) might halt this effect.

Finally, a persistent gap in the understanding of social exchange is that it cannot explain failures of the established norm (usually, reciprocity). In other words, this theory does not explain why people neglect to return fair treatment or interact with an aggressor in a positive way. One theory that specifically addresses inaction is the theory of planned behavior. In this theory, subjective norms, attitudes towards the behavior, and perceived behavioral control predict a behavioral intention, which in turn predicts a behavior. However, the intention does not always lead to behavior, depending upon barriers towards the behavior and the presence of preferred alternative behaviors. Although a few studies have integrated social exchange theory and the theory of planned behavior, they typically emphasize the normative component of each theory (e.g., subjective norms are conceptualized as the norm of reciprocity). Future research on the behavior–intention gap (i.e., barriers, the availability of alternative behaviors, competing norms, and values) following the best practices identified in previous research (Cropanzano et al., 2017) would address this concern.

REFERENCES

Adams, J. S. (1963). Towards an understanding of inequity. *Journal of Abnormal and Social Psychology*, *67*(5), 422–436.

Adams, J. S. (1965). Inequity in social exchange. In L. Berkowitz (Ed.), *Advances in experimental social psychology* (Vol. 2, pp. 267–299). Academic Press.

Ambrose, M. L., & Schminke, M. (2009). The role of overall justice judgments in organizational justice research: A test of mediation. *Journal of Applied Psychology*, *94*(2), 491–504.

Andersson, L. M., & Pearson, C. M. (1999). Tit for tat? The spiraling effect of incivility in the workplace. *Academy of Management Review*, *24*(3), 452–471.

Appels, A. (1997). Exhausted subjects, exhausted systems. *Acta Physiologica Scandinavica Supplementum*, *640*, 153–154.

Aust, B., Peter, R., & Siegrist, J. (1997). Stress management in bus drivers: A pilot study based on the model of effort–reward imbalance. *International Journal of Stress Management*, *4*(4), 297–305.

Bellé, N., & Cantarelli, P. (2019). Do ethical leadership, visibility, external regulation, and prosocial impact affect unethical behavior? Evidence from a laboratory and a field experiment. *Review of Public Personnel Administration*, *39*(3), 349–371.

Bies, R. J., & Tripp, T. M. (1996). Beyond distrust: "Getting even" and the need for revenge. In R. M. Kramer & T. R. Tyler (Eds), *Trust in organizations: Frontiers of theory and research* (pp. 246–260). Sage.

Blau, P. M. (1964). *Exchange and power in social life.* John Wiley.

Colquitt, J. A. (2001). On the dimensionality of organizational justice: A construct validation of a measure. *Journal of Applied Psychology, 86*(3), 386–400.

Cropanzano, R., Anthony, E. L., Daniels, S. R., & Hall, A. V. (2017). Social exchange theory: A critical review with theoretical remedies. *Academy of Management Annals, 11*(1), 479–516.

Cropanzano, R., & Mitchell, M. S. (2005). Social exchange theory: An interdisciplinary review. *Journal of Management, 31*(6), 874–900.

Emerson, R. M. (1976). Social exchange theory. *Annual Review of Sociology, 2,* 335–362.

Farthing, A. M. (2011). Cognitions and emotions-testing the tenets of Fairness Theory. Unpublished manuscript.

Fiske, A. P. (1992). The four elementary forms of sociality: Framework for a unified theory of social relations. *Psychological Review, 99*(4), 689–723.

Foa, U. G., & Foa, E. B. (1974). *Societal structures of the mind.* Charles C. Thomas.

Folger, R., & Cropanzano, R. (2001). Fairness theory: Justice as accountability. In J. Greenberg & R. Cropanzano (Eds), *Advances in Organizational Justice.* Stanford University Press.

Fox, S., Spector, P. E., & Miles, D. (2001). Counterproductive work behavior (CWB) in response to job stressors and organizational justice: Some mediator and moderator tests for autonomy and emotions. *Journal of Vocational Behavior, 59*(3), 291–309.

Gouldner, A. W. (1960). The norm of reciprocity: A preliminary statement. *American Sociological Review, 25*(2), 161–178.

Greenberg, J. (1984). On the apocryphal nature of inequity distress. In *The sense of injustice* (pp. 167–186). Springer.

Hauenstein, N. M. A., McGonigle, T., & Flinder, S. W. (2001). A meta-analysis of the relationship between procedural justice and distributive justice: Implications for justice research. *Employee Responsibilities and Rights Journal, 13*(1), 39–56.

Homans, G. C. (1958). Social behavior as exchange. *American Journal of Sociology, 63,* 597–606.

Irie, M., Tsutsumi, A., Shioji, I., & Kobayashi, F. (2004). Effort–reward imbalance and physical health among Japanese workers in a recently downsized corporation. *International Archives of Occupational and Environmental Health, 77*(6), 409–417.

Jones, D. A., & Skarlicki, D. P. (2013). How perceptions of fairness can change: A dynamic model of organizational justice. *Organizational Psychology Review, 3*(2), 138–160.

Kivimäki, M., Virtanen, M., Elovainio, M., Kouvonen, A., Väänänen, A., & Vahtera, J. (2006). Work stress in the etiology of coronary heart disease: A meta-analysis. *Scandinavian Journal of Work, Environment and Health, 32*(6), 431–442.

Kuper, H., Singh-Manoux, A., Siegrist, J., & Marmot, M. (2002). When reciprocity fails: Effort–reward imbalance in relation to coronary heart disease and health functioning within the Whitehall II study. *Occupational and Environmental Medicine, 59*(11), 777–784.

Lawler, E. E. (1968). Equity theory as a predictor of productivity and work quality. *Psychological Bulletin, 70*(6), 596–610.

Leventhal, G. S. (1976). The distribution of rewards and resources in groups and organizations. *Advances in Experimental Social Psychology, 9,* 91–131.

Lind, E. A., Kray, L., & Thompson, L. (2001). Primacy effects in justice judgments: Testing predictions from fairness heuristic theory. *Organizational Behavior and Human Decision Processes, 85*(2), 189–210.

Lind, E. A., & van den Bos, K. (2002). When fairness works: Toward a general theory of uncertainty management. In B. M. Staw & R. M. Kramer (Eds), *Research in organizational behavior: An annual series of analytical essays and critical reviews* (pp. 181–223) Elsevier Science/JAI Press.

Malinowski, B. (1932). Pigs, Papuans, and police court perspective. *Man, 32*, 33–38.

Mitchell, M. S., Cropanzano, R. S., & Quisenberry, D. M. (2012). Social exchange theory, exchange resources, and interpersonal relationships: A modest resolution of theoretical difficulties. In *Handbook of social resource theory* (pp. 99–118). Springer.

Molm, L. D., Takahashi, N., & Peterson, G. (2000). Risk and trust in social exchange: An experimental test of a classical proposition. *American Journal of Sociology, 105*(5), 1396–1427.

Organ, D. W. (1990). The motivational basis of organizational citizenship behavior. *Research in Organizational Behavior, 12*(1), 43–72.

Siegrist, J. (1996). Adverse health effects of high-effort/low-reward conditions. *Journal of Occupational Health Psychology, 1*(1), 27–41.

Siegrist, J. (2012). Effort–reward imbalance at work: Theory, measurement and evidence. Department of Medical Sociology, University of Dusseldorf.

Siegrist, J. (2016). Stress in the workplace. In W. Cockerham (Ed.), *The new Blackwell companion to medical sociology* (pp. 268–285). Blackwell.

Tang, T. L., Furnham, A., & Davis, G. M. W. (2002). The meaning of money: The money ethic endorsement and work-related attitudes in Taiwan, the USA and the UK. *Journal of Managerial Psychology, 17*(7), 542–563.

Tsutsumi, A., & Kawakami, N. (2004). A review of empirical studies on the model of effort–reward imbalance at work: Reducing occupational stress by implementing a new theory. *Social Science and Medicine, 59*(11), 2335–2359.

van Vegchel, N., De Jonge, J., Bosma, H., & Schaufeli, W. (2005). Reviewing the effort–reward imbalance model: Drawing up the balance of 45 empirical studies. *Social Science and Medicine, 60*(5), 1117–1131.

Vermunt, R., & Steensma, H. (2005). How can justice be used to manage stress in organizations? In J. Greenberg & J. A. Colquitt (Eds), *Handbook of organizational justice* (pp. 383–410). Lawrence Erlbaum Associates.

Wu, S. J., & Paluck, E. L. (2021). Having a voice in your group: Increasing productivity through group participation. Unpublished manuscript.

Zhang, Y., LePine, J. A., Buckman, B. R., & Wei, F. (2014). It's not fair … or is it? The role of justice and leadership in explaining work stressor–job performance relationships. *Academy of Management Journal, 57*(3), 675–697.

Zhou, X., Vohs, K. D., & Baumeister, R. F. (2009). The symbolic power of money: Reminders of money alter social distress and physical pain. *Psychological Science, 20*(6), 700–706.

7. Social information and evaluations

Social cognitive theories marked a period of transition, moving from the study of *intra*personal (e.g., behaviorist, cognitive, justice) processes, towards *inter*personal processes. In other words, allostasis, emotions, and appraisals mostly occur within the person, but other people also influence how we learn and maintain behaviors. Social learning, social information processing, and emotions-as-social-information theories describe processes such as these and can help inform the study of job stress.

Social factors also impact psychology, and job stress in particular, through perceived social evaluation. Theories about social evaluations have considered the role of positive evaluations from various perspectives, including as inherent need, a way to feel good about ourselves, or a signal that we are belonging (or not). Ultimately, it feels good to receive positive evaluations from others and we are motivated to do that. When this positive social evaluation is thwarted, we experience strain. This process is described within theories of ego threat, need for belonging, identity, stress as offense to self (SOS), and social support.

SOCIAL LEARNING THEORIES

Social learning theories describe how behaviors can be acquired from experiences with other people. This is a departure from behaviorism, which holds that individuals acquire behavior only from rewards and punishment. Conversely, social learning theories state that behaviors can be learned through observation and mimicry, or vicariously through other people's rewards and punishment. For example, Bandura's (Bandura & Walters, 1977) social learning theory, and later, his social cognitive theory, explained how social behavior is learned by imitating the behavior of others. He stated that people were able to learn behaviors from observing role models (as opposed to directly via rewards and punishments) when the behavior was observed, retained in memory, physically able to be reproduced, and adequately motivated. Person factors (e.g., cognitive ability) are central to social learning theory, which assumes that an individual is both an agent of and a recipient of behavior patterns. Five basic cognitive abilities were identified, including the capability to engage in symbolizing, forethought, vicarious learning, self-regulation, and self-reflection. Biological factors act as predisposing conditions impacting on behavior and learning.

Self-efficacy is a particularly important person factor. Self-efficacy refers to an individual's belief in whether their skills are sufficient to cope with a specific situation. Consistent with Bandura's propositions, self-efficacy has been shown to relate to a multitude of benefits, including learning processes and outcomes, amount and quality of performance, motivation, wellbeing, the ability to withstand failure, and training quality (e.g., Bandura & Locke, 2003). Judgments of personal efficacy are believed to be based on vicarious experience, verbal persuasion, and physiological state (or emotional arousal), but mostly closely informed by successful direct experience.

Other social learning theories developed at about the same time. For example, a book entitled *Social Learning and Imitation* (Miller & Dollard, 1941) proposed that biological drives innervate behavior, which is in turn reinforced by social interaction. Another social learning theory is depicted in Rotter's (1954) book, *Social Learning and Clinical Psychology*, which describes the importance of a person's behavioral expectancy regarding whether their actions affect their situations. Like Bandura, Rotter wrote his book in the behaviorist tradition, but it is seen as bridging the gap to more modern cognitively mediated theories of learning and behavior. Specifically, Rotter developed the term *locus of control* to describe people's beliefs about how much agency they have over their lives, which can range from internal (i.e., self-determined) to external (i.e., based on luck, fate, or other people). To illustrate, a person with an internal locus of control might think that their resume is sufficient/insufficient to be hired for a particular position, whereas a person with an external locus of control might think their resume doesn't matter – hiring depends on who you know, or being in the right place at the right time. Generally, internal locus of control is associated with better performance and wellbeing. However, when a person does not actually have control (e.g., after a break-up), internal locus of control is associated with more anxiety or inability to detach from stressors.

Research and Practical Implications

Bandura and Walters' (1977) social learning theory has been cited more than 70,000 times. When it was initially written, the majority of processes discussed within behavior theories were needs, drives, and subconscious psychodynamic impulses, all internal to the person. Bandura argued for the importance of looking outside of the person for a variety of reasons, including empirical testing. The components of some previous theories, such as psycho-dynamics and the mechanisms of action within classical conditioning, were unable to be observed and were frequently ignored (e.g., Hull & Spencer's stimulus response model). Despite his desire to create a more testable model, self-efficacy is highly confounded with actual ability.

Applied to work stress, social learning theory may explain coping choices. For example, employees might model the coping of other organization members or choose coping methods that they think will be successful. In one study, individuals were slightly more likely to drink alcohol in response to work stressors when they lacked better coping options and when they believed (i.e., expected) that alcohol improved mood (Cooper, Russell, & Frone, 1990). Due to its applicability, Bandura's social learning theory has prompted the development of several workplace stress management interventions that train self-efficacy and enhance behavioral expectancies for appropriate coping behaviors (e.g., muscle relaxation; Cheek & Miller, 1983).

This theory has also been applied to social media (e.g., Bingham & Conner, 2010). Specifically, this theory suggests that social media can be used to transfer knowledge among people and connect organizational stakeholders in a more natural way. In other words, social media can be used to deliver information more comfortably than classroom lectures or other typical intervention formats. Consequently, information shared via social media might be more likely to transfer into behavior. Coping behaviors like breathing exercises can be taught informally and less intrusively than within a workshop, for example. This might also subtly normalize targeted behaviors. This is valuable because typical attempts to change subjective norms can cause reactivity that makes employees unwilling to engage in change (Röttger et al., 2017).

Theoretical Extension: Social Cognitive Theory

Social cognitive theory (Bandura, 1986) is a clarification and expansion of social learning theory. Specifically, social cognitive theory also states that learning can occur by observing a behavior, but adds that the manifestation of behavior is regulated by the *reciprocal determinism* between personal (e.g., cognitive) factors, the environment (e.g., reinforcement), and the behavior. Social cognitive theory also clarified the importance of perception in self-efficacy, which was described more commonly as "expectations of personal efficacy" in social learning theory. That said, the distinctions between the theories are unclear. Overall, both theories describe the way in which people acquire and maintain behavior by considering the individual's past experiences (i.e., reinforcement, expectancies) and the social environment in which behaviors are performed. This is appreciated because the maintenance of behavior, and not just initiation of behavior, is the goal of most interventions. There are, nonetheless, limitations to social cognitive theory. For one, the loose causal structure does not satisfyingly explain how to effect behavior change. The overly ambitious inclusion of person, environment, and behavioral characteristics, interacting in an indeterminate dynamic process, would be impractical to comprehensively test.

Recent applications of social cognitive theory include positive psychology and health promotion. However, misapplications of self-efficacy have contributed to the tyranny of positive thought, perpetuating lay beliefs that positive thinking can cure all ills, literally and figuratively (e.g., Ehrenreich, 2009). Research on post-traumatic growth, for example, does show that certain person–situation combinations result in positive outcomes following traumatic events. However, post-traumatic growth does not often occur and does not fully compensate for negative outcomes. The emphasis on self-efficacy can lead to victim blaming (i.e., "mind over matter"), as keeping a positive attitude has even been (incorrectly) suggested as a cure for cancer (see Ehrenreich, 2009).

SOCIAL INFORMATION PROCESSING THEORY

Whereas social cognitive theory describes how other people affect an individual's behavior through mimicry and vicarious rewards/punishments, social information-processing theory describes (more or less) how other people's thoughts affect an individual's thoughts. In other words, people gather information from observations and interactions with coworkers in order to understand events, develop attitudes, and determine behavioral expectations (Salancik & Pfeffer, 1978). This is because uncertainty is uncomfortable, but inherent in day-to-day life. Consequently, people look to others for social information, especially during times of excessive uncertainty (e.g., at the beginning of the COVID-19 pandemic). This is surprising given that this information typically comes from other laypeople who have no expert knowledge or facts.

People also use social information for referencing and validation, sometimes leading to conformity. *Social referencing* is the use of social information to resolve gaps in understanding and inform job attitudes. *Social validation* is a type of conformity, often operationalized as an individual difference, that occurs when people look to others before making a decision, forming an attitude, or engaging in a behavior. For example, when students are asked "Was a homework assigned yesterday?" by a substitute teacher, they may look around for social information before answering. Similarly, students may look around a chemistry classroom to see if others are wearing their goggles before donning their own. There are a few reasons why people seek social validation, including the desire to avoid norm breaking (e.g., in the previous example, "I don't want to be the only one wearing goggles"). Similarly, people also feel more "correct" when others agree, even if the others are not experts or particularly well informed (e.g., "I'm not sure if we are using dangerous chemicals today, but these must be safe because no one else has goggles on").

Research and Practical Implications

This theory has been tested in the workplace, particularly regarding normative behavior. Empirical research shows that social information informs attitudes regarding job characteristics, work hazards, and other work characteristics (e.g., McLain, 2014). Although it is generally understood that management should model safe and appropriate behavior, this theory describes one mechanism (i.e., social information) through which supervisors' behaviors affect their subordinates.

Support for this theory is evidenced from research on gossip. In one study, longitudinal panel data regarding interpersonal deviance shows that social information about a coworker's interpersonal deviance predicts interpersonal deviance by another employee at a later time (Ferguson & Barry, 2011). Furthermore, when employees are aware of their coworkers' deviance and then personally engage in deviant behaviors, this creates more social information, and in turn leads to further deviance. However, only indirect knowledge (i.e., gossip) was associated with later deviance. Direct observation of deviance did not predict later deviance, possibly because only those who participate in gossip are more likely to engage in deviant behaviors, or because direct observation may create heightened empathy for the victim. Organizations concerned about a gossip problem might want to first address the root cause of the perceptions, but also intervene in the cyclical social information process by encouraging empathy and understanding. For example, if employees are gossiping or venting about poor equipment, management might provide transparency about the reasons for the shortage, steps taken to diagnose the problem, and attempts to procure more equipment. That said, other research has shown that constructive gossip can help employees recall and make salient the beneficial aspects of the workplace, shaping a shared, positive perception of work (e.g., Yun, Roach, Do & Beehr, 2020). So, gossip may not have inherently negative qualities.

Theoretical Extension: Social Comparison Theory

Social comparison theory was developed by Festinger (1954), one of Kurt Lewin's students, and was among the theories that contributed to social information-processing theory. Social comparison theory states that people are motivated to compare themselves to others, their opinion to objective facts, but when objective information is not available, they will compare their ideas to those of similar others. In his theory of cognitive dissonance, he clarified that when the comparison is not favorable, the individual may be motivated to cognitively emphasize differences from the referent others, thus dismissing those comparisons as irrelevant (Festinger, 1957). For example, if a person is playing video games with a friend and the friend wins very soundly, the person may think "Well, they don't work so they can practice a lot more than I do." In fact, *self-enhancement* (e.g., processes by which people increase their self-esteem by emphasizing positive qualities and minimizing negative information about themselves) is well supported as an important motive. Furthermore, self-enhancement is linked to lower acute stress responses, more rapid cardiovascular recovery, and lower baseline cortisol levels (Taylor et al., 2003).

Despite the notoriety of this theory, it did not receive much attention for the first decades after its inception, partially because it was abandoned by Festinger. He was more interested in cognitive dissonance than conformity (see Goethals, 1986). Furthermore, research by his colleague, Schachter, showed that social comparison was more a function of anxiety and affiliation than information seeking. Specifically, Schachter (1959), well known for his research on misattribution of arousal (i.e., the shaky bridge experiment) and the related Schachter–Singer two-factor theory of emotion, found that individuals under stress seek out similar others for comfort. He described this effect with a modification to a turn of phrase: "misery loves miserable company." Further refinement to Schachter's affiliation hypothesis accommodates the finding that affiliative tendencies are nullified in conditions of embarrassment. In this study, Morris et al. (1976) randomly assigned participants into one of three rooms, which were characterized by fear (hazardous electric equipment), embarrassment (contraceptives and books about sexually transmitted infections), and a neutral condition (boxes of forms). The fear condition elicited the most affiliation and the embarrassment condition the least, although participants in both groups reported a great deal of anxiety. This oft-cited study did have a major limitation – there were only five groups per condition and some of the people in the fear groups were already friends.

Although it did not start out this way, the research on social comparison led to better understanding about self-enhancement and affiliation. For example, when self-esteem is threatened, people might engage in downward comparisons by comparing themselves to lower-status referents to restore their perception of themselves (Wills, 1981). Making downward comparisons also plays a role in the coping process. For example, one study showed that nurses under stress engaged in downward comparisons to feel better about themselves (Buunk, Collins, Taylor, VanYperen, & Dakof, 1990). Although threats to self-esteem are certainly a stressor, and diminished job performance certainly a strain, the theory is more frequently applied outside of the job stress literature. For example, a study on leader–member exchange shows social comparisons (e.g., "I have a better relationship with my manager than most others in my work group") correlate positively with job performance and organizational citizenship behavior (Vidyarthi, Liden, Anand, Erdogan, & Ghosh, 2010).

Further testing within a job stress context, perhaps including validated buffer variables, will help determine the applicability of social comparison to stress management in the workplace.

Theoretical Extension: Emotions as Social Information

Emotions as social information originates from Frijda's (1986) social-functional approach to emotion, which states that emotional expressions provide social information to observers and influence their behavior. This can happen through inferential or affective processes (Van Kleef, De Dreu, & Manstead, 2004). *Inferential processes* refer to the information that other people's emotions tell the observer about their own behaviors. For example, if an employee perceives that their coworker is expressing anger, the employee might infer that they did something wrong and will change their behavior. On the other hand, *affective reactions* directly affect observer behaviors through emotional contagion (e.g., mirror neurons) or social signals (e.g., expressions of happiness increase relationship quality). Inferences and affective reactions encourage behaviors, and these behavioral reactions are influenced by social-relational factors, such as the nature of the interpersonal relationship, cultural norms, and display rules (e.g., expectations for emotional expression). The social context can also affect behavioral reaction by modifying the processing of emotional information. For example, in competitive settings, people rely more heavily on inference (rather than affective) reactions, but the reverse is true in cooperative settings (Van Kleef et al., 2004).

EGO THREAT

Social interactions provide information that people use in order to inform their own attitudes and behaviors. Additionally, social interactions are important because they contribute to a person's self-esteem and evaluation of themselves. This is sometimes studied in terms of ego threat. It is difficult to define ego threat theory, as theorists and researchers have historically used the terms *ego* and *ego threat* in broad and varied ways, resulting in a jingle fallacy. Initially, ego threat was implicated in cognitive, emotional, and behavioral phenomena from Freud's early writings, when he defined ego threat as the ego's reactions to events that challenge its ability to negotiate the demands of the id and super-ego. Social psychologists later became interested in the effects of ego threats on people's emotions, self-images, and social interactions. Most recently, ego threat is implicated in behavioral self-regulation (balancing personal desires, biological urges, and the demands of other people and society; or simply successful performance on controlled tasks); or a person's self-image or *self-esteem* (i.e., a person's subjective evaluation of their value).

Similarly, ego is sometimes meant to represent conceitedness. For example, when using this definition, narcissism is characterized by tenuous or low levels of self-esteem (i.e., self-evaluation) and high levels of ego or egotism (e.g., pridefulness, conceit). In colloquial English, the term *ego* does not distinguish among these different meanings.

Most contemporary studies that attempt to induce an ego threat do so by challenging a person's positive self-image or self-esteem in a variety of ways (e.g., priming thoughts of low self-esteem, using deception to indicate that a future event might harm the participant's self-esteem; Leary, Terry, Batts Allen, & Tate, 2009). In fact, manipulations of ego threat that involve negative reactions from other people are indistinguishable from manipulations that researchers use to study reactions to negative social interactions (e.g., ostracism; Williams, 2007). Consequently, even when operationalized as a threat to self-esteem, the research on ego threat is still confounded, unstandardized, and difficult to interpret.

Research and Practical Implications

Within the context of job stress, ego is most relevant through the theory of threatened egotism and aggression (Baumeister, Smart, & Boden, 1996). This theory posits that the combination of inflated self-esteem and an ego threat causes aggression. This has contributed to our understanding of counterproductive work behavior (CWB). Specifically, research has shown that narcissism exacerbates the detrimental relationship between organizational constraints and CWB (e.g., Meurs, Fox, Kessler, & Spector, 2013; Penney & Spector, 2002). Furthermore, narcissism leads to anger, which in turn leads to CWB. However, the correlation between narcissism and CWB was not consistently significant, and the leadership/authority facet of narcissism correlated negatively with CWB, so selection based on narcissism is not recommended. Instead, minimizing stressors continues to be a good strategy for minimizing strain – in this case, CWB.

Theoretical Extension: Need for Belonging

Ego threat might be understood within the context of the need for belonging and affiliation. The fundamental *need for belonging* can be met via regular and affectively pleasurable interpersonal connections that are characterized by long-term stability and affective consideration (Baumeister & Leary, 1995). Similarly, due to the *need for affiliation*, people are driven to have relationships with others and thus form friendships, develop attachments, join organizations, and attend social gatherings (e.g., McClelland, 1961). Ego threat may signal the inability to meet these needs. Failure to meet this need may result in *loneliness*, which is characterized by a self-reinforcing cycle of painful interpersonal experiences due to dysfunctional cognitions and hypervigilance regarding social threats (Baumeister & Leary, 1995). Due to this maladaptive cycle, it becomes difficult to experience rewarding interpersonal interactions. Consequently, loneliness and the thwarted need for belonging are associated with less associative and helping behavior in the workplace.

IDENTITY AND STRESS AS OFFENSE TO SELF (SOS) THEORY

According to identity theory, multiple social roles (e.g., parent, teacher, community member) form the basis of an individual's *identity* or sense of self (e.g., Thoits, 1991). These social roles consist of normative expectations for behavior, and meeting these expectations has implications for self-evaluation. In other words, people make comparisons between their "preferred" level of role performance and their "actual" level as part of a cybernetic control system (Burke, 1991). Discrepancies in this self-other comparison damage self-evaluation and incur stress. Therefore, stressors that interfere with role performance are proposed to negatively impact wellbeing, and the strength of this impact depends upon individual differences in the importance (i.e., salience) of a particular role (Thoits, 1991). As such, job stressors are more strongly associated with employee wellbeing when the job role is important (often measured as job involvement) for self-identification (e.g., Probst, 2000).

SOS (Semmer, Jacobshagen, Meier, & Elfering, 2007) theory reflects a workplace application of identity theory. Specifically, professional roles tend to become part of people's identity and, thus, part of the self. People often have high salience for their professional roles, so threats to the professional role are generalized to their overall self-esteem, thus inhibiting wellbeing. Furthermore, SOS distinguishes between the personal self and social self, such that strain is related to poor evaluations by the self and others (respectively). To elaborate, when a person does not believe they meet their own standards for behavior and performance, they incur stress from poor personal-self evaluations. On the other hand, the social self causes stress when the person does not feel appreciated or belonging, which is conceptualized as *stress as disrespect*.

SOS has been applied to social support (e.g., Beehr, Bowling, & Bennett, 2010). Although social support is typically considered a resource or buffer against strain (e.g., Cohen & Wills, 1985), social support given without regard for esteem can be a stressor. For example, well-intentioned coworkers might suggest quick and simple solutions to an issue. These suggestions, however, imply that the employee had not already considered quick and simple alternatives. Consequently, the employee might feel incompetent (i.e., a threat to the personal self) or that the coworker believes the employee to be incompetent (i.e., a threat to the professional self).

Research and Practical Implications

Semmer and colleagues (2019) integrate SOS theory with resource models of job stress. These consider self-esteem to be a resource, or even a key resource (e.g., Halbesleben, Neveu, Paustian-Underdahl, & Westman, 2014), but self-esteem is central within SOS theory. In this paper, Semmer and colleagues describe the application of SOS theory to best practices within negative feedback. Specifically, supervisors may take efforts to deliver feedback constructively, use a helpful tone, and avoid making personal attributions, but continue to overlook subtle offenses. However, only minimal cues are required to direct people's attention to undermining aspects of a communication (Leary & Baumeister, 2000), so it is likely that unintentional offenses will occur. For example, when delivering feedback, supervisors are encouraged to provide examples of employee behavior to illustrate the negative evaluation. These repeated examples may feel like overkill. Semmer instead recommends the principle of "minimally invasive negative feedback" (Semmer & Jacobshagen, 2010). Related, because unintentional offenses are likely to occur despite good intentions, managers should proactively consider methods for restoring esteem. Future research on minimally invasive negative feedback and restoring esteem would better inform practical suggestions.

Similarly, it might be beneficial to develop training interventions within the context of SOS theory. First, critical incidents of esteem-building and esteem-threatening social support or feedback could be used to identify high-quality communications. These critical incidents could then be content analyzed into themes. Training could target these themes for practice and overlearning. Ideally, overlearning could result in the automatic use of esteem-building social support or feedback, so that unintentional offenses are less likely. This SOS intervention might be particularly useful for diversity training. Specifically, modern racism is often subtle and unconscious. There is already a variety of diversity training that focus on what not to say or do. Instead, SOS-based training might better facilitate esteem-building communications by automating the right things to say.

Theoretical Integration: Social Support Theory

Social support includes both emotional and tangible resources provided by others to meet demands and is a central component of some job stress theories, including the job demands-control-support model. Social support includes emotional, instrumental, informational, and reappraisal resources (French,

Dumani, Allen, & Shockley, 2018). However, there are other measurement methods, including social network analysis, which describes the quantity, and to some extent the quality (e.g., centrality, density), of interpersonal relationships in a person's social network. This measure thus provides information regarding potential social support or the availability of interpersonal support (Cohen & Wills, 1985).

Measurement of social support is relevant to social support theory, which posits that broad measures of social support are better predictors of strain than narrow measures. Broad measures accommodate the varied types and potential sources of social support available to the employee (Cohen & Wills, 1985). Consistent with the bandwidth fidelity and matching hypotheses, specific types of support only match similar, narrow demands. A large, cross-national meta-analysis provides evidence that broad sources of support were more strongly related to work–family conflict than were specific sources of support (French et al., 2018). Furthermore, moderator analysis of cultural and economic contexts shows that social support is most beneficial in contexts in which it fits (e.g., is perceived as useful).

Social support is one of the most commonly studied buffers of the stressor-strain response, but there is debate over whether social support has, instead, a direct or mediating effect on outcomes. There is also robust evidence that poorly applied social support can result in a reverse buffering (i.e., exacerbating, negative moderating) effect (e.g., Beehr et al., 2010). This can occur via co-rumination, stress as offense, detrimental social information, poor fit between desired and actual social support, and other reasons (see Jolly, Kong, and Kim, 2021 for a review and best practices).

Part of the disconnect between early research showing positive effects and later research questioning the buffering capability of social support is that earlier theorizing assumed social support was effective and beneficial, and this is evidenced in the measurement of social support. One such measure, described as "one of the most commonly used" (Beehr et al., 2010, p. 50) includes items such as "How much can your [support person] be relied on when things get tough at work?" However, employees do indicate unwanted social support (e.g., "My [support person] seems to try to help me regardless of whether I want it or not") with at least some frequency, as the mean for unwanted social support was 2.46 on a seven-point scale, and correlated with strains such as physical symptoms and emotional exhaustion (Beehr et al., 2010). Further evidence that typical social support items are written to capture only positive social support can be seen in the negative correlation with unwanted social support. That is to say, the unwanted social support items were written to reflect poor social support and should have some negative correlation with neutral social support items. However, the correlation between poor social support and typical social support was as high as −0.59 (depending on the subfacet), suggesting that typical social support is rather the opposite of poor social support, and not a good coverage of the entire domain of potential types of social support.

CONCLUDING REMARKS

Overall, the theories regarding social information, self-esteem threats from social evaluations, and social support are empirically supported despite concerns about the methods and measurements used across many of these studies. For example, self-efficacy is well supported as a key resource and predictor of job stress. However, Bandura was explicit that self-efficacy is based on the task and not an individual difference. Nonetheless, research on stable, generalized self-evaluations shows similar results, contrary to self-efficacy theory. Overall, research on many of these social constructs is inherently confounded with variables such as embarrassment, ambiguity, and poor performance. This is particularly true within ego threat, precluding consensus about these models. An exception is the theory of threatened egotism and aggression, which seems to accurately describe the manifestation of certain stressors in aggressive responses.

Despite the limitations of testing, the role of social information in job stress warrants further attention. This is because social information and evaluation is inherent in the perception of job stressors and strain. For example, an employee likely seeks information about their coworkers' abilities to manage their workloads before making judgments about their own level of work overload. Employees may also look to others to determine if their strain reactions are appropriate. In general, the research is clear that behavioral, normative, and emotional information from other people inform employee perceptions and expectations, and ultimately their behaviors. Better understanding of these processes can lead to organizational suggestions for training and managing gossip, social support, feedback, and the stressor-strain environment.

REFERENCES

Bandura, A. (1986). *Social foundations of thought and action: A social cognitive theory*. Prentice-Hall.
Bandura, A., & Locke, E. A. (2003). Negative self-efficacy and goal effects revisited. *Journal of Applied Psychology, 88*, 87–99.
Bandura, A., & Walters, R. H. (1977). *Social learning theory* (Vol. 1). Prentice-Hall.
Baumeister, R. F., & Leary, M. R. (1995). The need to belong: Desire for interpersonal attachments as a fundamental human motivation. *Psychological Bulletin, 117*, 497–529.

Baumeister, R. F., Smart, L., & Boden, J. M. (1996). Relation of threatened egotism to violence and aggression: The dark side of high self-esteem. *Psychological Review*, *103*(1), 5–33.

Beehr, T. A., Bowling, N. A., & Bennett, M. M. (2010). Occupational stress and failures of social support: When helping hurts. *Journal of Occupational Health Psychology*, *15*(1), 45–59.

Bingham, T., & Conner, M. (2010). *The new social learning: A guide to transforming organizations through social media*. Berrett-Koehler Publishers.

Burke, P. J. (1991). Identity processes and social stress. *American Sociological Review*, *56*(6), 836–849.

Buunk, B. P., Collins, R. L., Taylor, S. E., VanYperen, N. W., & Dakof, G. A. (1990). The affective consequences of social comparison: Either direction has its ups and downs. *Journal of Personality and Social Psychology*, *59*(6), 1238–1249.

Cheek, F. E., & Miller, M. D. (1983). The experience of stress for correction officers: A double-bind theory of correctional stress. *Journal of Criminal Justice*, *11*(2), 105–120.

Cohen, & Wills, T. A. (1985). Stress, social support, and the buffering hypothesis. *Psychological Bulletin*, *98*(2), 310–357.

Cooper, M. L., Russell, M., & Frone, M. R. (1990). Work stress and alcohol effects: A test of stress-induced drinking. *Journal of Health and Social Behavior*, *31*(3), 260–276.

Ehrenreich, B. (2009). *Bright-sided: How the relentless promotion of positive thinking has undermined America*. Metropolitan Books.

Ferguson, M., & Barry, B. (2011). I know what you did: The effects of interpersonal deviance on bystanders. *Journal of Occupational Health Psychology*, *16*(1), 80–94.

Festinger, L. (1954). A theory of social comparison processes. *Human Relations*, *7*(2), 117–140.

Festinger, L. (1957). *A theory of cognitive dissonance* (Vol. 2). Stanford University Press.

French, K. A., Dumani, S., Allen, T. D., & Shockley, K. M. (2018). A meta-analysis of work–family conflict and social support. *Psychological Bulletin*, *144*(3), 284–314.

Frijda, N. H. (1986). *The emotions*. Cambridge: Cambridge University Press.

Goethals, G. R. (1986). Social comparison theory: Psychology from the lost and found. *Personality and Social Psychology Bulletin*, *12*(3), 261–278.

Halbesleben, J. R., Neveu, J. P., Paustian-Underdahl, S. C., & Westman, M. (2014). Getting to the "COR" understanding the role of resources in conservation of resources theory. *Journal of Management*, *40*(5), 1334–1364.

Jolly, P. M., Kong, D. T., & Kim, K. Y. (2021). Social support at work: An integrative review. *Journal of Organizational Behavior*, *42*(2), 229–251.

Leary, M. R., & Baumeister, R. F. (2000). The nature and function of self-esteem: Sociometer theory. In M. P. Zanna (Ed.), *Advances in experimental social psychology* (Vol. 32, pp. 1–62). Academic Press.

Leary, M. R., Terry, M. L., Batts Allen, A., & Tate, E. B. (2009). The concept of ego threat in social and personality psychology: Is ego threat a viable scientific construct? *Personality and Social Psychology Review*, *13*(3), 151–164.

McClelland, D. (1961). *The achieving society*. Van Nostrand Company.

McLain, D. L. (2014). Sensitivity to social information, social referencing, and safety attitudes in a hazardous occupation. *Journal of Occupational Health Psychology*, *19*(4), 425–436.

Meurs, J. A., Fox, S., Kessler, S. R., & Spector, P. E. (2013). It's all about me: The role of narcissism in exacerbating the relationship between stressors and counterproductive work behavior. *Work and Stress, 27*(4), 368–382.

Miller, N. E., & Dollard, J. (1941). *Social learning and imitation.* Yale University Press.

Morris, W. N., Worchel, S., Bois, J. L., Pearson, J. A., Rountree, C. A., Samaha, G. M., Wachtler, J., & Wright, S. L. (1976). Collective coping with stress: Group reactions to fear, anxiety, and ambiguity. *Journal of Personality and Social Psychology, 33*(6), 674–679.

Penney, L. M., & Spector, P. E. (2002). Narcissism and counterproductive work behavior: Do bigger egos mean bigger problems? *International Journal of Selection and Assessment, 10*(1), 126–134.

Probst, T. M. (2000). Wedded to the job: Moderating effects of job involvement on the consequences of job insecurity. *Journal of Occupational Health Psychology, 5*(1), 63–73.

Rotter, J. B. (1954). *Social learning and clinical psychology.* Prentice-Hall.

Röttger, S., Maier, J., Krex-Brinkmann, L., Kowalski, J. T., Krick, A., Felfe, J., & Stein, M. (2017). Social cognitive aspects of the participation in workplace health promotion as revealed by the theory of planned behavior. *Preventive Medicine, 105*, 104–108.

Salancik, G. R., & Pfeffer, J. (1978). A social information processing approach to job attitudes and task design. *Administrative Science Quarterly, 23*(2), 224–253.

Schachter, S. (1959). *The psychology of affiliation: Experimental studies of the sources of gregariousness.* Stanford University Press.

Semmer, N. K., & Jacobshagen, N. (2010). Illegitimate tasks and counterproductive work behavior. *Applied Psychology, 59*(1), 70–96.

Semmer, N., Jacobshagen, N., Meier, L., & Elfering, A. (2007). Occupational stress research: The stress-as-offense-to-self perspective. In S. McIntyre & J. Houdmont (Eds), *Occupational health psychology: European perspectives on research, education and practice* (Vol. 2, pp. 41–58). Nottingham University Press.

Semmer, N. K., Tschan, F., Jacobshagen, N., Beehr, T. A., Elfering, A., Kälin, W., & Meier, L. L. (2019). Stress as offense to self: A promising approach comes of age. *Occupational Health Science, 3*, 205–238.

Taylor, S. E., Lerner, J. S., Sherman, D. K., Sage, R. M., & McDowell, N. K. (2003). Are self-enhancing cognitions associated with healthy or unhealthy biological profiles? *Journal of Personality and Social Psychology, 85*(4), 605–615.

Thoits, P. A. (1991). On merging identity theory and stress research. *Social Psychology Quarterly, 54*(2), 101–112.

Van Kleef, G. A., De Dreu, C. K. W., & Manstead, A. S. R. (2004). The interpersonal effects of emotions in negotiations: A motivated information processing approach. *Journal of Personality and Social Psychology, 87*(4), 510–528.

Vidyarthi, P. R., Liden, R. C., Anand, S., Erdogan, B., & Ghosh, S. (2010). Where do I stand? Examining the effects of leader–member exchange social comparison on employee work behaviors. *Journal of Applied Psychology, 95*(5), 849–861.

Williams, K. D. (2007). Ostracism. *Annual Review of Psychology, 58*, 425–452.

Wills, T. A. (1981). Downward comparison principles in social psychology. *Psychological Bulletin, 90*(2), 245–271.

Yun, M., Roach, K. N., Do, N., & Beehr, T. A. (2020). It's not how you say it, but what you say: Communication valence in the workplace and employees' reactions. *Occupational Health Science, 4*, 357–374.

8. Theories about job demands and resources

Throughout the early (and perhaps middle) stages of industrial organizational psychology, the topic of job stress was largely unwanted, likely because of the overlap with clinical psychology (Beehr, 1998). However, the 1970s were met with an explosion of job stress research, marked by the publishing of a relevant book (Cooper & Payne, 1978), and a comprehensive review of the literature cobbled together from the nebulous studies from across psychology and medical studies of stress (Beehr & Newman, 1978). The general trend of early job stress theories was to include a demand and one or more resources that acted as a buffer. Certainly, many other theories have included demands (e.g., inequity) or resources (e.g., self-efficacy), but the theories in this lineage did so overtly and specifically within the context of job stress. Initially, the job demands-control model (Karasek, 1979) focuses on any demand (in principle, although uncertainty and time pressure were the most common operationalizations) and a single resource – control. The adaptation of this (the job demands-control-support theory) focuses on demands and two resources. The theory was further modified to include any demands and resources (job demands-resources model; Demerouti, Nachreiner, Bakker, & Schaufeli, 2001).

The job demands-resources model is currently one of the most inclusive and adaptable frameworks for understanding work stress. This theory, which states that stressors or demands only result in strain when they are not offset by resources, runs parallel to other job stress theories. The effort-recovery model holds that efforts deplete resources and must be recovered, either passively over time (through stressor detachment) or actively through relaxation or nonwork resource crossover (e.g., mastery or control experiences). The stressor-detachment process is further elaborated within mindfulness-to-meaning theory, suggesting that mindfulness training can strengthen detachment.

THE JOB DEMANDS-CONTROL MODEL

According to the job demands-control model (Karasek, 1979), highly demanding jobs that offer too little control over work will induce strain. Demands are often operationalized as *uncertainty* (i.e., a lack of job-related information that is needed to perform well) or *time pressure* (i.e., running out of time to complete tasks). Both of these demands predict negative outcomes, including frustration, job dissatisfaction, and decreased wellbeing. Conversely, control is typically operationalized as *decision latitude*, which reflects the employees' authority to make decisions and ability to carry out those decisions. Traditionally, job control has been seen as decision latitude to meet or reduce demands, thus protecting against strain and facilitating coping. Strain is measured in a variety of ways, including level of physiological arousal and impaired psychological wellbeing, among others.

Four job conditions are proposed to describe the demands-control relationship. Within jobs with high job control, employees might experience low demands (i.e., *low strain* condition) or high demands (i.e., *active* condition). Within low-control jobs, employees might have low demands (i.e., *passive* condition) or high demands (i.e., *high strain* condition). The *strain hypothesis* states that when demands are additively increased and control decreased, the likelihood of strain increases, such that wellbeing will be worse within the high strain condition. These four conditions, however, reflect a deficient model as many job demands and resources are omitted. Furthermore, despite a large amount of testing, there is weak empirical support for a multiplicative effect (i.e., interaction). Thus, researchers expanded the model to include another resource – social support.

Theoretical Extension: The Job Demands-Control-Support Model

As an update to the original model, Karasek and Theorell (1990) clarified the job demands-control model and proposed the addition of social support as a resource. Altogether, the job demands-control-support model includes three key variables. *Job demands* constitute physical, social, or organizational aspects of the job that require physical or mental effort. Consistent with arousal theory, job demands that are too high or too low are expected to result in strain. However, like with arousal theory, this curvilinear effect has not been empirically supported. Instead, job demands relate to strain in a positive linear relationship. Next, *job control* describes an employee's evaluation of their ability to effect a change within their work environment. Finally, *workplace social support* is believed to reflect tangible and intangible job-related assistance from others that can reduce the burden on the employee's personal resources. This again has weak support for the interaction effect.

This theory has been further refined. In one such modification, authors assert that the model is valid when the types of job demands, control, and support match. For example, interpersonal conflict is better resolved by interpersonal resources than financial resources. The matching effect does seem to result in more support for the model, but begins to approximate person-job fit theory. In other words, the hypothesis that the characteristics of the job should match employee characteristics, including knowledge, skills, abilities, and other characteristics, is more aligned with person–job fit than with the job demands-control-support model (Fila, 2016). In another modification, the three-way interaction within job demands-control-support was proposed to be valid for hindrance, but not challenge stressors (Dawson, O'Brien, & Beehr, 2016). Because challenge stressors evoke resource investment, and hindrance stressors prompt conservation of resources, resources were likely to be expended when facing challenge stressors.

Research and Practical Implications

Reviews of the job demands-control(-support) interaction are generally pessimistic (e.g., in one review, 29 of 97 articles support the job demands-control interaction; in another review, only 7 of 52 showed the three-way job demands-control-support interaction; Häusser, Mojzisch, Niesel, & Schulz-Hardt, 2010). There are a few potential reasons for this. First, the model with buffering effects might simply be incorrect and the rare studies that provide evidence for the buffering hypotheses might reflect Type I errors. Second, the effect sizes of the multiplicative effects might be substantially lower than the effect sizes for additive effects, making it difficult to detect in hierarchical regression. Third, there may be additional boundaries to this model. For example, it may only work for hindrance stressors or when the demands and resources fit.

Considering the relative lack of support for interactive effects found in previous research, de Lange, Taris, Kompier, Houtman, and Bongers (2003) conducted a review using "high-quality" studies. Overall, only 19 studies were qualified, in which eight studies showed support for strain hypothesis and only one study showed support for the interactive effect hypothesis, concluding that high-quality studies do not provide stronger support. In another review, Häusser and colleagues (2010) assessed the role of study methodology in 87 studies and identified methodological characteristics that affect the detection of an effect. For one, a sufficiently large sample (i.e., power) is associated with nearly unilateral support for additive effects of demands, control, and social support, as per the additive strain hypothesis. Although adequate statistical power ensures detection of any effect, even those meaningless in magnitude (i.e., Meehl's 1990 "crud factor"), the large sample sizes provide confidence that the effect is in the expected direction and robust. Also, additive effects were consistently lower in longitudinal studies than cross-sectional studies, possibly due to noise introduced over time or reverse-causal effects being included in the cross-sectional studies. A less flattering explanation would be that the cross-sectional studies contain more common method variance, artificially inflating the effect sizes. Indeed, evidence for interactive effects was again sparse: 30 percent provide partial support for demands-control interaction, 13 percent provide full support, and 6 percent show a three-way interaction. Finally, models that reflected the job demands-control-support model received less support than models that only included job demands and control, possibly due to the increased difficulty of detecting three-way interactions.

The existence of additive effects has been established beyond doubt, precluding the need for additional studies that demonstrate only zero-order correlations (see Beehr, Glaser, Canali, & Wallwey, 2001). However, "if main effects are all that constitute the theory, then demands and lack of control are simply a set of independent stressors with no necessary relationship to each other" (Beehr et al., 2001, p. 117). In other words, job demands, control, and support are not a model, just some variables that predict wellbeing. It is truly unusual that a model with so little empirical support continues to receive attention, with a substantial proportion of the research dedicated to showing how incorrect it is. Part of the reason for this might be that this is an older theory, and replications and null effects used to be more publishable than they are now. On the other side, proponents of the job demands-control model and the job demands-control-support model argue that the basic premise is supported if demands, control, (and support) separately exert main effects on strain, which is well documented. After all, implications for job redesign are equivalent whether effects are additive or multiplicative.

JOB DEMANDS-RESOURCES MODEL

Various modifications have been made to the job demands-control model over time. The largest of these was to broaden the buffer variable to include any resource, not just control, leading to the development of the job demands-resources model (Demerouti et al., 2001). The primary tenet of this model is that work contexts with high job demands and low job resources necessitate greater depletion and induce strain (e.g., reduced employee motivation, burnout; Demerouti et al., 2001). Within this theory, *job demands* refer to "physical, social, or organizational aspects of the job associated with certain physiological or psychological costs due to required sustained effort" (Demerouti et al., 2001, p. 501). *Job resources*, on the other hand, refer to aspects of the job that may facilitate the achievement of work goals, prevent job demands, reduce the impact of job demands on strain, or promote personal growth.

Research and Practical Implications

This model has garnered better empirical support than its predecessors. However, evidence for the interactions is again weak (e.g., Hu, Schaufeli, & Taris, 2011) and has been abandoned by some (e.g., Schaufeli, 2017). For example, one study of employees working in home care organizations found that job demands are positively associated with the exhaustion component of burnout, whereas job resources are negatively related to cynicism and positively related to professional efficacy (Bakker, Demerouti, Taris, Schaufeli, & Schreurs, 2003). Another study found positive correlations between job demands and burnout, as well as negative correlations between resources and physical and emotional exhaustion, in a sample of coal miners (Li & Wang, 2009). Similarly, Schaufeli (2017) states that job demands and resources contribute to burnout and engagement, and that increasing resources hits two birds with one stone. This is different from a multiplicative effect, in which a zero level of either variable should predict no outcome (e.g., no improvement to engagement), because zero (e.g., resources) multiplied by anything (e.g., demands) is zero (e.g., engagement). Nonetheless, it is clear that both job demands and resources impact strain, at least in an additive way.

The current iteration of this model is strong and has robust empirical support (see Schaufeli, 2017, for a historical account). One optimal feature is the inclusion of eustress, typically operationalized as engagement in this model. Another strength is the relatively specific definition of resources (i.e., they must be goal-relevant), as opposed to the rather tautological definitions used within other contexts (i.e., anything of value). That said, the definition of demands (i.e., any aspect of the job that has costs due to sustained effort) is somewhat circular because "costs" are very nearly the definition of strain, or at least depletion. Other weaknesses in the model have been addressed with the model changing over time to reflect empirical findings, adding to its strength. For one, the interaction has been largely abandoned (e.g., Schaufeli, 2017; Xanthopoulou, Bakker, Demerouti, & Schaufeli, 2009). Also, the conceptualization of resources has been modified to include *personal resources*, defined as a person's self-evaluation that they can successfully control and influence their environment, similar to outcome and self-efficacy expectancies. To elaborate, trait resources (e.g., locus of control) predict demands and resources, whereas state levels of personal resources (e.g., self-efficacy) mediate the relationship between job resources and outcomes (Xanthopoulou et al., 2009). This concept, and others like "engaging leadership," have been integrated into certain iterations of the job demands-resources model from self-determination theory. Finally, a measure entitled the Energy Compass has been developed in order to specifically measure job demands, job resources, personal resources, and both distress- and eustress-related outcomes (Schaufeli, 2017).

Altogether, the dynamic processes are of central importance, as the recipro-cal unfolding of these stressor–strain relationships over time is what makes this a model. Otherwise, these are just some variables that relate to strain (Beehr et al., 2001). Despite strong empirical support, this model fails to meet criteria for a theory, as it does not really explain why stressors lead to strain. Nonetheless, this model is valuable because it informs practical decisions. For a com-prehensive review of current findings regarding the job demands-resources model, and the application thereof to stress interventions, see Schaufeli (2017). Schaufeli's (2017) cyclical model is much like Lewin's action research model, which is often applied to organizational change. Lewin's model emphasizes collaboration with organizational stakeholders within each stage of a cyclical process, starting with problem identification, then developing a hypothesis, followed by hypothesis testing, and then data interpretation. This cycle is repeated until the aims are satisfied. In Schaufeli's (2017) model, aims and the research team guide customization of the Energy Compass, which is used in a communication campaign prior to sending out the survey to establish individual baseline measures. Then, responses are subjected to priority anal-ysis and reported to top management in survey feedback. Then, team- and organization-level measures are discussed with top management to inform interventions (e.g., update the organization's training curriculum to meet the needs of the employees). Some time after the intervention is completed, out-comes are evaluated in a follow-up measure. If desired, the follow-up can be used to help guide aims for another organizational change attempt, restarting the cycle.

Theoretical Extension: Success-Resource Model of Job Stress

Like the job demands-resources model, the success-resource model also emphasizes resources, in this case, subjective success. The primary tenet is that subjectively experienced success at work promotes health and wellbeing, and buffers the effect of job stressors on strain (Grebner, Elfering, & Semmer, 2010). This model integrates aspects of the cognitive theory of emotion (Lazarus, 1991) and affective events theory (Weiss & Cropanzano, 1996). *Subjective occupational success* describes positive, meaningful work events resulting from the employees' behaviors that are relevant to their personal work goal attainment or progress. According to this model, it is the subjective perception, appraisal, meaning, and interpretation of job-related events that determines responses.

CROSSOVER OF RESOURCES

Crossover explains how resources expended or gained can affect another person. *Crossover* involves the transmission of states (resources, stressors, strains) between closely related people (Westman, 2002). For example, vigor and dedication expressed by one partner affected the other partner, even when controlling for relevant aspects of the work and home environments (Bakker, Demerouti, & Schaufeli, 2005). Engagement can even cross over a larger group of people and contribute towards a *vigorous organization*, which describes an organization that fosters employee vigor and directs vigor towards organizational goals (Shirom, 2011). This interpersonal resource transmission can occur via direct (e.g., empathy) or indirect processes (e.g., interpersonal resource caravan). For example, if an employee receives instrumental support from a coworker, they may be able to dedicate more time and energy towards supporting their spouse at home. Crossover of resources can also be explained using self-expansion theory (Aron, Aron, Tudor, & Nelson, 1991), wherein people in an intimate relationship increasingly integrate their partners' characteristics into their own self-concept. Thus, resources like self-esteem can become incorporated into the other person's identity (e.g., Neff, 2012).

Furthermore, a person's stress at work may lead to their partner's stress at home. This is unlike work–family conflict, which refers to a transfer of states within a person – from work to home. For example, one study shows that high job demands require employees to devote more resources (e.g., time, emotional labor) to work, leaving them with fewer resources to devote to their family (Xanthopoulou, Bakker, Oerlemans, & Koszucka, 2018). Thus, the employee is unable to devote resources to home, leaving their partner to expend additional resources to maintain the household. Furthermore, it is possible that depletion results in decreased frustration tolerance, so that the partner must also expend resources to maintain civil relationships.

Crossover can be integrated with stressor-detachment theory. Specifically, resource loss via crossover is cyclical, such that resource loss at work can impact resource loss at home and can thereby incur future resource loss at work. To stop the cycle, nonwork time can be used to recover resources expended during work. To elaborate, the recovery of strain and allostatic load during the nonwork time can allow detachment and relaxation and enable physical recovery from heightened arousal at work. Detachment can be inhibited by use of information communication technology during nonwork time (e.g., Park, Liu, & Headrick, 2020) and social undermining (e.g., bickering; Bakker, Westman, & van Emmerik, 2009), so this suggestion, like many others, is simple but not easy.

EFFORT-RECOVERY MODEL

The effort-recovery model, based on the load-capacity model from exercise physiology, emphasizes resource replenishment (e.g., Meijman & Mulder, 1998). According to this model, employees mobilize psychological resources (e.g., effort, energy) to engage in job activities and cope with demands. This resource mobilization then leads to both task performance and depleted resources. Recovery then occurs when the work-related processes end (usually at the end of the work day) or the employee incurs negative effects (e.g., exhaustion). *Energy* is the key resource within this model and encompasses both physical energy (i.e., capacity to perform work) and energetic activation (i.e., subjective feeling of being energized; Hunter & Wu, 2016). Motivation and concentration are other relevant resources, and all of these have finite amounts that vary day to day (Hunter & Wu, 2016). According to the effort-recovery model, resources that are depleted and replenished must be recovered through the activation of the opponent stress process, an extension of how the parasympathetic nervous system must be activated in order to dampen the acute stress response. Recovery allows the physiological and affective systems to return to pre-stressor levels (Meijman & Mulder, 1998).

Recovery experiences are the mechanisms through which recovery processes occur (Sonnentag & Fritz, 2007). The four most researched recovery experiences are *psychological detachment*, which involves abstaining from thinking about work during nonwork time; *relaxation*, which describes maintaining a low activation level; *mastery*, which involves facing a positive challenge to learn something new; and *control*, which reflects perceptions of autonomy during nonwork time (Sonnentag & Fritz, 2007). Detachment and relaxation can be used to decrease autonomic nervous system activity and arousal, facilitating the physiological replenishment of neurotransmitters, prevent desensitization to these neurotransmitters (i.e., tolerance, accommodation), and allow other allostatic processes to return the body to baseline. On the other hand, mastery experiences reduce activation from work, but also increase personal resources such as competence. Similarly, control can be used to build self-efficacy in nonwork areas (Sonnentag & Fritz, 2007). To summarize, psychological detachment and relaxation reduce activation from work and provide time to replenish resources, whereas mastery and control both increase other resources that might cross over to work via resource caravans (Hobfoll, 2001).

Research and Practical Implications

A meta-analysis on recovery experiences tested the effects of challenge and hindrance demands on vigor and fatigue. In this study, vigor and fatigue were conceptualized as separate affective dimensions per the circumplex model, rather than low and high levels of a single construct. This meta-analysis found that challenge demands were associated with both fatigue and vigor, whereas hindrance demands were only associated with more fatigue (Bennett, Bakker, & Field, 2018). Other surprising findings were delineated, which the authors interpreted to mean that (1) people with more challenge demands have vigor but may be fatigued due to not adequately seeking relaxation activities and (2) employees do not simply avoid thinking about negative aspects of the job but instead prefer to seek meaning in other areas. Consequently, organizations could offer training so that employees can understand, monitor, and adjust their recovery experiences (Bennett et al., 2018). Similarly, organizational policies that discourage working during nonwork hours (e.g., disallowing emails sent outside of business hours) can encourage segmentation and recovery.

Theoretical Extension: Stressor-Detachment Model

The stressor-detachment model is an offshoot of the effort-recovery model and states that employees who encounter more job stressors benefit more from detachment activities but are less able to do them (Sonnentag & Fritz, 2015). This model integrates the cognitive activation theory of stress and the allostatic load model to describe how sustained activation (occurring even when the stressor is no longer present) leads to strain. Herein, self-control is considered to be the key resource, which is presumed to relate to physiological arousal (e.g., cardiovascular reactivity) and ego depletion (e.g., reduced self-regulation, fatigue). These inhibit stressor detachment by impeding the ability to disregard intrusive work-related thoughts, inhibit inappropriate emotions, and ignore distractions. In other words, these negative feelings and arousal induced by engaging in self-control at work encourage anticipation, rumination, and hypervigilance of intrusive work-related cognitions, thereby impairing psychological detachment. Empirical research supports the spillover of ego depletion from work to home, as well as from the employee to their partner at home (Germeys & De Gieter, 2017). Because of this pervasive and cyclical effect, the implication is that employees and organizations should take dedicated steps to intervene in the process by prioritizing segmentation and stressor detachment (perhaps via mindfulness), especially when work is particularly stressful (i.e., arousing).

Theoretical Extension: Mindfulness-to-Meaning Theory

Stressor detachment is clearly important for wellbeing and reducing allostatic load. Mindfulness may also improve stress modulation through stressor detachment and other recovery activities (e.g., relaxation, mastery).

Mindfulness-to-meaning theory is a mechanism by which mindfulness might promote a sense of *eudemonic meaning* (i.e., Maslow's self-actualization, more or less) in the face of adversity, overlapping to some degree with Fredrickson's (2001) broaden and build theory. Specifically, mindfulness allows the employee to move away from stress appraisals into a *meta-cognitive* (thinking about thinking) state of awareness, inducing broadened attention to new information and encouraging reappraisal of life circumstances (Garland, Farb, Goldin, & Fredrickson, 2015). Through meta-cognitive training, mindfulness can facilitate the savoring of positive environmental conditions, which enriches reappraisal. Positive reappraisal then motivates values-driven behavior and finds eudemonic meaning in life. Mindfulness improves a person's ability to experience the meta-cognitive state. Therefore, mindfulness training strengthens adaptive coping through both decentering and reappraisal (Garland et al., 2015).

There is also evidence of a neural mechanism in the mindfulness-to-meaning relationship. Specifically, according to the neurobiological stress-buffering model, mindfulness meditation increases the capacity to regulate attention, behavior, and emotions through relevant neuronal activation (Creswell & Lindsay, 2014). This is supported by empirical research showing that among people with mindfulness training, there is greater mass in the prefrontal cortex, as well as less mass and activity in the amygdala (Guendelman, Medeiros, & Rampes, 2017). Consequently, mindfulness is proposed to act directly and indirectly as a resource in the job demands-resources model (e.g., Bakker & Demerouti, 2017; Bartlett et al., 2019).

Implications

Well-structured mindfulness-based stress reduction interventions have genererally positive, or at least neutral, outcomes (see Bartlett et al., 2019). For example, Haun, Nübold, and Bauer (2018) found that mindfulness at work and at home moderated the relation between job demands and detachment. Job demands only impaired employees' detachment when mindfulness levels at work or at home were low. Therefore, the implication is that mindfulness at both work and home can facilitate detachment from job demands.

CONCLUDING REMARKS

The application of the stressor-strain model to the workplace manifested in a series of job stress theories describing job demands (i.e., stressors) and strains (typically burnout or cardiovascular disease) as moderated by one or more resources. In contrast to the job demands-control model, which emphasizes task-level control, the effort-reward imbalance model highlights the rewards given to employees. These two models affect different aspects of occupational stress and the health effects of the two models are independent of each other (Tsutsumi, Kayaba, Theorell, & Siegrist, 2001). So, although there are similarities, there is no reason to collapse or retire either theory.

Of the theories reviewed, the job demands-resources theory continues to receive the most empirical attention and support. In fact, analysis has become quite complex and the theory has been refined and supported even in longitudinal meta-analysis (Lesener, Gusy, & Wolter, 2019). Specifically, both initial and reciprocal effects have been evidenced, such that job demands lead to burnout, and resources lead to decreased burnout and increased engagement. Reciprocal effects are demonstrated as burnout leads to later job demands and decreased resources, whereas engagement leads to later resources. The interactive effects, however, remain generally elusive, and future testing of the model should adopt a dynamic, reciprocal approach but perhaps abandon the interactive effect. However, a model in which demands and resources additively predict burnout and engagement, which predict later demands and resources, is likely better described as conservation of resources theory (Hobfoll, 2001). Although conservation of resources theory does not discuss demands, in many cases, a demand can reflect a lack of resources (e.g., role ambiguity or conflict could be a lack of role clarity, quantitative overload may reflect a lack of time, abusive supervision is a lack of civility).

Given the tremendous importance of stressor detachment evidenced in the empirical literature, it may be worthwhile to practice recovery techniques (e.g., progressive muscle relaxation, breathing exercises) or mindfulness. These may help initiate parasympathetic nervous system responses and otherwise reduce allostatic load and return the body to homeostasis. This may be particularly helpful for people faced with challenge stressors, or other people who have difficulty detaching from work. However, this has not been tested. In fact, mindfulness is meta-analytically linked to reduced depression, but has been shown to be ineffective for clinical levels of anxiety (Strauss, Cavanagh, Oliver, & Pettman, 2014). The other caveat is that proper mindfulness training truly requires expert guidance and practice. The naive understanding of mediation and mindfulness may suggest "imagining yourself on a nice beach," but this is more consistent with guided imagery. Mindfulness is instead a state of awareness and acceptance of the present moment and internal states (e.g., bodily sensations, emotions, thoughts). In a departure from the mindfulness-to-meaning theory, mindfulness does not inherently encourage positive reappraisal, simply nonjudgmental acceptance.

REFERENCES

Aron, A., Aron, E. N., Tudor, M., & Nelson, G. (1991). Close relationships as including other in the self. *Journal of Personality and Social Psychology, 60*(2), 241–253.

Bakker, A. B., & Demerouti, E. (2017). Job demands-resources theory: Taking stock and looking forward. *Journal of Occupational Health Psychology, 22*(3), 273–285.

Bakker, A. B., Demerouti, E., & Schaufeli, W. B. (2005). The crossover of burnout and work engagement among working couples. *Human Relations, 58*(5), 661–689.

Bakker, A B., Demerouti, E., Taris, T. W., Schaufeli, W. B., & Schreurs, P. J. G. (2003). A multigroup analysis of the job demands-resources model in four home care organizations. *International Journal of Stress Management, 10*(1), 16–38.

Bakker, A. B., Westman, M., & van Emmerik, H. I. (2009). Advancements in crossover theory. *Journal of Managerial Psychology, 24*(3), 206–219.

Bartlett, L., Martin, A., Neil, A. L., Memish, K., Otahal, P., Kilpatrick, M., & Sanderson, K. (2019). A systematic review and meta-analysis of workplace mindfulness training randomized controlled trials. *Journal of Occupational Health Psychology, 24*(1), 108.

Beehr, T. A. (1998). Research on occupational stress: An unfinished enterprise. *Personnel Psychology, 51*(4), 835–844.

Beehr, T. A., Glaser, K. M., Canali, K. G., & Wallwey, D. A. (2001). Back to basics: Re-examination of demand-control theory of occupational stress. *Work and Stress, 15*(2), 115–130.

Beehr, T. A., & Newman, J. E. (1978). Job stress, employee health, and organizational effectiveness: A facet analysis, model, and literature review. *Personnel Psychology, 31*(4), 665–669.

Bennett, A. A., Bakker, A. B., & Field, J. G. (2018). Recovery from work-related effort: A meta-analysis. *Journal of Organizational Behavior, 39*(3), 262–275.

Cooper, C., & Payne, R. (1978). *Stress at Work*. Somerset, NJ: Wiley.

Creswell, J. D., & Lindsay, E. (2014). How does mindfulness training affect health? A mindfulness stress buffering account. *Current Directions in Psychological Science, 23*(6), 401–407.

Dawson, K. M., O'Brien, K. E., & Beehr, T. A. (2016). The role of hindrance stressors in the job demand-control-support model of occupational stress: A proposed theory revision. *Journal of Organizational Behavior, 37*(3), 397–415.

de Lange, A. H., Taris, T. W., Kompier, M. A. J., Houtman, I. L. D., & Bongers, P. M. (2003). The very best of the millennium: Longitudinal research and the demand-control-(support) model. *Journal of Occupational Health Psychology, 8*(4), 282–305.

Demerouti, E., Nachreiner, F., Bakker, A. B., & Schaufeli, W. B. (2001). The job demands-resources model of burnout. *Journal of Applied Psychology, 86*(3), 499–512.

Fila, M. J. (2016). The job demands, control, support model: Where are we now? *TKM International Journal for Research in Management, 1*(1), 15–44.

Fredrickson, B. L. (2001). The role of positive emotions in positive psychology: The broaden-and-build theory of positive emotions. *American Psychologist, 56*(3), 281–226.

Garland, E. L., Farb, N. A. R., Goldin, P., & Fredrickson, B. L. (2015). Mindfulness broadens awareness and builds eudaimonic meaning: A process model of mindful positive emotion regulation. *Psychological Inquiry, 26*(4), 293–314.

Germeys, L., & De Gieter, S. (2017). Clarifying the dynamic interrelation of conflicts between the work and home domain and counterproductive work behaviour. *European Journal of Work and Organizational Psychology*, *26*(3), 457–467.

Grebner, S., Elfering, A., & Semmer, N. K. (2010). The success resource model of job stress. In P. L. Perrewé & D. C. Ganster (Eds), *New developments in theoretical and conceptual approaches to job stress* (pp. 61–108). Emerald.

Guendelman, S., Medeiros, S., & Rampes, H. (2017). Mindfulness and emotion regulation: Insights from neurobiological, psychological, and clinical studies. *Frontiers in Psychology*, *8*(220), 1–23.

Haun, V. C., Nübold, A., & Bauer, A. G. (2018). Being mindful at work and at home: Buffering effects in the stressor-detachment model. *Journal of Occupational and Organizational Psychology*, *91*(2), 385–410.

Häusser, J., Mojzisch, A., Niesel, M., & Schulz-Hardt, S. (2010). Ten years on: A review of recent research on the job demand-control(-support) model and psychological well-being. *Work and Stress*, *24*(1), 1–35.

Hobfoll, S. E. (2001). The influence of culture, community, and the nested-self in the stress process: Advancing conservation of resource theory. *Applied Psychology: An International Review*, *50*(3), 337–421.

Hu, Q., Schaufeli, W. B., & Taris, T. W. (2011). The job demands-resources model: An analysis of additive and joint effects of demands and resources. *Journal of Vocational Behavior*, *79*(1), 181–190.

Hunter, E. M., & Wu, C. (2016). Give me a better break: Choosing workday break activities to maximize resource recovery. *Journal of Applied Psychology*, *101*(2), 302–311.

Karasek, R. A. (1979). Job demands, job decision latitude, and mental strain: Implications for job redesign. *Administrative Science Quarterly*, *24*(2), 285–308.

Karasek, R. A., & Theorell, T. (1990). *Healthy work: Stress, productivity, and the reconstruction of working life*. Basic Books.

Lazarus, R. S. (1991). Cognition and motivation in emotion. *American Psychologist*, *46*, 352–367.

Lesener, T., Gusy, B., & Wolter, C. (2019). The job demands-resources model: A meta-analytic review of longitudinal studies. *Work and Stress*, *33*(1), 76–103.

Li, N. W., & Wang, X. F. (2009). The job demands-resources model of coal miners job burnout. *Chinese Mental Health Journal*, *23*(7), 515–520.

Meehl, P. E. (1990). Why summaries of research on psychological theories are often uninterpretable. *Psychological Reports*, *66*(1), 195–244.

Meijman, T. F., & Mulder, G. (1998). Psychological aspects of workload. In P. J. D. Drenth, H. Thierry, & C. J. de Wolff (Eds), *Handbook of work and organizational: Work psychology* (Vol. 2, 2nd Ed., pp. 5–33). Psychology Press/Erlbaum.

Neff, A. (2012). What's mine is yours: The crossover of job-related self-evaluations within working couples. Doctoral dissertation.

Park, Y., Liu, Y., & Headrick, L. (2020). When work is wanted after hours: Testing weekly stress of information communication technology demands using boundary theory. *Journal of Organizational Behavior*, *41*(6), 518–534.

Schaufeli, W. B. (2017). Applying the job demands-resources model. *Organizational Dynamics*, *2*(46), 120–132.

Shirom, A. (2011). Vigor as a positive affect at work: Conceptualizing vigor, its relations with related constructs, and its antecedents and consequences. *Review of General Psychology*, *15*(1), 50–64.

Sonnentag, S., & Fritz, C. (2007). The recovery experience questionnaire: Development and validation of a measure for assessing recuperation and unwinding from work. *Journal of Occupational Health Psychology, 12*(3), 204–221.

Sonnentag, S., & Fritz, C. (2015). Recovery from job stress: The stressor-detachment model as an integrative framework. *Journal of Organizational Behavior, 36*(51), 72–103.

Strauss, C., Cavanagh, K., Oliver, A., & Pettman, D. (2014). Mindfulness-based interventions for people diagnosed with a current episode of an anxiety or depressive disorder: A meta-analysis of randomised controlled trials. *PLOS One, 9*(4), e96110.

Tsutsumi, A., Kayaba, K., Theorell, T., & Siegrist, J. (2001). Association between job stress and depression among Japanese employees threatened by job loss in a comparison between two complementary job-stress models. *Scandinavian Journal of Work, Environment and Health, 27*(2), 146–153.

Weiss, H. M., & Cropanzano, R. (1996). Affective events theory. *Research in Organizational Behavior, 18*, 1–74.

Westman, M. (2002). *Crossover of stress and strain in the family and workplace: Historical and current perspectives on stress and health* (2nd Ed.). Emerald Group Publishing.

Xanthopoulou, D., Bakker, A. B., Demerouti, E., & Schaufeli, W. B. (2009). Reciprocal relationships between job resources, personal resources and work engagement. *Journal of Vocational Behavior, 74*(3), 235–244.

Xanthopoulou, D., Bakker, A. B., Oerlemans, W. G., & Koszucka, M. (2018). Need for recovery after emotional labor: Differential effects of daily deep and surface acting. *Journal of Organizational Behavior, 39*(4), 481–494.

9.   Conservation of resources theory

Conservation of resources (COR) theory differs from other theories due to its exclusive focus on resources. Nonetheless, COR has been well tested and generally supported, and notably led to the development of the challenge-hindrance model (e.g., Cavanaugh, Boswell, Roehling, & Boudreau, 1998). Challenge stressors allow an opportunity for mastery or growth (i.e., net gain of resources), whereas hindrance stressors necessarily interfere with goal attainment and provide no opportunity for growth (i.e., net loss or resources). The challenge-hindrance model works well as a prescriptive model (e.g., minimize hindrance stressors, don't give too many challenge stressors). However, much like COR theory, it is not well suited for describing how a stressor or demand will be appraised.

In both models, there is debate over the importance of the objective conditions versus the appraisal thereof (see Frese & Zapf, 1999; Perrewé & Zellars, 1999; Schaubroeck, 1999). This is because COR does not account for cognitive mediation, having been developed based on Cannon's work on emotion and physiological stress (Hobfoll, 1989). Specifically, according to the Cannon theory of emotion, a person could have a physiological reaction without emotion or vice versa. Similarly, people might have a stress reaction (e.g., sweating palms or racing heart rate) without reporting anxiety.

CONSERVATION OF RESOURCES THEORY

There are many misunderstandings about COR theory, resulting in overgeneralizations and misapplications of the model. It is described as "a motivational theory that explains much of human behavior based on the evolutionary need to acquire and conserve resources for survival" (Hobfoll, Halbesleben, Neveu, & Westman, 2018, p. 104). This broad model is more accurate when integrated with a more narrow theory relevant to the particular resources or contexts of interest (Hobfoll et al., 2018).

The basic tenet of COR theory is that people strive to accumulate resources that are valuable to them. Stress (i.e., strain) results regardless of whether resource loss is threatened or incurred, and actual or perceived. *Resources* were initially defined as objects (e.g., car), personal characteristics (e.g., self-esteem), conditions (e.g., social status), or energies (e.g., time and money) that people desire. More recently, the definition was narrowed to include only those resources that support goal achievement, given findings that certain ostensible resources can engender strain (e.g., conscientiousness and social support; Hobfoll et al., 2018). Appraisal of a resource is not typically measured. Instead, resources must be considered within their cultural context. Other variables are measured, including psychological stress (often operationalized as burnout; e.g., Lee & Ashforth, 1996). Although there is no tidy parallel to stressors, presumed (i.e., unmeasured) culturally determined demands or resource loss may fit in most contexts. These terms (demand, stressor, resource loss) are sometimes used interchangeably (e.g., Hobfoll, 2001), but were later differentiated (Hobfoll et al., 2018). Specifically, stressors or demands incur objective resource loss, and thus are included in the loss–strain relationship.

Beyond the basic tenet of COR theory, there are several principles and corollaries (see Hobfoll, 2001; Hobfoll et al., 2018). In the latest explication of the tenets (Hobfoll et al., 2018), the first principle states that, because of negative saliency (i.e., negativity bias, positive–negative asymmetry), resource loss is more salient than resource gain. This is referred to as the "primacy of loss hypothesis." The second principle posits that people must invest resources in order to gain, retain, and grow resources, as well as to recover from resource loss. The third principle is that resource gain is more salient in the context of resource loss. The corollary is that, because resources can be invested into gaining more resources, people with greater resources are less vulnerable to resource loss and more able to invest in hopes of gain. Related, the fourth principle states that depleted individuals are likely to adopt a defensive posture with their resources and invest less. This is believed to be the most explanatory principle but the least tested (Hobfoll et al., 2018). There are two additional corollaries of these principles, which state that initial loss begets future loss in a loss spiral, and that initial gain begets future gain in a resource caravan. These are also testable hypotheses unique to COR.

Research and Practical Implications

COR is one of the most frequently studied theories in job stress research. Some of its components have received excellent empirical support, including the broadest premise that the loss of resources has deleterious effects on outcomes (e.g., Lee & Ashforth, 1996). Furthermore, resource investment affects job performance, safety behaviors, turnover, and absenteeism (Hobfoll et al., 2018). The premise of resource caravans and loss spirals also seems promising, but at least partially because dynamic processes are difficult to test, these have received only limited empirical testing using appropriate methods (e.g., Demerouti, Bakker, & Bulters, 2004). A notable omission, however, is testing on the relative importance of actual resource loss versus the appraisal of resource loss (Hobfoll, 2002). The exclusion of appraisal is highly contentious, but little research has specifically addressed Hobfoll's assumption that the impact of actual resource loss, rather than perceived resource loss, is more important to strain. In general, the relative importance of objective measurement and subjective appraisal (typically of the stressor or demand) should be further investigated. One such study found that the perception of social support was more important than objective social support (Sarason, Shearin, Pierce, & Sarason, 1987). Carefully designed methods and measures will be necessary in order to disentangle resource loss from the appraisal of resource loss. For example, an experimental design that manipulates resource loss and appraisal, or a thoughtfully designed survey that separately measures resource loss and appraisal (perhaps using relative weights analysis) would contribute to the resolution of a very lengthy debate on the importance of objective loss versus subjective appraisal (e.g., Perrewé & Zellars, 1999; Schaubroeck, 1999).

To elaborate, Hobfoll (e.g., 2001) states that appraisals proximally predict strain but do not meaningfully vary within or between persons. Whether the employee appraises three weekly meetings or 20 weekly meetings as a stressor (or demand, or resource loss), meetings positively predict strain. Instead, Hobfoll (2001) states that appraisals are culturally based, such that measurement is unnecessary. This assumption has not received much empirical exploration. Therefore, targeted empirical testing (e.g., comparing variance in appraisals within and between cultures) may shed some light on the validity of this assumption. One such study found that autonomy was significantly related to reduced frustration ($B = -0.08$ and -0.17) and increased job satisfaction ($B = 0.11$ and 0.24) in both American and Chinese samples (respectively; Liu, Spector, & Shi, 2007). However, the qualitative inquiry showed that the American sample reported lack of job control as a stressor more so than the Chinese sample, even though the American employees (quantitatively) reported more job autonomy. Overall, it seems that autonomy is more salient to American employees, but because of cultural and normative appraisal, these differences may not be readily viewed in quantitative data. Consequently, testing of cultural differences in appraisal may perhaps be more insightful if measured qualitatively.

There are implications for the workplace and broader society based on this theory, perhaps chief among them being the need to invest resources into those who are resource depleted. This is to say, people cannot pull themselves up by the bootstraps if they do not have bootstraps in the first place. From an organizational perspective, employees cannot invest their time and energy into new projects or training if they are already depleted. Replacing resources (e.g., limiting involvement in other projects that require time or energy) can help. Alternatively, job crafting can allow for resource caravans.

Autonomy almost always helps, to a point (e.g., Chung-Yan, 2010), such that job control is one of the most well-supported resources or buffers against strain. A *buffer* variable is a moderator that renders a stressor-strain response less strong. In this case, a link between, say, interpersonal conflict and anger might be mitigated (i.e., less strong, buffered) for people who have the autonomy to avoid the offending coworkers (see Figure 9.1). Consistent with this theory, autonomy may buffer against strain or promote wellbeing by allowing employees to invest resources where needed. Continuing the above analogy, people cannot pull themselves up by the bootstraps if they do not have the autonomy to do so.

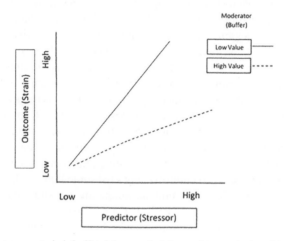

Note: The stressor–strain is buffered (i.e., weaker) for employees who have higher levels of the moderator.

Figure 9.1   Buffering effect

THE COR AND TRANSACTIONAL THEORY DEBATE

Although COR and transactional theory have some common features, they are fundamentally incompatible (Hobfoll, 2001), opposite (Hobfoll et al., 2018), or at least orthogonal. For example, Hobfoll specifically states that resource loss, and not the appraisal, is relevant. Lazarus, on the other hand, views COR as reductive behaviorism. Their arguments were explicated in a point–counterpoint (see Hobfoll, 2001; Lazarus, 2001). In fact, iterations of this debate have been rehashed several times. For example, when translating the COR/transactional theory discourse to the person–situation debate, the appraisal of a demand is informed by personal factors and the objective resources are the situational factor. Hobfoll does not seem to pay much mind to the person, except inasmuch as personality may act as a resource (e.g., conscientiousness; Hobfoll et al., 2018) or confound (e.g., Hobfoll, 2001). Further arguments are delineated below, integrating Hobfoll's writings into those of Lazarus's (2001) response to COR, using quotes from their writings when appropriate to convey tone or specific arguments.

The Role of Resources

Hobfoll (2001) and Lazarus (2001) agree on the definition of resources, and that resources are pivotal to the experience of strain. However, they disagree about which stage of the stress process resources are relevant. To begin, Lazarus (1999) states that stressful person–environment relationships are a function of the balance between environmental demands and the person's resources for dealing with them. In this model, then, resources are relevant in the secondary appraisal (i.e., evaluation of available resources) or coping behaviors. COR theory does not frequently invoke the terms "stressor" or "demand," and is more concerned about the resources associated with stressful events than the event itself (e.g., a layoff event predicts strain via objective factors like employability, financial savings, availability of new positions; Hobfoll et al., 2018). In other words, the resources are said to be directly predictive of strain within this model, rather than offsetting a demand. COR is not interested in the precipitating event that creates the need for resources like employability, so resources are the first part of the COR model. In fact, Hobfoll does not include demands in his model because of its overlap with coping (i.e., resources), stating that:

> The balance model is tautological because it does not separately define demand or coping capacity, the two sides of the model. Demand is that which is offset by coping capacity. Yet, coping capacity is that which offsets threat or demand. Clearly, this reasoning is circular and evolves from the sole emphasis on perceptions … Demand and coping capacity are conceptualized post hoc. We only know that a resource aids coping capacity after it is observed to counteract some demand. (Hobfoll, 1989, p. 515)

Unfortunately, his goal to create a theory that was not "tautological, overly complex, and not given to rejection" (Hobfoll, 1989, p. 515) was hampered, perhaps, by an overly inclusive definition of resources. He acknowledges that "it is arguable that resources are limitless and that as such the theory has circumscribed utility because it is too general" (Hobfoll, 2001, p. 360). To minimize this, he has created a measure assessing 74 resources, and encourages future research on key culturally held resources (e.g., self-efficacy, energy, social support). In doing so, he says, "we have attempted to avoid the slippery slope of devaluing resources until everything that is good is a resource. This vigilance against trivialising resources will need to continue if resource theories are to remain meaningful," (Hobfoll, 2001, p. 360). An alternative definition of resources emphasizing the relevance of resources to goal attainment was later incorporated into COR (Hobfoll et al., 2018). Based on job demands-resource theory, the definition states that job resources include aspects of the job that may facilitate the achievement of work goals, reduce job demands or buffer the effect of job demands on strain, or promote personal growth (Demerouti, Bakker, Nachreiner, & Schaufeli, 2001). The middle component (e.g., "reduces job demands or the deleterious effects of job demands") is again tautological, so perhaps there may be inherent difficulties with identifying resources.

Appraisals

Beyond resources, COR and transactional theory differ in the way that individual appraisals are included via two separate arguments here that are often conflated. The first is the primacy of the objective environment over individual appraisal, and the second is that objective measurement is more valuable than subjective measurement. Regarding the first argument, both authors agree that process (e.g., appraisal) has a place in stress models and that appraisal is the most proximal cause of behavior (Lazarus, 2001). However, Hobfoll points out that if *only* the process is measured, research will be deficient, lacking the ability to predict dysfunction based on environmental risk factors or to compare across organizations. Furthermore, "although perceptions will play a role, [objective resources] will be the prevailing influences on any outcome" (Hobfoll et al., 2018, p. 104). Lazarus replies by asking if "we define 'stressors' in a probabilistic sense, that is, as events or conditions that increase the risk of a reaction in terms of strain? The emphasis on risk is important, as not everyone reacts to the same event or condition in the same way" (Lazarus, 1999). He similarly states, "Thus, an appraisal can be said to be shared only if we settle for a vague statement that all these persons are under stress" (Lazarus, 2001, p. 387). In other words, if research neglects appraisal, we cannot determine if an environmental characteristic is a stressor for each person in a relevant population (e.g., each employee within an intervention), only that it is a stressor for most people. This argument is particularly relevant within clinical psychology, or when applied to tertiary interventions. However, this argument likely falls flat within primary interventions, which intentionally target those probabilistically at risk of strain.

Additionally, Hobfoll et al. (2018) raise concerns about victim blaming due to appraisal. Interventions that target appraisal put the burden on the stressed employee to adjust their appraisals and simply change their minds about the stressor. In a similar argument, Hobfoll et al. (2018, p. 104) state microaggressions are objectively stressful, and "subtle racist and sexist behavior is real and not just perceived by the victim." However, this finding may also suit the reverse argument – stress is certainly in the eye of the beholder, as observers might not recognize a microaggression when it occurs. For example, if a woman is interrupted in a meeting, this might not meet the criteria for a microaggression, but be perceived as one depending upon past experiences, group context, tone of interruption, or other idiosyncratic factors. Nonetheless, because resources are mostly agreed upon within a culture, we are able to have measures that simply list life events, instead of asking whether each is stressful (e.g., Holmes & Rahe, 1967). Hobfoll (1989, p. 514) specifically questions a scale that Lazarus collaborated on, asking "how would it be possible to construct finite lists of minor irritations and hassles (Kanner, Coyne, Schaefer, & Lazarus, 1981), the most perception-bound kinds of stressors?"

Regarding the objective measurement, Lazarus (and most other researchers) agree there is no "universal truth," and that objective measurement usually just reflects a common perception, such that "the word 'objective' can only refer to a subjective consensus among a sample of people about how they appraise a given reality" (Lazarus, 2001, p. 385). Hobfoll instead suggests that objective truth is important and that attempts should be made to even measure self-perceptions objectively. "It would be worthwhile to have clinicians, for example, assess people's self-efficacy and to examine whether this measurement is consistent with individuals' own appraisal of their self-efficacy" (Hobfoll, 2002, p. 319). Regarding behavioral outcomes, Hobfoll (1988) states "objective measurement can be drawn from performance tests, observation, or reliable peer reports." It seems unlikely that another person would be able to provide a more accurate report of personality, self-esteem, or certain (e.g., covert) behaviors than the person themself (unless motivated to represent themself untruthfully). That said, objectivity of measurement lies on a continuum, and other-reports are not necessarily more objective than self-reports (although they mitigate the risk of common method variance; e.g., Schaubroeck, 1999).

For his part, Lazarus (2001, p. 385) states "I can't believe that I still must defend the concept of appraisal, which I first began defending in the 1950s and 1960s in the era of radical behaviorism and operationism." Hobfoll (1989) addressed this, stating that COR is different from behaviorism, as reinforcement theory does not differentially weigh rewards (i.e., positive reinforcement) and punishments (perhaps negative punishment, or the removal of a valued stimulus in order to decrease an unwanted behavior). However, this statement is dated, as the majority of reinforcement theory now converges upon an understanding that positive reinforcement is far more effective than punishment, and that punishment leads to fear and distrust. Integrating the two perspectives, perhaps punishment is more salient than reward, and punishment is more feared and offensive than reward or a lack of reward (i.e., negative salience).

Individual Differences

In an argument that parallels those within the larger person–situation debate (see Gerhart, 2005), Hobfoll, clearly a situationist, dismisses the role of personality and other individual differences. Specifically, he states that individual differences matter, but have no predictive power beyond that of their objective and cultural components. He states, for example, "neuroticism and introversion may play a role by exposing people to greater loss events and decreasing their ability to recover from losses, but resource loss has a robust effect over and above the impact of these personality traits" (Hobfoll, 2001, p. 360). Furthermore, he points out that a resilient person might interpret stressors as a challenge, such that they do not recognize the demands placed upon them. Meanwhile, their coworkers may see these same demands as burdensome. Hobfoll (1989, p. 515) asks, "has no demand been placed on the hardy individuals because they failed to pay it heed, or is it a demand that their strong resources quickly overcame?"

On the other hand, Lazarus (2001, p. 388) states "If Hobfoll regards the theory of appraising to be overly concerned with individuals, as he says, I respond that this is his most serious error, especially when he speaks of the objective environment." Lazarus sees the emphasis on the situation, rather than the person residing within it, to be a problem with psychology more broadly. Instead of emphasis on norms and "central tendencies," he believes we should give more attention to variation between persons. Lazarus further encourages researchers to "put the 'person' back into personality research" and emphasize the study of a whole, dynamic, interactive, self-determined, and goal-determined person (Smith & Lazarus, 1990, p. 632). A more practical argument is that even though appraisals are idiosyncratic, understanding individual differences or other predictors of appraisal would allow hiring managers to perhaps select more resilient employees or develop an overcommitment intervention (e.g., Siegrist, 1996) that targets only dysfunctional appraisals.

Resource Loss

The concept of resource loss is central to Hobfoll's approach and "distinguishes COR theory from appraisal theory" (2001, p. 343). Lazarus (2001) states that harm/loss is one of the three key appraisals in his model, such that he is doubtful that "Hobfoll's definition of loss can contain more information than what [Lazarus means] by harm/loss." However, Lazarus (2001) uses concepts like the loss of a loved one and grief, which are quite different from the concept of resource loss. Replacing resource loss with loss of a loved one within the second corollary of COR would approximate "death begets more death." Instead, Hobfoll's concept of resource loss is different in that resource loss directly, perhaps automatically, invokes a stress response. Of course, the death of a loved one could cause inability to fulfill the need for belonging, meet financial responsibilities, or interfere with the attainment of other resources. Only in this case, as an event that causes resource loss, would a death be relevant within COR theory.

Predictive Power

Perhaps Hobfoll's most consistent argument, maintained from the early writings through the most recent, is that the major weakness of transactional theory is its inability to predict due to emphasis on idiosyncratic and proximal appraisals. Specifically, appraisal "limits the predictive strength and provides few insights into groups or systems" (Hobfoll, 2001, p. 341). Furthermore, "[Transactional theory], however, is limited, because by definition one has to wait until after an event has occurred to recognize it as stressful. This simple fact makes stress-appraisal theories either idiographic or nonpredictive" (Hobfoll et al., 2018, p. 104). Meanwhile, Lazarus (2001) argues that COR theory is unable to predict strain better than appraisal theory. A review of the literature, however, shows that the tenets of COR and transactional theory are both predictive of stress (e.g., Lee & Ashforth, 1996; Webster, Beehr, & Love, 2011).

CHALLENGE-HINDRANCE STRESSORS

The objective–appraisal argument has carried over into the discussion of challenge and hindrance demands. However, the concept that some demands have positive outcomes (e.g., growth) whereas others are unilaterally detrimental has been discussed for decades. For example, Beehr, Walsh, and Taber (1976, p. 42) state:

> overload might increase the motivation to work if the work load is experienced as a challenge, because challenging work increases intrinsic rewards to be gained from successful performance … Role ambiguity, on the other hand, might reduce overall motivation to work by reducing either the expectation that effort leads to performance or the expectation that performance leads to valued outcomes.

This basis in expectancy theory would now be called a challenge or hindrance stressor, and has been studied as such (e.g., LePine, Podsakoff, & LePine, 2005).

In particular, Cavanaugh et al. (1998) proposed that *challenge stressors* "are work-related demands or circumstances that, although potentially stressful, have associated potential gains for individuals" (Cavanaugh et al., 1998, pp. 6–7). These gains can be intrinsic outcomes themselves (e.g., satisfaction) or be useful for promoting future work achievement (e.g., learning and development). Common challenge stressors include job demands and time pressures. Additionally, Cavanaugh et al. (1998) specifically proposed a curvilinear relationship between challenge demands and positive outcomes (e.g., wellbeing), such that at the highest levels of challenge stressors, these stressors will become overwhelming, resulting in a resource loss that will not be offset by resource gains (thus overruling net positive outcomes of the challenge stressor). By contrast, *hindrance stressors* "are work related demands or circumstances that tend to constrain or interfere with an individual's work achievement, and which do not tend to be associated with potential gains for the individual" (Cavanaugh et al., 1998, p. 8). Hindrances are considered an unmitigated source of stress because no significant gains are achieved that offset the resources expended. Unlike with challenge stressors, the authors do not propose a clear curvilinear relationship, noting that although the relationship between hindrance-related stress and negative outcomes might plateau at some point, employees are likely to leave if hindrance stressors become overwhelming. Consequently, because challenge stressors have a curvilinear relationship with outcomes, and hindrance stressors a linear negative relationship, hindrance stressors are expected to have a stronger relationship with outcomes than challenge stressors.

Research and Practical Implications

Overall, these propositions have been supported in that hindrance stressors tend to be more consistently and strongly related to outcomes than challenge stressors. Specifically, meta-analytic evidence from LePine and colleagues (2005) shows that hindrance stressors were more strongly related to strain ($r = 0.56$, 95 percent confidence interval 0.50 to 0.62) than were challenge stressors ($r = 0.40$, 95 percent confidence interval 0.34 to 0.47), such that their confidence intervals do not even overlap. Additionally, hindrance stressors were strongly negatively related to job satisfaction ($r = -0.57$, 95 percent confidence interval -0.61 to -0.52), but challenge stressors had a near-zero relationship with job satisfaction ($r = -0.02$, 95 percent confidence interval -0.10 to 0.05). Furthermore, the distinctions between challenge and hindrance stressors are robust and have been used to refine other job stress theories (e.g., job demands-control-support model; Dawson, O'Brien, & Beehr, 2016).

The potential mechanisms are explored in a study in which day-to-day variations in arousal were expected to play a role in the distinction between challenge and hindrance stressors (Downes, Reeves, McCormick, Boswell, & Butts, 2021). Hindrance stressors may be less likely to vary across time, such that daily variances may cause additional strain. Also, hindrance demands may simply be more arousing than challenge demands because of secondary stressors or emotions (e.g., frustration, worry). Conversely, the effort-recovery model posits that recovery activities are most effective when they induce detachment or relaxation, but also mastery or control. Because challenge stressors may include more opportunities for mastery and control, there may be a built-in "recovery" aspect to challenge stressors.

A point–counterpoint within this topic closely parallels, and at times invokes, the COR-transactional theory debate. This is because Cavanaugh et al. (1998) initially base the challenge-hindrance framework on COR theory, stating that stress leads to positive (e.g., job satisfaction) or negative (e.g., burnout) outcomes depending on whether the stressor involves a net gain or loss of resources. However, later tests (e.g., LePine et al., 2005) are framed within transactional theory. The central focus of the challenge-hindrance model debate is whether appraisals are generalizable enough to be assumed, or specific enough to necessitate measurement. There is valuable evidence for each side of the debate (see Mazzola & Disselhorst, 2019; O'Brien & Beehr, 2019). To summarize two decades of empirical research, appraisals add a layer of granularity and understanding. However, it is clear that organizations should attempt to minimize stressors that are probably perceived as hindrances. The differential outcomes between challenge and hindrance stressors are not particularly contentious;[1] instead, the methodology used to categorize stressors as challenge or hindrance is under scrutiny.

CONCLUDING REMARKS

COR theory and the challenge hindrance model are well supported but not useful for describing whether a stressor will be appraised as a challenge or a hindrance. To elaborate, COR states that appraisals exist but are proximal, idiosyncratic, and somewhat automatic. This contentious claim needs empirical exploration. For example, subjective appraisals are expected to be varied and meaningful when the stressor is ambiguous, objective stressors are not salient, the stressor is not clearly biologically or culturally harmful, and the appraisal is not a challenge to the appraiser's self-identity (Hobfoll, 2001). This is a testable hypothesis that would provide strong evidence in support of this theory.

Arguably, a weakness of the theory is the reliance on objective measurement, as it is sometimes impossible, impractical, inappropriate, or unethical to measure some constructs objectively. At least anecdotally, it seems that some researchers prefer the objective measurement but also dismiss COR theory as seriously deficient due to exclusion of subjective appraisal. The logical conclusion, therefore, is to include both objective and subjective measures when appropriate. However, objective measurement is not always meaningful and accessible, and can be deficient (e.g., absences to measure withdrawal). Ostensibly objective measurement like peer or supervisor reports must still pass through subjective filters like mood, acquiescence, social desirability, and others (Spector, 2006). On the other hand, subjective appraisals (i.e., "This situation is a hindrance"; Webster et al., 2011) are probably redundant with most measures of stressors (e.g., "How often do you find it difficult or impossible to do your job because of organizational constraints"; Spector & Jex, 1998) and therefore overly burdensome for participants. It is ethically inadvisable to overburden participants, so care must be taken to choose only relevant measures.

Common method variance is frequently cited as a reason to avoid subjective measurement, but this argument mistakes subjective measurement for self-report data, and objective measurement for pretty much all other reporting sources. Common method variance is defined as systematic variance associated with a method of data collection (see Spector, 2006). Although all methods have method variance, concerns about method variance are almost exclusively applied to self-report data (especially when cross-sectional), presumably due to acquiescence or mood biases. The best method to minimize common method variance (barring the ability to collect data from multiple sources) is likely to vary the response scale (e.g., five points or seven points from strongly disagree to strongly agree) to decrease bias from cognitive consistency (Podsakoff, Whiting, Welsh, & Mai, 2013).

NOTE

1.   Although Mazzola and Disselhorst (2019) purport no significant difference in burnout for challenge and hindrance stressors, their analytic method was not reported in the paper. A Fisher's r-to-z test indicates that challenge and hindrance demands are, in fact, differentially related to burnout ($z = -8.43, p < .01$).

REFERENCES

Beehr, T. A., Walsh, J. T., & Taber, T. D. (1976). Relationships of stress to individually and organizationally valued states: Higher order needs as a moderator. *Journal of Applied Psychology, 61*(1), 41–47.

Cavanaugh, M. A., Boswell, W. R., Roehling, M. V., & Boudreau, J. W. (1998). "Challenge" and "hindrance" related stress among US managers. Unpublished technical report.

Chung-Yan, G. A. (2010). The nonlinear effects of job complexity and autonomy on job satisfaction, turnover, and psychological well-being. *Journal of Occupational Health Psychology, 15*(3), 237–251.

Dawson, K. M., O'Brien, K. E., & Beehr, T. A. (2016). The role of hindrance stressors in the job demand-control-support model of occupational stress: A proposed theory revision. *Journal of Organizational Behavior, 37*(3), 397–415.

Demerouti, E., Bakker, A. B., & Bulters, A. J. (2004). The loss spiral of work pressure, work–home interference and exhaustion: Reciprocal relations in a three-wave study. *Journal of Vocational Behavior, 64*(1), 131–149.

Demerouti, E., Bakker, A. B., Nachreiner, F., & Schaufeli, W. B. (2001). The job demands-resources model of burnout. *Journal of Applied Psychology, 86*(3), 499–512.

Downes, P. E., Reeves, C. J., McCormick, B. W., Boswell, W. R., & Butts, M. M. (2021). Incorporating job demand variability into job demands theory: A meta-analysis. *Journal of Management, 47*(6), 1630–1656.

Frese, M., & Zapf, D. (1999). On the importance of the objective environment in stress and attribution theory: Counterpoint to Perrewé and Zellars. *Journal of Organizational Behavior, 20*(5), 761–765.

Gerhart, B. (2005). The (affective) dispositional approach to job satisfaction: Sorting out the policy implications. *Journal of Organizational Behavior, 26*(1), 79–97.

Hobfoll, S. E. (1988). *The ecology of stress.* Hemisphere Publishing Corp.

Hobfoll, S. E. (1989). Conservation of resources: A new attempt at conceptualizing stress. *American Psychologist, 44*(3), 513–524.

Hobfoll, S. E. (2001). The influence of culture, community, and the nested-self in the stress process: Advancing conservation of resources theory. *Applied Psychology, 50*(3), 337–421.

Hobfoll, S. E. (2002). Social and psychological resources and adaptation. *Review of General Psychology, 6*(4), 307–324.

Hobfoll, S. E., Halbesleben, J., Neveu, J. P., & Westman, M. (2018). Conservation of resources in the organizational context: The reality of resources and their consequences. *Annual Review of Organizational Psychology and Organizational Behavior, 5*, 103–128.

Holmes, T. H., & Rahe, R. H. (1967). The social readjustment rating scale. *Journal of Psychosomatic Research, 11*(2), 213–218.

Kanner, A. D., Coyne, J. C., Schaefer, C., & Lazarus, R. S. (1981). Comparison of two modes of stress measurement: Daily hassles and uplifts versus major life events. *Journal of Behavioral Medicine, 4*(1), 1–39.

Lazarus, R. S. (1999). *Stress and emotion: A new synthesis.* Springer Publishing.

Lazarus, R. S. (2001). Conservation of resources theory (COR): Little more than words masquerading as a new theory. *Applied Psychology, 50*(3), 381–391.

Lee, R. T., & Ashforth, B. E. (1996). A meta-analytic examination of the correlates of the three dimensions of job burnout. *Journal of Applied Psychology, 81*(2), 123–133.

LePine, J. A., Podsakoff, N. P., & LePine, M. A. (2005). A meta-analytic test of the challenge stressor-hindrance stressor framework: An explanation for inconsistent relationships among stressors and performance. *Academy of Management Journal, 48*(5), 764–775.

Liu, C., Spector, P. E., & Shi, L. (2007). Cross-national job stress: A quantitative and qualitative study. *Journal of Organizational Behavior, 28*(2), 209–239.

Mazzola, J. J., & Disselhorst, R. (2019). Should we be "challenging" employees? A critical review and meta-analysis of the challenge-hindrance model of stress. *Journal of Organizational Behavior, 40*(8), 949–961.

O'Brien, K. E., & Beehr, T. A. (2019). So far, so good: Up to now, the challenge-hindrance framework describes a practical and accurate distinction. *Journal of Organizational Behavior, 40*(8), 962–972.

Perrewé, P. L., & Zellars, K. L. (1999). An examination of attributions and emotions in the transactional approach to the organizational stress process. *Journal of Organizational Behavior, 20*(5), 739–752.

Podsakoff, N. P., Whiting, S. W., Welsh, D. T., & Mai, K. M. (2013). Surveying for "artifacts": The susceptibility of the OCB–performance evaluation relationship to common rater, item, and measurement context effects. *Journal of Applied Psychology, 98*(5), 863–874.

Sarason, B. R., Shearin, E. N., Pierce, G. R., & Sarason, I. G. (1987). Interrelations of social support measures: Theoretical and practical implications. *Journal of Personality and Social Psychology, 52*(4), 813–832.

Schaubroeck, J. (1999). Should the subjective be the objective? On studying mental processes, coping behavior, and actual exposures in organizational stress research. *Journal of Organizational Behavior, 20*(5), 753–760.

Siegrist, J. (1996). Adverse health effects of high-effort/low-reward conditions. *Journal of Occupational Health Psychology, 1*(1), 27–41.

Smith, C. A., & Lazarus, R. S. (1990). Emotion and adaptation. In L. A. Pervin (Ed.), *Handbook of personality: Theory and research* (p. 632). Guilford Press.

Spector, P. E. (2006). Method variance in organizational research: Truth or urban legend? *Organizational Research Methods, 9*(2), 221–232.

Spector, P. E., & Jex, S. M. (1998). Development of four self-report measures of job stressors and strain: Interpersonal conflict at work scale, organizational constraints scale, quantitative workload inventory, and physical symptoms inventory. *Journal of Occupational Health Psychology, 3*(4), 356–367.

Webster, J. R., Beehr, T. A., & Love, K. (2011). Extending the challenge-hindrance model of occupational stress: The role of appraisal. *Journal of Vocational Behavior, 79*(2), 505–516.

10. Person-environment theories

There are several frameworks that describe person–situation interactions as they relate to job stress, including person-environment (PE) fit theory, trait activation theory, and the person–situation debate. All of these more or less originate from Kurt Lewin's field theory. The theory had a major impact on psychology, introducing an understanding of how the environment and individual traits interrelate to cause behavior. Field theory is so named because it posits that a person's life is divided up into multiple distinct spaces (i.e., fields). There are many forces that push a person toward their goal, but it requires them to traverse several fields to achieve it. A corollary is that even if people share the same goal, their fields may vary. Not only do experiences differ between people, but because fields are constantly changing, there are within-person differences in experiences as well. Paraphrased for clarity, Lewin's (1939, p. 888) field theory states:

> It is possible to link a variety of facts about psychology that seem to have very little in common by characterizing objects and events in terms of interdependence rather than their similarity or dissimilarity. Generally, it is more difficult to describe a fact in terms of its effect on others and its being affected by others. However, if one characterizes an object or event by the way it affects the situation, every type of fact becomes interrelated to any other relevant fact that affects the situation. The simple truth is that both facts influence the same situation.

Fields vary in terms of size and strength, and some fields overlap or have disparate impacts (see Figure 10.1). Overall, people are influenced by multiple fields and behavior is informed by the "totality of coexisting facts." PE fit research reflects this breadth by considering fit as an algebraic combination of environmental fields. Consequently, PE fit is the sum of person–vocation, person–job (PJ), person–organization (PO), person–group, and person–person fits (Jansen & Kristof-Brown, 2006). Thus, relevant PE comparisons first include *person–vocation fit* as the broadest level of the work environment. For example, people may choose their job based on their self-identity. *PO fit* (e.g., personal values and organizational climate) and *PJ fit* (usually compares a person's competencies against the job requirements) may inform a person's acceptance of a job offer per Schneider's (1987) attraction-selection-attrition (ASA) model. *Person–group fit* describes the compatibility between people and their work groups, which may influence helping or aggressive behaviors.

Person–person fit is concerned with the alignment between a person's preferences and the values, beliefs, statements, and actions of others. Generally, people prefer similar others (i.e., supplemental fit) based on the similarity–attraction paradigm (Byrne, 1997). Only rarely do opposites attract (i.e., complementary fit). Person–person fit is not typically studied by PE fit researchers, likely due to the granularity of information, and is instead studied within the specific domains of the dyad. However, it seems like an integration would benefit both literatures. Among the literature on person–person comparisons, the most commonly studied comparisons include mentors with protégés or supervisors with subordinates.

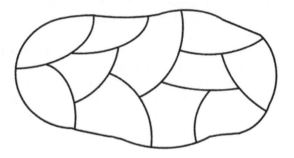

Note: The nature of various fields within an environment are pictured.

Figure 10.1   Lewin's field theory

PERSON–ENVIRONMENT FIT

PE fit theory states that mismatch between the person and environment (e.g., organization, group) causes strain (e.g., French, Rodgers, & Cobb, 1974). This is a reciprocal relationship, with the person influencing the environment and vice versa. Furthermore, either objective (e.g., knowledge, skills, abilities; number of hours worked) or subjective (e.g., self-efficacy; quantitative overload) characteristics can be considered. High PE fit is achieved via attraction, selection, and attrition, which in turn creates a homogenous environment (ASA model; Schneider, 1987). Specifically, people will be *attracted* to work at organizations with which they perceive fit. These people will not be *selected* into the company unless the company perceives fit and vice versa. Finally, if the person notices misfit after joining the company, they may choose to leave or be asked to leave (i.e., *attrition*), either due to poor performance or other reasons related to misfit.

Fit can be conceptualized in a number of ways,[1] typically as the difference between organizational resources and personal goals (supply–values fit) or between task requirements and competencies (demand–abilities fit). *Supply–values fit* refers to the fit of personal desires (e.g., goals, values) with resources provided by the environment (e.g., opportunities, rewards), and reflects a process in which people cognitively evaluate the surrounding environment based on their personal values. Supply–values misfit is associated with poor wellbeing. *Demand–abilities fit*, on the other hand, describes the fit of personal characteristics (e.g., knowledge, skills, abilities) with job requirements and infers a process whereby employees adjust to the demands of their environment by activating their competencies. Demand–abilities misfit can result in poor performance. Empirical investigations have sometimes minimized the distinctions between these models by conflating both types of misfit as interchangeable predictors of the same set of strains. Because both types of misfit do inherently reflect goal frustration, they are both ultimately associated with strain.

Various iterations of PE fit theory have been published since the 1930s. For example, Lewin (1939) defines PE fit as a mathematical formula in which individual *behavior* results in the best outcomes when it is a *function* of the *person* and *environment*, represented as $B = f(P,E)$. In another example, the McGrath (1970) four-step stress model (environmental stressor, cognitive appraisal, physiological stress response, behavioral strain) is a largely cognitive theory, stating that stress is a subjective appraisal of a demand. When met with the appropriate skills, the demand is less stressful. Again, according to Karasek's (1979) job demands-control model, job demands that are met with control are less stressful. Additionally, Cummings and Cooper (1979) showed that a disparity between individuals' preferred and actual state leads to a negative feedback loop and strain. Transactional theory similarly states that stressors are evaluated, and those that are appraised to be manageable are less stressful (e.g., Lazarus & Folkman, 1984). In part, this pervasiveness is due to the conceptual advantages of fit over simpler approaches, including those that view stress as an objective event (e.g., life events scale) or as an automatic physiological response. In fact, PE fit is applied to other outcomes (e.g., job performance) regularly. For example, some research shows that people who fit the organization share values with the organization, such that helping the organization will benefit the individual (i.e., goal alignment; Jansen & Kristof-Brown, 2005).

Research and Practical Implications

The theoretical development of PE fit theory has been robust compared to the empirical support, likely due to practical challenges in the measurement of fit. PE fit is a natural extension of existing stress theories, including need theories and person–situation theories, and provides more nuance than physiological stress, resource, and job design theories. It is clear that PE fit guided a large number of theories across a variety of contexts (e.g., job performance, turnover, wellbeing). However, assessing each person's level of need and fulfillment is onerous, as it is difficult to ascertain whether fit at the organization, job, or group level is most important.

Improvements to the PE fit theorizing and conceptualization have been largely methodological as many common forms of measurement are so poor as to prohibit interpretation. For example, creating difference scores as an index of fit by subtracting participant scores from environment scores causes breakdown of psychometric quality (e.g., reliability, normality, independence of observations) and precludes interpretation, as scores are not anchored to a meaningful metric (e.g., Edwards, 2001). For example, a score of −3 on a scale of autonomy ranging from 1–7 could mean that the environment has a great deal of autonomy (7) and that the individual only perceives a moderate amount (4), or that the environment offers middling autonomy (4), and the individual perceives almost none (1). Failure to distinguish among these possibilities will make it difficult to draw clear implications. Nonetheless, this process continues to be used unconcernedly in PE fit research and remains possibly the most common measure of fit (Zhang, Yan, Wang, & Li, 2017).

There are few good alternatives. For example, categorizing fit based on dichotomization or trichotomization of difference scores (e.g., underestimators, overestimators) has similar inadequacies as well as restricted range and reduced power. Asking the employee if they perceive fit is seen as overly subjective, disposed to common method variance, and potentially biased. The best option is response surface analysis using polynomial regression. In this methodology, the x-axis represents one report (say, the employee) and the y-axis represents the other report (e.g., organization). A z-axis is used to plot the dependent variable (e.g., wellbeing, job performance), creating response surfaces of various shapes. Although this methodology is now easier than when it increased in visibility approximately 30 years ago, it is nonetheless a specialized skill (see Shanock, Baran, Gentry, Pattison, & Heggestad, 2014). Altogether, the required methods, sources of data collection, and analyses complicate the study of PE fit.

The robust theoretical implications nonetheless lend insight into organizational management. For one, management should recognize and respect individual differences, given the finding that people may respond to a job demand or characteristic in different ways. Furthermore, due to the reciprocal relationship between the person and environment, another suggestion is to design jobs to fit people, instead of selecting or training people to fit jobs. Careful job design or redesign, informed by subject matter experts (probably job incumbents), can increase organizational outcomes and individual outcomes simultaneously. Job design and redesign do not have to be expensive, time consuming, and disruptive. Sometimes small, inexpensive changes as desired by employees (e.g., job characteristics like more/less feedback built into the work processes) can improve fit and resultant outcomes.

PERSON–ORGANIZATION FIT

PO fit describes fit between the person and organization, but the development of a literature on this topic has been hindered by nebulous conceptualizations and ambiguous distinction from other forms of PE fit (Kristof, 1996). One conceptualization is *needs–supply fit*, which overlaps with supply–values fit and describes whether an organization meets the wants and needs of its members. *Demand–abilities fit* describes whether an individual has the competencies necessary to fulfill organizational requirements. Within these two comparisons are *supplementary fit*, which occurs when a person is similar to comparable others in an environment, and *complementary fit*, which occurs when a person's characteristics fill gaps left by others.

The constructs of interest within PO fit have also been operationalized in a variety of ways (Westerman & Cyr, 2004). This includes assessing fit as the supplementary match (i.e., consistency) of fundamental characteristics, like values and organizational culture, between the organization and its employees. Or, another type of supplementary fit might reflect an employee's goal congruence with coworkers and leaders. Alternatively, the needs–supply perspective might describe fit between individual needs/wants and their organizational system (e.g., need press theory, theory of work adjustment; Kristof, 1996).

In addition to nebulous conceptualizations and operationalizations of PO fit, there is also a variety of disparate methodological treatments. For example, PO fit can be measured *directly*, by asking people explicitly whether they believe that a good fit exists, or *indirectly*, in which a comparison is made between individual ratings and organization-level characteristics (Sekiguchi, 2004). This can be accomplished using cross-level measurement (i.e., comparing individual ratings with a single organizational score for that characteristic) or individual-level measurement (i.e., asking employees about their level of the characteristic, as well as their organization's level of the characteristic).

There are some criticisms of both conceptualizations. Direct measurement has weaknesses including confounds between the constructs of the person and environment, thereby violating the assumption of independence underlying parametric statistics. Also, some researchers are less concerned with personal perception of the environment than the objective environment. On the other hand, indirect cross-level measurement assumes that organizational indices are "correct," but objectivity falls on a continuum, and many attempts to use objective measurement are simply "more objective" than explicit perceptions. For example, an employee might be asked to report if they are overloaded (a perceptual measurement). The objective counterpart might be to ask about the number of hours worked or number of "works" to be completed (however defined). This objective measurement must still pass through a personal filter, such that an overloaded person might be hypervigilant to additional work, or working inefficiently due to fatigue, thus reporting more hours worked. Overcommitment (e.g., Van Vegchel, De Jonge, Bosma, & Schaufeli, 2005) might also cause greater reports of objective work if employees feel compelled to engage in organizational citizenship behavior or illegitimate tasks. Conversely, supervisor reports of workload can be used. However, supervisors are often detached from the day-to-day operations of employees. Employees who stay late, skip social events, or keep their door closed might not be visible to the supervisors. The alternative, individual-level indirect measurement, is not inherently better as it is optimistic to assume that individuals within the organization view it in a homogeneous way. That is to say, group or department perceptions may color the employees' views of the organization, such that individual-level indirect measurement may be inaccurate.

Research and Practical Implications

Despite these conceptual difficulties, empirical tests of PO fit demonstrate numerous employee benefits. This includes enhanced work attitudes of job satisfaction and organizational commitment using supplementary fit and needs–supply fit (Westerman & Cyr, 2004). A review of PO fit (Kristof, 1996) indicates that positive outcomes include decreased turnover intentions and physiological stress, and increased prosocial work behaviors (e.g., organizational citizenship behaviors, teamwork, ethical behavior). However, several theorists have suggested that high levels of PO fit produce negative outcomes at the organizational level, including a lack of creativity (Farabee, 2011).

PO fit was initially posited as true fit, such that both a deficit and excess of a characteristic can cause strain (Edwards, 1991). A review of research on fit between actual and preferred characteristics considered the misfit between organizational characteristics (e.g., amount of autonomy offered) and employee preference (e.g., the amount of autonomy desired). Positive outcomes might result from a surplus of "actual" characteristics when excess characteristics can be saved for a later time or used to fulfill another need. However, excess "actual" characteristics can hinder the future preferences (e.g., too much autonomy at first can result in fewer degrees of freedom and autonomy for later decisions) or interfere with the fulfillment of other preferences (e.g., too much autonomy can lead to too much responsibility). Consequently, fit likely takes the shape of a curvilinear association with outcomes (see Edwards, 1994 for more visualizations of PO fit). More research is required on these early models of fit, as the current evidence indicates that personal characteristics only result in strain when they are not at sufficient levels to cope with the environment. Negative effects of typically beneficial characteristics (e.g., an excess of qualifications) are rarely shown. For example, perceived overqualification results in less helping behavior when PO fit is low (e.g., Erdogan, Tomás, Valls, & Gracia, 2018), but certain deleterious effects (e.g., reduced job satisfaction) can be ameliorated with empowerment (Erdogan & Bauer, 2009).

OTHER LEVELS OF FIT

Fit can be applied in a variety of contexts, including person–team, mentor–protégé, and person–job comparisons. In terms of person–team fit, teams function better when all group members have similar (preferably high) levels of conscientiousness (i.e., supplementary fit), to ensure similar work values (Prewett, Walvoord, Stilson, Rossi, & Brannick, 2009). However, teams may function better when only some are extraverted (i.e., complementary fit). This ensures enough people are willing to speak up, but also prevents members from competing for airtime. On the other hand, research on mentor–protégé matching is often touted as very necessary, but rarely studied. A few studies have investigated fit in terms of demographics, personality, values (Eby, Butts, Lockwood, & Simon, 2004), and self-disclosure (Wanberg, Welsh, & Kammeyer-Mueller, 2007).

PJ fit is studied more often, and refers to the congruence between the employee and their job (Edwards, 1991), such that the employees' skills match the specific job requirements (demand–abilities fit), or when their needs are aligned with the resources available (needs–supply fit). Similar to other levels of fit, PJ fit is related to better job attitudes, job performance, and wellbeing. Furthermore, newer research recognizes that fit is a dynamic, reciprocal process, with features of both employees and jobs changing over time (e.g., Tinsley, 2000). Thus, research on PJ fit is still making novel contributions (e.g., Vleugels, De Cooman, Verbruggen, & Solinger, 2018).

TOO-MUCH-OF-A-GOOD-THING EFFECT

"Too much" is thought to reflect poor fit (e.g., Edwards, 1991), and the too-much-of-a-good-thing (TMGT) effect describes how commonly valued characteristics (e.g., resources) have a positive relationship with outcomes until they reach a certain point, after which the relationship plateaus or becomes negative (Pierce & Aguinis, 2013). To illustrate, challenge stressors include those stressors that help the employee develop or reach mastery, but in excessive amounts, become overwhelming and harmful. Other ordinarily beneficial resources (e.g., empowerment, financial growth rate) surprisingly lead to negative outcomes at a certain level, suggesting that these detrimental outcomes occur in a variety of situations. However, when the resource can be saved for a later time or to fill a gap in another area, poor fit is unlikely to result in detrimental outcomes. This is intuitive, as "too much money" is a rare complaint. Nonetheless, organizational identity, organizational citizenship behavior, morale, trust, autonomy, team, and group size were all found to have curvilinear effects with performance (e.g., Pierce & Aguinis, 2013).

Research and Practical Implications

This principle is easily applied to job stress theory, with clear translations to allostasis (i.e., some stability through change is adaptive, but after repeated or prolonged exposure can be depleting), arousal theory (e.g., Yerkes-Dodson Law), PE fit, equity theory (e.g., entitlement versus benevolence), and over-commitment (e.g., effort–reward imbalance). In fact, this observation has already been explicated within Warr's (1987) vitamin model, which holds that psychological features of the environment (e.g., job characteristics) relate to wellbeing in a nonlinear manner. The analogy is that vitamins can help our physical health to a point, after which the vitamin has no effect or becomes harmful.

The main theoretical implication of the TMGT effect is that theory-testing efforts should predict not only whether the commonly valued characteristic will relate to positive outcomes, but also the precise amount at which the relationship will plateau or turn negative. This will require more statistical power than we typically achieve. Adding to this concern, job stress domains may inherently be hampered by restriction of range. Stressor–strain relationships are likely to be constrained by norms, expectancies, and contingencies (e.g., payment) that will result in attrition (e.g., voluntary or involuntary turnover). Thus, a disattenuated stressor–strain relationship might not be visible. In addition to testing problems, the biggest limitation of TMGT is that it is unlikely that TMGT adds to our understanding beyond fit.

CYBERNETIC THEORY

Cybernetics or control theory describes how systems can self-regulate through a negative feedback loop. This theory posits that people make comparisons between their current status and some referent, and when there is poor fit, they will have strain. Specifically, a sensor first receives input from the environment and transmits the signal to a comparator. The comparator evaluates the signal against a reference criterion. If there is a discrepancy, an output function attempts to modify either the environment or reference criterion in order to rectify the discrepancy. Within Edwards's (1992) cybernetic theory specifically, stress is a discrepancy between an employee's perceived and desired states, which must be judged to be important. Stress affects psychological and physical health (i.e., wellbeing) and coping, which can influence wellbeing directly or by modifying the determinants of stress (i.e., the perceived state, desired state, or perceived importance of the discrepancy).

Like PE fit, this likely meets the criteria for a formal meta-theory, as it includes higher-order principles that can be applied across a number of different theories. For example, cybernetic mechanisms (i.e., a feedback mechanism) can be applied to Festinger's social comparison (with cognitive dissonance being evidence of changes to a reference criterion), Bandura's self-regulation theory, and, perhaps, goal-setting theory. If people recognize that their efforts result in performance clearly exceeding their goals (i.e., a discrepancy), they may decide to decrease performance or increase their goal (i.e., reference) in the future. Within job stress specifically, role stress theory, Cummings and Cooper's (1979) framework, and McGrath's (1976) model of stress include cybernetic features (Edwards, 1992).

TRAIT ACTIVATION THEORY

Trait activation theory (Tett & Guterman, 2000), like PE fit theory, explains the relationship between the person and their environment in an interactive, dynamic, and reciprocally causal way. This theory posits that intrinsic motivation drives individuals to behaviorally manifest their traits (i.e., personality) when trait-relevant situational features (i.e., cues, activators) are present. People high on a trait are expected to be more sensitive to trait-relevant cues and require less trait activation to express their traits than those who are lower on a trait. Cues occur at different levels (task, social, and organizational) and compete for trait expression. For example, a person who is introverted but conscientious might struggle to speak up at a professional meeting, as introversion may be expressed as aversion to public speaking, but conscientiousness may drive behaviors associated with visibility. There are a variety of such trait-relevant cues, such as *demands*, which contribute positively to trait expression, and *distractors*, which contribute negatively to trait expression. Other cues include *constraints*, which limit trait expression, *releasers* to counteract constraints, and *facilitators* that amplify trait-relevant cues. In the above example, constraints might include discomfort with the people at the meeting, but a releaser might include being told that this is a safe space. A facilitator might include the format of the meeting (e.g., online, face to face).

Furthermore, people alter their environment to increase or decrease trait-activating cues based on a feedback loop. For example, a person who is very timid might avoid customer service jobs to increase their likelihood of success. This proposition conceptually overlaps with PE fit theory. Trait activation theory is often applied to job performance, but has implications in job stress as well. It is unique from, and probably inconsistent with, traditional job stress theory because the trait is viewed as the predictor, not a buffer or moderator of a stressor–strain relationship.

Research and Practical Implications

Although trait activation theory is rarely applied to job stress, the tenets of this theory were upheld in a study of counterproductive work behaviors resulting from job stressors (O'Brien, Henson, & Voss, 2021). Understanding the activation of personality might allow attempts to mitigate detrimental expressions of personality by minimizing trait-activating cues or placing constraints to restrict trait expression. Cue management is expected to prevent behavioral manifestations of other stress-related traits or job situations, as well. For example, negative affectivity could be diminished through positive feedback. Instead of (or in addition to) requesting that customers or clients provide criticism, publicly posting compliments might facilitate the expression of competing positive affect.

However, trait activation theory has not been adequately applied to nonbehavioral manifestations, like physiological stress and ruminative thoughts. For example, failure to express an activated trait may thwart fulfillment of identity needs, thus damaging wellbeing. Empirical testing on this would be highly informative. Additionally, testing of the varied levels of cues (i.e., task, social, organizational) would mirror the research on PE fit and ecological systems theory. It is curious whether proximal but limited task cues (e.g., job demands) or distal but pervasive organizational cues (e.g., espoused values) would be more relevant within job stress.

PERSON–SITUATION DEBATE

The person–situation debate is also relevant when considering the interaction between people and the environment as it describes a philosophical and empirical conflict regarding the relative strength of personal characteristics and the environment (see Gerhart, 2005). Simply put, it asks *is a person's behaviour stable across situations?* Clearly, personality theory would not exist without some stable contribution of individual differences. In fact, it has been said that the person–situation debate is 98 percent over (Funder, 2001). However, this point is still debated today within organizational psychology and job stress research. For example, Hobfoll (2001) takes a clearly situationist approach, admitting only that person factors probably play some uninteresting role. Similarly, Maslach, who witnessed the Stanford Prison Experiments, says that any person can be changed by power, expectations, social norms, motivated reasoning, and situational embeddedness. Lazarus (2001), on the other hand, considers personal perception to be fundamental and wholly essential to the understanding of psychological stress, particularly as person factors interact (or transact) with the environment. Other personalists point out that there is a stable (albeit limited) effect of personality on job satisfaction, organizational commitment, organizational citizenship behavior, counterproductive work behavior, burnout, and wellbeing. Even genetics, certainly a person factor, influence job satisfaction (Judge, Ilies, & Zhang, 2012).

Ultimately, both dispositional and situational factors influence job attitudes, strain, and stress perceptions. In a *Journal of Organizational Behavior* point–counterpoint, Gerhart (2005) argues on behalf of situationists by pointing out gaps in the understanding of person–situation contributions to behavior. He states that, to increase our understanding of person-related contributions to job attitudes and behavior, predictive design and inclusion of moderators such as occupation, industry, and organizational culture are required. For their part, personalists (represented by Staw & Cohen-Charash, 2005) also suggest room for synthesis. They acknowledge that traits are not robust predictors of attitudes and behaviors across contexts. For example, someone who is extraverted may be no more likely than an introvert to command attention at a funeral, but extraversion may predict a distribution of behaviors over time and context that is different from the distribution of behaviors for an introvert. That is to say, individual behaviors have poor cross-situational consistency but high consistency across time, which is explained by distributions around a mean level of a trait.

CONCLUDING REMARKS

As a construct, PE fit transcends theory. Fit can be applied to nearly any other job stress theory. For example, when a person has an acute stress response due to environmental alarm, their characteristics (e.g., age, physical fitness) may mitigate strain. When a person interprets social information, they do so through the filter of their previous interactions with the social group. PE fit is therefore a broad, expansive, and ambiguous application to narrow or idiosyncratic criterion (e.g., how this person will react in this situation).

PO fit has clear applications to organizational culture, for example. *Organizational culture* is a shared understanding of the way things work in an organization (Schein, 1990) and is expressed in a variety of ways, including visible artifacts (e.g., signage), explicit values (e.g., mottos, policies), and subtle behavioral norms. Organizational culture is established by influential leaders via a period of socialization, after which organizational culture has a direct effect on employees and is resistant to change. Thus, culture is stable, guides employee behavior, and reduces ambiguity. In a test of organizational culture using PO fit theory, individual enactment of behavioral norms (i.e., "actual" level) was compared to the extent the employee believes the behavioral norm "should exist" (i.e., "preferred" level; Arbour, Kwantes, Kraft, & Boglarsky, 2014). Organizational cultures were compared according to the Cooke and Rousseau (1988) model. *Constructive* cultures encourage employees to work in ways that will help them achieve higher-order goals, *passive/ defensive* cultures encourage employees to work in a way that will not threaten their own comfort, and *aggressive/defensive cultures* encourage employees to act forcefully to protect their status. On average, employees preferred a more constructive culture and a less passive/defensive culture than they actually had, and the discrepancy predicted job satisfaction. Beyond organizational culture alone, PO fit regarding behavioral norms provided an additional 10.4 percent of variance in job satisfaction and an additional 13.3 percent of variance in intention to stay, but was not related to stress.

In another example, PJ fit is sometimes applied within the context of job characteristics theory via job scope. Job scope is typically an additive index of the five job characteristics (e.g., Xie & Johns, 1995). That is to say, according to job characteristics theory (Hackman & Oldham, 1980), five core job characteristics (skill variety, task identity, task significance, autonomy, and feedback) contribute towards three critical psychological states (i.e., meaningfulness, responsibility, and knowledge of results), which in turn predict motivation and wellbeing. Low levels of job scope can prohibit meaningfulness at work (supply–values misfit). Conversely, high levels of job scope can lead to stress via overload (demand–abilities misfit). Thus, the relationship between job scope and stress (operationalized as emotional exhaustion and anxiety) is curvilinear. However, subjective perception of fit between job demands and ability might moderate the curvilinear relationship between job scope and stress for three reasons (Schuler, 1980). First, ability decreases stress by reducing an individual's perception of uncertainty. Second, high-ability individuals can choose a better strategy to deal with stressors than low-ability individuals. Third, Schuler (1980) points out that high-ability individuals may perceive stressors as challenges, rather than hindrances (although he did not use these terms).

That said, PE fit provides a useful framework for guiding research and practice with at least three messages. For one, the ASA framework shows that both employees and employers consider fit during the organizational entry process, although there is much less evidence that this process incurs harmful organizational homogeneity as originally proposed by Schneider (1987). Perhaps Schneider underestimated the degree to which organizations and prospective employees would consider complementary fit when making decisions. For example, a person might prefer to take a job in which they can flex their skills, or the organization is likely to specifically look for people who can fill gaps. Ultimately, the pool of applicants and available opportunities may be too small, such that practical concerns (e.g., finding a job in the same town) override fit considerations.

NOTE

1. On a side note, it seems that both singular and plural forms of supplies, values, demands, and abilities are used when describing fit, which adds an additional layer of complication to database searches for literature reviews.

REFERENCES

Arbour, S., Kwantes, C. T., Kraft, J. M., & Boglarsky, C. A. (2014). Person–organization fit: Using normative behaviors to predict workplace satisfaction, stress and intentions to stay. *Journal of Organizational Culture, Communications and Conflict, 18*(1), 41–64.

Byrne, D. (1997). An overview (and underview) of research and theory within the attraction paradigm. *Journal of Social and Personal Relationships, 14*(3), 417–431.

Cooke, R. A., & Rousseau, D. M. (1988). Behavioral norms and expectations: A quantitative approach to the assessment of organizational culture. *Group and Organization Studies, 13,* 245–273.

Cummings, T. G., & Cooper, C. L. (1979). A cybernetic framework for studying occupational stress. *Human Relations, 32*(5), 395–418.

Eby, L., Butts, M., Lockwood, A., & Simon, S. A. (2004). Protégés negative mentoring experiences: Construct development and nomological validation. *Personnel Psychology, 57*(2), 411–447.

Edwards, J. R. (1991). *Person–job fit: A conceptual integration, literature review, and methodological critique.* John Wiley & Sons.

Edwards, J. R. (1992). A cybernetic theory of stress, coping, and well-being in organizations. *Academy of Management Review, 17*(2), 238–274.

Edwards, J. R. (1994). The study of congruence in organizational behavior research: Critique and a proposed alternative. *Organizational Behavior and Human Decision Processes, 58*(1), 51–100.

Edwards, J. R. (2001). Ten difference score myths. *Organizational Research Methods, 4*(3), 265–287.

Erdogan, B., & Bauer, T. N. (2009). Perceived overqualification and its outcomes: The moderating role of empowerment. *Journal of Applied Psychology, 94*(2), 557.

Erdogan, B., Tomás, I., Valls, V., & Gracia, F. J. (2018). Perceived overqualification, relative deprivation, and person-centric outcomes: The moderating role of career centrality. *Journal of Vocational Behavior, 107,* 233–245.

Farabee, A. M. (2011). *Person–organization fit as a barrier to employee creativity.* Unpublished manuscript, University of Missouri-Saint Louis.

French, J. R. P., Rodgers, W., & Cobb, S. (1974). Adjustment as person–environment fit. In G. V. Coelho (Ed.), *Coping and adaptation* (pp. 316–333). Basic Books.

Funder, D. C. (2001). *The personality puzzle* (2nd Ed.). Norton.

Gerhart, B. (2005). The (affective) dispositional approach to job satisfaction: Sorting out the policy implications. *Journal of Organizational Behavior, 26*(1), 79–97.

Hackman J. R., & Oldham G. R. (1980). *Work redesign.* Addison-Wesley.

Hobfoll, S. E. (2001). The influence of culture, community, and the nested-self in the stress process: Advancing conservation of resources theory. *Applied Psychology: An International Review, 50*(3), 337–421.

Jansen, K. J., & Kristof-Brown, A. L. (2005). Marching to the beat of a different drummer: Examining the impact of pacing congruence. *Organizational Behavior and Human Decision Processes, 97*(2), 93–105.

Jansen, K. J., & Kristof-Brown, A. L. (2006). Toward a multidimensional theory of person–environment fit. *Journal of Managerial Issues, 18*(2), 193–212.

Judge, T. A., Ilies, R., & Zhang, Z. (2012). Genetic influences on core self-evaluations, job satisfaction, and work stress: A behavioral genetics mediated model. *Organizational Behavior and Human Decision Processes, 117*(1), 208–220.

Karasek, R. A. (1979). Job demands, job decision latitude, and mental strain: Implications for job redesign. *Administrative Science Quarterly, 24*, 285–308.

Kristof, A. L. (1996). Person–organization fit: An integrative review of its conceptualization, measurement, and implications. *Personnel Psychology, 49*, 1–49.

Lazarus, R. S. (2001). Conservation of resources theory (COR): Little more than words masquerading as a new theory. *Applied Psychology: An International Review, 50*(3), 381–391.

Lazarus, R. S., & Folkman, S. (1984). *Stress, appraisal, and coping.* Springer.

Lewin, K. (1939). Field theory and experiment in social psychology: Concepts and methods. *American Journal of Sociology, 44*(6), 868–896.

McGrath, J. E. (1970). A conceptual formulation for research on stress. In J. E. McGrath (Ed.), *Social and psychological factors in stress* (pp. 10–21). Holt, Rinehart, & Winston.

McGrath, J. E. (1976). Stress and behavior in organizations. In M. D. Dunnette (Ed.), *Handbook of industrial and organizational psychology* (pp. 1351–1395). Rand McNally.

O'Brien, K. E., Henson, J. A., & Voss, B. E. (2021). A trait–interactionist approach to understanding the role of stressors in the personality–CWB relationship. *Journal of Occupational Health Psychology, 26*(4), 350–360.

Pierce, J. R., & Aguinis, H. (2013). The too-much-of-a-good-thing effect in management. *Journal of Management, 39*(2), 313–338.

Prewett, M. S., Walvoord, A. A., Stilson, F. R., Rossi, M. E., & Brannick, M. T. (2009). The team personality–team performance relationship revisited: The impact of criterion choice, pattern of workflow, and method of aggregation. *Human Performance, 22*(4), 273–296.

Schein, E. H. (1990). *Organizational culture.* American Psychological Association.

Schneider, B. (1987). The people make the place. *Personnel Psychology, 40*(3), 437–453.

Schuler, R. S. (1980). Definition and conceptualization of stress in organizations. *Organizational Behavior and Human Performance, 25*(2), 184–215.

Sekiguchi, T. (2004). Person–organization fit and person–job fit in employee selection: A review of the literature. *Osaka Keidai Ronshu, 54*, 179–196.

Shanock, L. R., Baran, B. E., Gentry, W. A., Pattison, S. C., & Heggestad, E. D. (2014). Erratum to: Polynomial regression with response surface analysis: A powerful approach for examining moderation and overcoming limitations of difference scores. *Journal of Business and Psychology, 1*(29), 161.

Staw, B. M., & Cohen-Charash, Y. (2005). The dispositional approach to job satisfaction: More than a mirage, but not yet an oasis. *Journal of Organizational Behavior, 26*(1), 59–78.

Tett, R. P., & Guterman, H. A. (2000). Situation trait relevance, trait expression, and cross-situational consistency: Testing a principle of trait activation. *Journal of Research in Personality, 34*(4), 397–423.

Tinsley, H. E. (2000). The congruence myth: An analysis of the efficacy of the person–environment fit model. *Journal of Vocational Behavior, 56*(2), 147–179.

Van Vegchel, N., De Jonge, J., Bosma, H., & Schaufeli, W. (2005). Reviewing the effort–reward imbalance model: Drawing up the balance of 45 empirical studies. *Social Science and Medicine, 60*(5), 1117–1131.

Vleugels, W., De Cooman, R., Verbruggen, M., & Solinger, O. (2018). Understanding dynamic change in perceptions of person–environment fit: An exploration of competing theoretical perspectives. *Journal of Organizational Behavior, 39*(9), 1066–1080.

Wanberg, C. R., Welsh, E. T., & Kammeyer-Mueller, J. (2007). Protégé and mentor self-disclosure: Levels and outcomes within formal mentoring dyads in a corporate context. *Journal of Vocational Behavior, 70*(2), 398–412.

Warr, P. (1987). *Work, unemployment, and mental health*. Oxford University Press.

Westerman, J. W., & Cyr, L. A. (2004). An integrative analysis of person–organization fit theories. *International Journal of Selection and Assessment, 12*(3), 252–261.

Xie, J. L & Johns, G. (1995). Job scope and job stress: Can job scope be too high? *Academy of Management Journal, 38*(5), 1288–1309.

Zhang, M., Yan, F., Wang, W., & Li, G. (2017). Is the effect of person–organisation fit on turnover intention mediated by job satisfaction? A survey of community health workers in China. *British Medical Journal Open, 7*(2), e013872.

11. Role-related stress theories

A *role* is a set of expected behaviors within a specific field or system (Kahn, Wolfe, Quinn, Snoek, & Rosenthal, 1964). According to identity theory (see Chapter 7, this volume), people are inherently motivated to successfully meet role expectations and failure to do so can result in frustration, anxiety, and poor self-evaluation. Because the work role is so important to many people, inability to understand and perform role expectations can be especially harmful. Employees learn about the rights, responsibilities, and standards for their roles from role messages sent by other members of their role sets. Attempts have been made to understand role stressors, including role ambiguity (i.e., unclear role expectations) and role conflict (i.e., incompatible role expectations). Boundary and border theories help explain inter-role stress, which occurs between different roles that a person might occupy. Inter-role conflict can occur, for example, when employees occupy boundary-spanning roles (e.g., developing friendly relationships with work clients) that they must maintain. Another form of inter-role conflict is work–family conflict, which occurs when role expectations from the work and family environments are incompatible. In other words, the work role makes it difficult to fulfill the family role or vice versa.

ROLE THEORY

Role theory is primarily a framework regarding interpersonal communication and posits that people learn about their roles (e.g., rights, requirements, norms, expectations) from communication (e.g., role messages, role pressures) sent by members of their role sets (Kahn et al., 1964). Specifically, the role episode model states that role messages are sent to a focal person from role senders who comprise the role set. Because people are intrinsically motivated to perform their roles successfully, they must navigate a process in which they differentiate their roles. This cyclical process is influenced by the focal person, organization, and interpersonal factors. *Role stress* (role conflict and role ambiguity) describes the discomfort that employees experience when they do not understand or cannot learn the relevant behaviors needed to succeed in the organization and perform their roles well. Initial conceptualization describes role dysfunction as having objective and subjective components, which may reflect stressors and strains, respectively. That said, this model was conceived before job stress terminology and conceptualization (e.g., the stressor-strain model) were established, such that attempts to resolve overlap among variables or describe causal relationships were not made until later (see King & King, 1990).

Role conflict reflects various types of incompatible expectations. First, *intrasender conflict* describes contradictory role messages sent from one individual within the role set. An example might be when a supervisor encourages an employee to work both quickly and safely. *Intersender conflict* occurs when two or more members of the role set send incompatible messages, like when a patient asks a nurse for more pain medication, but the doctor states that the patient is not due for more medication yet. *Inter-role conflict* describes incompatibilities between various roles held by the individual (e.g., employee and parent). Finally, *person–role conflict* reflects discrepancies between role requirements and the goals and values of the employee. A fifth category, entitled *other complex conflicts*, includes interactions among the other conflicts, such as role overload.

Role ambiguity describes insufficient or unclear information about role behaviors and originates from both environmental and individual sources. In terms of environmental contributions to role stress, rapidly changing environments may preclude complete information, thus leading to lack of clarity about what constitutes successful role behaviors. Individual contributions to role ambiguity include poor communication from role senders or the focal person's inability to understand role sender signals. There are various types of role ambiguity, which reflect lack of clarity regarding task-related (e.g., scope of responsibilities, role behaviors needed to fulfill responsibilities, and which role senders must be obeyed) and socioemotional expectations (e.g., consequences to the self or organization of role performance).

The two types of dysfunction, role conflict and role ambiguity, were expected to be more or less orthogonal. Each, therefore, is associated with unique strains, such that role conflict causes anxiety and job dissatisfaction, whereas ambiguity causes hopelessness and poor self-evaluations. For example, withdrawal can occur when employees attribute their role stress to other people in their role set. Withdrawal includes behaviors and cognitions such as turnover, absenteeism, reducing communication with role message senders (e.g., avoiding a coauthor to whom you owe some writing), or by cognitively re-evaluating overwhelming or contradictory role messages as unimportant (e.g., dismissing negative feedback). However, some research has tested positive effects of role overload due to the expectancy that it would serve as a challenge demand (e.g., Beehr, Walsh, & Taber, 1976).

Research and Practical Implications

Perhaps due to the age of this theory, as well as a validated measure of role stressors that facilitated theory testing (Rizzo et al., 1970), role stressors have been empirically scrutinized. Evidence that role stressors cause strain is robust, with one meta-analysis showing that, of 36 analyses (role ambiguity and role conflict with 18 criteria each), half were significant (Fisher & Gitelson, 1983). Strains related to both role ambiguity and role conflict included organizational commitment, job involvement, satisfaction with coworkers, and boundary spanning. Role ambiguity was also related to satisfaction with promotion, whereas role conflict was also related to satisfaction with pay, supervision, and self-rated performance. In another meta-analysis with 24 analyses (three role stressors with eight strains; e.g., emotional exhaustion, job satisfaction, job performance), only four were nonsignificant (Örtqvist & Wincent, 2006). In general, role conflict and role ambiguity were associated with more strains (and in greater magnitude) than role overload (Örtqvist & Wincent, 2006). They also found that role conflict and ambiguity were more clearly related to poor communication, as role overload is likely less amenable to resolution through role clarification. Overall, there is evidence that role stressors result in strain as expected, although there is some discussion over whether effects are direct or indirect (e.g., Jackson & Schuler, 1985).

There are some deviations from the negative outcomes of role stressors. For example, as noted above, role overload has fewer clearly negative outcomes than role ambiguity and conflict. Perhaps role overload acts as a challenge demand (especially when measured as quantitative workload and not as perception of overload), thereby mitigating negative effects on the employee. In a few cases, especially when an employee reports other types of quantitative overload, role ambiguity was associated with less strain. For example, role ambiguity may relieve the effects of citizenship pressure on organizational citizenship behavior fatigue, but role conflict may exacerbate the effects (Pohlman, Mann, & O'Brien, 2019). In this sense, *clearly* incompatible expectations may be worse than *ambiguously* incompatible expectations. This proposition, however, needs further investigation, because role conflict and role ambiguity usually have a small positive correlation (it is worth noting that most meta-analyses on the topic do not include a correlation between role ambiguity and role conflict). However, typical role stress measurement reflects a large domain (i.e., the whole work role) or general period of time. When considering messages about narrow role behaviors, role conflict and role ambiguity may instead have a negative correlation. It would be difficult to have both inadequate (i.e., ambiguity) and excessive (e.g., overload) messages about a single task.

Based on this theory, it seems that organizations interested in alleviating role stress might take care to establish effective leader behaviors (i.e., directive, supportive, participative, and achievement-oriented) as per path-goal theory, or initiate a role clarification intervention (Schaubroeck, Ganster, Sime, & Ditman, 1993). This is a type of role analysis intervention in which a responsibility chart is created to define performance standards and communication responsibilities. Managerial roles are explicated, including both expected outcomes and activities to reach those outcomes, to clarify expectations and increase accountability. In a field experiment with random assignment, role clarification was associated with reduced role ambiguity but not with reduced health symptoms or sick days (Schaubroeck et al., 1993). This process is similar to management by objectives, a type of organizational intervention informed by goal-setting theory (e.g., Raia, 1974).

However, employees who are from marginalized groups may be less likely to ask for or receive this information (e.g., Leong & Tang, 2016). According to relational-cultural theory, members of marginalized groups are evaluated critically for engaging in the same adaptive relational behaviors used by the majority group members (e.g., Miller, 1976). A majority group member who asks for clarification may be seen as proactive or conscientious, whereas a minority group member who does the same thing may be seen as needy or incompetent. Consequently, a marginalized group member may feel punished for seeking role clarification. In fact, role ambiguity is higher for token group members (Young & James, 2001), mixed-demographic supervisor–subordinate dyads (Tsui & O'Reilly, 1989), and those in organizations with worse diversity climates (Madera, Dawson, & Neal, 2013). It is important to further investigate the existence of this phenomenon as well as steps to resolve it through socialization, given that previous research has shown promising but mixed results that need further clarification. For example, collective socialization tactics (e.g., new employee orientation) were associated with less role ambiguity, but sequential tactics (e.g., discussing potential for future promotions) were related to more role ambiguity among information technology workers (King, Xia, Campbell Quick, & Sethi, 2005). However, serial and formal tactics were related to reduced role ambiguity for social workers (Jaskyte, 2005). Future research on when various socialization techniques resolve role stressors would be valuable.

Theoretical Extension: Boundary-Spanning Theory

Early research on boundary roles (e.g., Adams, 1976) clearly extends from the Kahn et al. (1964) role theory. Boundary role theory, or boundary-spanning theory, describes how employees of service organizations occupy boundary-spanning roles that involve friendly relationships with clients with whom the employee is similar in terms of organizational hierarchy. Although there are various conceptualizations of boundary spanning (e.g., communicating across cultures), *boundary spanning* originally referred to a position on the cusp of work and nonwork, in which service employees are responsible for processing and filtering information and representing the organization to the client. However, the close relationship with the clients may cause a conflict when clients and organizational interests do not align. This is supported by empirical research. For example, one study shows that discrepancies between a bank employee's *preferred* treatment of clients and description of their management's *actual* treatment of clients is related to role ambiguity and role conflict (Parkington & Schneider, 1979). The actual–preferred discrepancy and role stress perceptions, in turn, predicted frustration, organizational dissatisfaction, and reports of poor customer service.

In sum, boundary-spanning roles can incur role stress when economic relationships develop into trusting, loyal social relationships, as described in Blau's social exchange theory. Resultantly, it seems that boundary spanning is more relevant when service workers are paid (within a work role) to provide or display care (typically associated with social roles; e.g., teachers, healthcare, bartenders, hairstylists). More research on boundaries outside of customer service would help us to understand the job stress of boundary spanners.

Theoretical Integration: Adaptation Theory

Adaptation theory holds that people are able to adjust to both positive and negative situations with an eventual return to baseline (Diener, Lucas, & Scollon, 2006). Consequently, stressors should relate to short-term, but not long-term, strain. Similarly, positive events should lead to short-term, but not long-term, eustress. Role stress has been viewed within the perspective of adaptation theory, as recent testing has investigated the unfolding nature of role stressors over time. Some researchers suggest that strain worsens over time, as is consistent with conservation of resources (COR) theory or the job demands-resources model, but rigorously designed longitudinal studies show that strains are temporary, fluctuate sporadically over time, and may resolve themselves without intervention (Ritter, Matthews, Ford, & Henderson, 2016). In other words, when viewed cross-sectionally, role stress relates to strain, but over time, the relationship becomes null through adaptation. This research is important, perhaps paradigm shifting, because (arguably) the only unique contribution of COR theory is the dynamic "spiraling" hypothesis. Without the loss and gain spirals, COR theory only combines the observation that "good things are good" with the primacy of loss hypothesis. In other words, the mechanism by which resources are good (i.e., because they allow investment) cannot be valid if adaptation theory is true. Or, these spirals occur over relatively short periods of time, or must reflect a variety of stressors. A person is less likely to adapt to multiple stressors than just one type (e.g., Benini, Oliveira, Gomes-de-Souza, Rodrigues, & Crestani, 2020).

Intuitively, it seems that loss spirals cannot be endless as people rarely reach exhaustion (i.e., death) in Selye's general adaptation syndrome. Instead, it is known that the body *habituates* (i.e., the dampening of a physiological response after repeated exposures) to a wide variety of stimuli (e.g., scents, drugs), including stressors. Specifically, there is strong evidence that stress is subject to habituation and, separately, a negative feedback loop (i.e., the corticotropin-releasing hormone (CRH) and adrenocorticotropic hormone (ACTH) indirectly cause cortisol release, then cortisol blocks certain CRH and ACTH production; Grissom & Bhatnagar, 2009). In other words, chronic stress has self-limiting features. However, we also know that certain stressors can sensitize the stress response (e.g., the kindling hypothesis, see Chapter 3, this volume) and that the body can habituate to cortisol, thus interfering with the negative feedback loop. In these ways, sustained stressors can increase strain. Future attempts to resolve these propositions, perhaps through cognitive mediation or as modulated by the magnitude, type, or duration of stressor, would be extremely illuminating. Without further clarification, practical implications cannot be readily drawn regarding the long-term impact of stressors.

WORK-FAMILY CONFLICT THEORY

Work–family conflict refers to a type of inter-role conflict in which role requirements from the work and family environments are incompatible (Bakker et al., 2008). Conflict theory states that the work and family environments are incompatible because they have distinct norms and requirements (Zedeck & Mosier, 1990). These incompatibilities can cause *work interference with family*, in which role demands at work interfere with role demands at home, and *family interference with work*, in which role demands at home prohibit role fulfillment at work. Conflicts can arise due to time (e.g., the physical inability to be in two places at the same time), strain (e.g., strain in one role impedes progress in another role), or behaviors (e.g., behaviors in one domain are not adaptive in the other).

Research on the work–family interface has been plagued by jingle and jangle fallacies (see Casper, Vaziri, Wayne, DeHauw, & Greenhaus, 2018, for construct clean-up and best practices for research on the work–nonwork interface). For example, the family role and nonwork role are sometimes conceptualized as interchangeable, even though they have different meanings (Casper et al., 2018). To illustrate, someone who leaves work to go meet the plumber at home is having a nonwork conflict, but not a family conflict. Furthermore, some research on work–family balance actually studies a lack of work–family conflict. That is to say, work–family *balance* is distinct from the absence of work–family conflict, because balance describes a state of effectiveness and satisfaction with both work and family, as guided by the individual's overall life priorities (e.g., Wayne, Butts, Casper, & Allen, 2017). The distinction between conflict and balance can be seen in their differential prediction abilities: work–family balance is more strongly related to organizational commitment, job satisfaction, family satisfaction, turnover intentions, job performance, and family role performance than work–family conflict (Wayne et al., 2017). Future research can improve our understanding of the work–nonwork interface by standardizing construct definitions, including multiple reporting sources (e.g., the employee, supervisor, domestic partner), incorporating a greater variety of nonwork roles, and minimizing deficiency by using multidimensional measures and conceptualizing balance more broadly (Casper et al., 2018).

Earlier research on the work–nonwork interface also used the term *spillover*, which is again implicated in some conceptual ambiguities (Casper et al., 2018). Spillover refers to the transmission of positive and negative states from one domain (e.g., work, family) to another. However, negative spillover is indistinct from work–nonwork conflict, and positive spillover is not unique from enrichment. *Work–nonwork enrichment* occurs when experiences in one role improve (i.e., spillover into) the quality of life in another role. Some examples might include positive emotions from recognition at work carrying over into time at home, or skills learned at home (e.g., gently making requests of family members) transferring to the work domain. Enrichment is an antecedent of balance. Very early in conceptualizing the work–family interface, an alternative to spillover was considered. Herein, compensation describes an inverse relationship between work and family, such that people ensure that any gaps in one area (e.g., self-esteem) are addressed in the other domain, perhaps via fluid compensation (i.e., a cognitive redirection from an area of weakness to an area of strength) or skill investment resulting in performance increases (e.g., minimizing energy expended at work to enable better involvement and high-quality interactions with family after work). There is little empirical evidence to suggest that compensation occurs at meaningful levels.

Research and Organizational Implications

Like with other forms of role stress, work–family conflict is conceptualized as either a stressor (i.e., a situation that requires adaptation) or a strain (i.e., the negative outcomes of such a stressor). In fact, work–family conflict has qualities of both stressors and strains in a reciprocal manner (Nohe, Michel, & Sonntag, 2014). Antecedents to work–family conflict include job characteristics such as job stressors, role conflict, role overload, role demands, and social support; family characteristics such as family stressors, family role conflict, family role overload, family social support, and family climate; and individual differences including locus of control and negative affectivity (Michel, Kotrba, Mitchelson, Clark, & Baltes, 2011). Work–family conflict is associated with a variety of employee strains, including worsened job attitudes, absenteeism, burnout, reduced organizational citizenship behavior and job performance, and increased depression, anxiety, and drug use (Amstad, Meier, Fasel, Elfering, & Semmer, 2011). Furthermore, work–family conflict affects the employee's withdrawal behaviors (i.e., lateness, absenteeism), as well as their spouse's withdrawal behaviors at work, even when controlling for the spouse's level of work–family conflict (Hammer, Bauer, & Grandey, 2003). In other words, individual-level and crossover effects were found for work–family conflict on withdrawal behaviors.

That said, work–family conflict may result in positive wellbeing in the long run because of adaptation (Matthews, Wayne, & Ford, 2014). In other words, like other role stressors, work–family conflict seems to have deleterious short-term effects on wellbeing, but many people adapt over time and can regain positive wellbeing after experiencing work–family conflict (Matthews et al., 2014). This is beneficial because not all sources of work–family conflict can be eliminated (e.g., night shifts, emergency schedule changes). In these cases, organizations should instead work to provide employees with the resources that they need to meet their demands. Unfortunately, however, methods for ameliorating work–family conflict are unclear. Several interventions have been proposed, including (a) flexibility of time (e.g., flextime) and place (e.g., telecommuting), or both (e.g., results-oriented work environment), (b) training supervisors to understand and support employees experiencing conflict, and generally improving the organizational climate, and (c) offering and encouraging use of dependent care support (e.g., childcare). Another option is to train employees to identify and correct cognitive distortions about their work–nonwork interface (e.g., "This always happens" is black and white thinking; "My manager will be upset if I take time off" reflects mind reading, as it is impossible to know what your manager will think) in a cognitive-behavioral intervention delivered by a licensed clinical psychologist. Other relevant skills training can be offered (e.g., assertiveness training, time management coaching, mindfulness) although this may blame the victim, implying that lack of efficiency or skill, rather than excessive work demands, causes work–family conflict. Such training may also require time investment that employees, especially those with work–family conflict, may find is in short supply. Similarly, interventions designed to limit work hours (i.e., providing more time at home) may force employees to complete more work in less time (i.e., depleting energy at work; Grzywacz & Carlson, 2007). Furthermore, certain benefits (e.g., flextime) may be technically available, but discouraged formally or informally via norms. This illustrates the importance of complementing family-supportive policies with organizational culture and leadership. Specifically, providing employees with a variety of available resources, with the autonomy and supervisory support to choose among them, should be the most effective at reducing work–nonwork conflict.

WORK-FAMILY BORDER THEORY

Whereas conflict theory posits inherent incompatibilities between roles, border theory describes attempts to shape the boundaries that define roles, and the degree to which people accommodate inter-role intrusions. Boundaries, as they are defined in border theory, were initially conceptualized within the cognitive sociological boundary theory of Nippert-Eng (1996). This book quite literally describes how people separate their work and home roles (e.g., "Renee shows just how much someone may have to patrol the home–work boundary where money is concerned," p. 66) and generally reflects upon how people distinguish between their roles. Work-family border theory builds upon this and emphasizes how employees deliberately create and modify boundaries around their work and their personal life (Clark, 2000). Work-family border theory states that people cross borders between work and family domains on a daily basis, and in this process, people influence their environments, define their borders, and determine the relationship of the border crosser to their domains. Clark (2000) carefully delineated definitions and specific propositions pertaining to multiple aspects of the work–family interface in border theory. A *domain* represents a field with specific associated rules, thought patterns, and behaviors. *Borders* define the point at which domain-relevant behavior begins or ends and can take the form of physical, temporal, or psychological limits. Borders differ in how readily they can be crossed, depending on their levels of *permeability* (the extent to which elements from other domains may enter) and *flexibility* (the extent to which a border may contract or expand).

Aspects of the border crossers also influence the way that borders are maintained. *Central participants* (more so than their counterparts – *peripheral participants*) internalize the culture and values of their domain, demonstrate competence of role behaviors, connect with other central participants, and personally identify with the domain. Central participants have *influence* because of their competence and social affiliation, so they have more power to modify the domain and borders for domain participants. Some domain members who are especially influential in defining the domain and border are called *border keepers*. At work, this is often the supervisor; at home, often the spouse.

Research and Organizational Implications

Border theory is based on the socio-cognitive boundary theory of Nippert-Eng (1996), but this boundary theory also inspired Ashforth, Kreiner, and Fugate (2000) to develop a separate boundary theory at about the same time. Ashforth et al.'s (2000) boundary theory describes *micro role transitions* (i.e., day-to-day boundary-crossing activities) and how roles can be arranged on a continuum from segmented to integrated. Segmentation between roles increases the amount of change that occurs during transitions, but decreases role blurring. Integrating roles minimizes the magnitude of change required, but increases blurring such that boundary maintenance is more onerous.

To summarize, both Clark and Ashforth describe the way that people differentiate their roles. However, the similarities in title (i.e., *border* and *boundary*), timing (published in the year 2000), origin (based on Nippert-Eng's work), and concepts (e.g., border crossing, role transitions) have precipitated a jangle fallacy, in which the theories are used interchangeably or sometimes combined into "boundary/border theory" (e.g., Park, Liu, & Headrick, 2020). In fact, the research on border theory seems to have adopted the term "boundary" to refer to distinctions between roles (Allen, Cho, & Meier, 2014). This has led some researchers to take efforts to improve conceptualization based upon the extant empirical evidence. Specifically, Allen et al. (2014) differentiate boundary and border theories, summarize empirical evidence, and provide suggestions for best practices in testing these theories.

In terms of the most recent theoretical testing and developments, it seems that interest lies in investigating the degree to which people integrate or segment their work and nonwork domains, as well as their tactics for doing so. The bulk of the evidence indicates there is no best amount of integration or segmentation. Instead, this depends upon personal values and abilities, as well as organizational, job-related, and nonwork-related constraints. For example, a cluster analysis shows that there are four boundary management profiles, but segmentation is weak across all of them (Bulger, Matthews, & Hoffman, 2007). In fact, the cluster of people who did the most segmentation was the smallest, and the amount of segmentation that they reported was at about the midpoint of the segmentation–integration scale (on average). This suggests that strong segmentation is quite uncommon. Other clusters reflected (1) integration, (2) having the capability to leave work but rarely using it, and (3) allowing nonwork role expectations to enter the work domain but not vice versa. In other words, there are a variety of ways to separate boundaries, although no group seems to be doing a whole lot of it.

CONCLUDING REMARKS

Role stress is clearly relevant to employees, but early role stress theory had conceptual and measurement problems. Some early research (as well as some newer research in boundary theory, see Allen et al., 2014) is even tautological. For example, in one such study, items measuring role ambiguity included "Do you feel you are always as clear as you would like to be about what you have to do on this job," whereas tension was measured with items like "How often do you feel bothered by not knowing just what the people you work with expect of you" (Lyons, 1971, pp. 103–104). Despite limitations, it is clear that role ambiguity and role conflict have distinct but robust implications for performance management, socialization, and inclusion efforts. That is to say, explicit, dynamic, and reciprocal role communications result (directly or indirectly) in beneficial employee and organizational outcomes. Communication, therefore, may be particularly important for marginalized employees who might not receive role messages through typical social network transmission. It seems likely that various person (e.g., culture) and organization (e.g., voice climate) factors will influence the likelihood that role communications occur satisfactorily. Furthermore, it is unclear the extent to which formal communication and socialization policies can regulate role messages and mitigate disparities in role clarity. Although formal policies may be unpopular, they can protect employees who may not benefit from informal networking. There may be drawbacks to communication policies, so this should be further tested before practical implications should be drawn.

There are also conceptual distinctions that should be further clarified, including potential overlap between role ambiguity and lack of job-related knowledge (Jackson & Schuler, 1985). To explicate, role ambiguity is unique in that it reflects an interpersonal process characterized by inadequate communication. That is to say, improved communication between the employee and supervisor can resolve role ambiguity but not inadequate training. However, the nearly exclusive reliance on measurement from the employee's perspective has confounded perceived role ambiguity with a lack of competency. For example, a stablehand asked to tack up a horse should know exactly how to do this, but untrained employees may find these instructions to be unclear. The employee might be motivated to protect their self-evaluation by blaming the supervisor for lack of communication, rather than their own lack of skill. Consequently, in the field, it would be difficult to disentangle role ambiguity from confounds. Instead, experimental research in which the competency, self-efficacy, and clarity of role expectations are manipulated may allow clearer interpretation of the unique contribution of role ambiguity.

Beyond role clarity, role theory inspired research into boundary management (i.e., segmentation, integration). Segmentation is affected by the use of mobile technology for work-related communication during nonwork hours. Boundary management regarding work communications within the traditionally nonwork domain may be particularly important due to changes in the nature of work (e.g., Allen et al., 2014) and the COVID-19 pandemic. Due to expected wellbeing problems associated with inadequate recovery from work stressors, some attempts to limit work–nonwork interference are being implemented by organizations and governments. For example, contacting your employees after hours in France or Brazil could result in fines. There is some empirical evidence confirming that after-hours work communication is associated with deleterious effects. For example, when teachers received greater communication requests during nonwork hours, they were more likely to experience negative work rumination, negative affect, and insomnia (Park et al., 2020). Furthermore, technological boundary tactics (e.g., turning off notifications on the phone) were more effective than communicative boundary tactics (e.g., managing expectations about communication to the supervisor or parents in advance) at decreasing information communication technology demands. The principals and families served as border keepers, such that they increased or decreased (respectively) the effect of information communication technology demands on rumination. Overall, there is no right way to keep boundaries, but technological tactics are more effective than asking other people to adapt.

That said, segmentation is generally difficult or unpopular (e.g., Bulger et al., 2007), even though the benefits of stressor detachment and recovery activities are well documented. However, little research has investigated negative health and performance outcomes of weak boundaries (beyond the above-referenced study on communication requests; Park et al., 2020), so it is unclear when and how segmentation is deleterious. Based on Park et al. (2020), it seems possible that negative effects may be specific to failed attempts to segment. However, these observations may be obscured by reverse causal pathways. For example, if an employee perceives strain and then uses segmentation tactics to strengthen boundaries, but after-hours work demands continue (i.e., segmentation tactics fail), there may appear to be a proximal positive correlation between segmentation attempts and experiencing demands or strain. Consequently, research investigating these topics will need to carefully consider the most appropriate study designs (e.g., experience sampling methodology). Given COVID-19, research on segmentation and job stress may be more relevant than in the past, and there is sure to be intensified interest in this topic in the coming years.

REFERENCES

Adams, J. S. (1976). The structure and dynamics of behavior in organizational boundary roles. In M. D. Dunnette (Ed.), *Handbook of industrial and organizational psychology* (pp. 1175–1199). Rand McNally College Publishing.

Allen, T. D., Cho, E., & Meier, L. L. (2014). Work–family boundary dynamics. *Annual Review of Organizational Psychology and Organizational Behavior, 1*(1), 99–121.

Amstad, F. T., Meier, L. L., Fasel, U., Elfering, A., & Semmer, N. K. (2011). A meta-analysis of work–family conflict and various outcomes with a special emphasis on cross-domain versus matching-domain relations. *Journal of Occupational Health Psychology, 16*(2), 151–169.

Ashforth, B. E., Kreiner, G. E., & Fugate, M. (2000). All in a day's work: Boundaries and micro role transitions. *Academy of Management Review, 25*(3), 472–491.

Bakker, A. B., Demerouti, E., & Dollard, M. F. (2008). How job demands affect partners' experience of exhaustion: Integrating work–family conflict and crossover theory. *Journal of Applied Psychology, 93*(4), 901.

Beehr, T. A., Walsh, J. T., & Taber, T. D. (1976). Relationships of stress to individually and organizationally valued states: Higher order needs as a moderator. *Journal of Applied Psychology, 61*(1), 41–47.

Benini, R., Oliveira, L. A., Gomes-de-Souza, L., Rodrigues, B., & Crestani, C. C. (2020). Habituation of the cardiovascular response to restraint stress is inhibited by exposure to other stressor stimuli and exercise training. *Journal of Experimental Biology, 223*(8), jeb219501.

Bulger, C. A., Matthews, R. A., & Hoffman, M. E. (2007). Work and personal life boundary management: Boundary strength, work/personal life balance, and the segmentation–integration continuum. *Journal of Occupational Health Psychology, 12*(4), 365–375.

Casper, W. J., Vaziri, H., Wayne, J. H., DeHauw, S., & Greenhaus, J. (2018). The jingle-jangle of work–nonwork balance: A comprehensive and meta-analytic review of its meaning and measurement. *Journal of Applied Psychology, 103*(2), 182–214.

Clark, S. C. (2000). Work/family border theory: A new theory of work/family balance. *Human Relations, 53*(6), 747–770.

Diener, E., Lucas, R. E., & Scollon, C. N. (2006). Beyond the hedonic treadmill: Revising the adaptation theory of well-being. In F. Huppert, N. Baylis, & B. Keverne (Eds), *The science of well-being* (pp. 103–118). Springer.

Fisher, C. D., & Gitelson, R. (1983). A meta-analysis of the correlates of role conflict and ambiguity. *Journal of Applied Psychology, 68*(2), 320–333.

Grissom, N., & Bhatnagar, S. (2009). Habituation to repeated stress: Get used to it. *Neurobiology of Learning and Memory, 92*(2), 215–224.

Grzywacz, J. G., & Carlson, D. S. (2007). Conceptualizing work–family balance: Implications for practice and research. *Advances in Developing Human Resources, 9*(4), 455–471.

Hammer, L. B., Bauer, T. N., & Grandey, A. A. (2003). Work–family conflict and work-related withdrawal behaviors. *Journal of Business and Psychology, 17*(3), 419–436.

Jackson, S. E., & Schuler, R. S. (1985). A meta-analysis and conceptual critique of research on role ambiguity and role conflict in work settings. *Organizational Behavior and Human Decision Processes, 36*(1), 16–78.

Jaskyte, K. (2005). The impact of organizational socialization tactics on role ambiguity and role conflict of newly hired social workers. *Administration in Social Work*, *29*(4), 69–87.

Kahn, R. L., Wolfe, D. M., Quinn, R. P., Snoek, J. D., & Rosenthal, R. A. (1964). *Organizational stress: Studies in role conflict and ambiguity*. John Wiley.

King, L. A., & King, D. W. (1990). Role conflict and role ambiguity: A critical assessment of construct validity. *Psychological Bulletin*, *107*(1), 48.

King, R. C., Xia, W., Campbell Quick, J., & Sethi, V. (2005). Socialization and organizational outcomes of information technology professionals. *Career Development International*, *10*(1), 26–51.

Leong, F. T., & Tang, M. (2016). Career barriers for Chinese immigrants in the United States. *Career Development Quarterly*, *64*(3), 259–271.

Lyons, T. F. (1971). Role clarity, need for clarity, satisfaction, tension, and withdrawal. *Organizational Behavior and Human Performance*, *6*(1), 99–110.

Madera, J. M., Dawson, M., & Neal, J. A. (2013). Hotel managers' perceived diversity climate and job satisfaction: The mediating effects of role ambiguity and conflict. *International Journal of Hospitality Management*, *35*, 28–34.

Matthews, R. A., Wayne, J. H., & Ford, M. T. (2014). A work–family conflict/subjective well-being process model: A test of competing theories of longitudinal effects. *Journal of Applied Psychology*, *99*(6), 1173–1187.

Michel, J. S., Kotrba, L. M., Mitchelson, J. K., Clark, M. A., & Baltes, B. B. (2011). Antecedents of work–family conflict: A meta-analytic review. *Journal of Organizational Behavior*, *32*(5), 689–725.

Miller, J. B. (1976). *Toward a new psychology of women* (2nd Ed.). Beacon Press.

Nippert-Eng, C. (1996). *Home and work: Negotiating boundaries through everyday life*. University of Chicago Press.

Nohe, C., Michel, A., & Sonntag, K. (2014). Family–work conflict and job performance: A diary study of boundary conditions and mechanisms. *Journal of Organizational Behavior*, *35*(3), 339–357.

Örtqvist, D., & Wincent, J. (2006). Prominent consequences of role stress: A meta-analytic review. *International Journal of Stress Management*, *13*(4), 399–422.

Park, Y., Liu, Y., & Headrick, L. (2020). When work is wanted after hours: Testing weekly stress of information communication technology demands using boundary theory. *Journal of Organizational Behavior*, *41*(6), 518–534.

Parkington, J. J., & Schneider, B. (1979). Some correlates of experienced job stress: A boundary role study. *Academy of Management Journal*, *22*(2), 270–281.

Pohlman, R., Mann, K. J., & O'Brien, K. E. (2019). Above and beyond to down and out: The progression of OCB to citizenship fatigue. Paper presented at the annual meeting of the Society of Organizational Psychology, Washington, DC.

Raia, A. P. (1974). *Managing by objectives*. Foresman and Company.

Ritter, K., Matthews, R. A., Ford, M. T., & Henderson, A. A. (2016). Understanding role stressors and job satisfaction over time using adaptation theory. *Journal of Applied Psychology*, *101*(12), 1655–1669.

Rizzo, J. R., House, R. J., & Lirtzman, S. I. (1970). Role conflict and ambiguity in complex organizations. *Administrative Science Quarterly*, *15*(2), 150–163.

Schaubroeck, J., Ganster, D. C., Sime, W. E., & Ditman, D. (1993). A field experiment testing supervisory role clarification. *Personnel Psychology*, *46*(1), 1–25.

Tsui, A. S., & O'Reilly, C. A. (1989). Beyond simple demographic effects: The importance of relational demography in superior–subordinate dyads. *Academy of Management Journal*, *32*(2), 402–423.

Wayne, J. H., Butts, M. M., Casper, W. J., & Allen, T. D. (2017). In search of balance: A conceptual and empirical integration of multiple meanings of work–family balance. *Personnel Psychology*, *70*(1), 167–210.

Young, J. L., & James, E. H. (2001). Token majority: The work attitudes of male flight attendants. *Sex Roles*, *45*(5), 299–319.

Zedeck, S., & Mosier, K. L. (1990). Work in the family and employing organization. *American Psychologist*, *45*(2), 240.

12. Sociocultural systems perspectives

Sociocultural perspectives describe how people and their circumstances are influenced by social and cultural factors. *Culture* has been defined in various ways, including as a shared pattern of beliefs, attitudes, norms, role perceptions, and values (Triandis & Gelfand, 1998) or as collective programming that distinguishes members of different groups (Hofstede, 1980). In cross-cultural research, a jingle fallacy occurs in which cross-national differences are sometimes used to represent cross-cultural differences. However, a nation can have multiple heterogeneous cultures, and several countries can be comparatively homogeneous, so that the terms "national" and "cultural" comparisons should not be used interchangeably. Despite empirical limitations, a fair amount of research has demonstrated that the stressor-strain process is similar across cultures, but there may be differences in the way that people from different cultures perceive and cope with stressors (e.g., Liu, Spector, & Shi, 2007).

Culture is expected to lead to within-nation similarities and cross-national differences. Nonetheless, within-group variation is larger than between-group variation, such that average differences between groups are typically not large and the distributions overlap quite a bit. Although it seems like culture has a very weak effect on human behavior, salient intergroup differences certainly relate to increased stressors and, in turn, strains. In other words, people are not so different, but they are sometimes evaluated and treated as such. Perceived outgroup status can lead to *prejudice* (i.e., negative attitudes) and *discrimination* (i.e., unfair treatment). Despite the focus on workplace diversity, equity, and inclusion, there is little understanding of the unique experiences of minority or stigmatized group members within the job stress literature. Certainly, it is understood that being the member of a stigmatized racial, gender, age, or religious group can lead to disparate treatment, even though this is illegal in many countries. A substantial amount of the research in industrial/organizational psychology is devoted to these issues, in fact. However, there remains inadequate research incorporating minority stress into job stress theories, despite evidence that minority stress is quantitatively and qualitatively different from other indicators of resource loss or other stressors.

HOFSTEDE'S CULTURAL DIMENSIONS

Culture is a shared set of beliefs, values; norms, expectations, and behaviors that exists within large groups of people and is typically resistant to change over time. For some time, scientific understanding of culture included mostly nebulous accounts of specific cultural observations. In an attempt to quantify and explicate characteristics of culture, Hofstede (at the time a personnel researcher at IBM) analyzed employee attitude surveys from almost 117,000 workers across 66 countries at two different time points. The items he chose were expected to describe the employees' values, and between four and six dimensions were extracted from the surveys (see Hofstede, 1980). These dimensions are important, he argued, because culture is conditioned, and "we see the world in the way we learned to see it" (Hofstede, 1980, p. 50). Consequently, employee appraisals of working contexts are influenced by these higher-level cultural values.

Of the typology that emerged, the most studied cultural dimension is individualism versus collectivism. This describes whether a person's identity is based on their own characteristics (e.g., achievements) or their group's. *Individualism* reflects a preference for a loose social structure in which people are expected to look after only themselves and their immediate families. Conversely, *collectivism* is characterized by a preference for a close social structure in which people can expect loyalty and care from their ingroup (typically immediate and extended family). A second cultural dimension is *power distance*, which represents the degree to which the less powerful members of a society accept and expect that power is distributed unequally. High power distance is associated with a hierarchical order of people, whereas low power distance is associated with attempts to equalize the distribution of power and remedy social inequalities. Next, *masculinity/femininity* refers to the amount that a society values achievement, assertiveness, and material rewards for success. Masculine cultures are more competitive, whereas feminine cultures value cooperation and quality of life. Another dimension, *uncertainty avoidance*, is the degree to which members of a society are comfortable with the unknown, and this manifests in how they manage change. Strong uncertainty avoidance is associated with rigid codes of belief and behavior that are intolerant of nonconformity. Cultures with low uncertainty avoidance are more flexible, and behavioral practices are considered more important than stated principles (a cultural idiom that describes this characteristic might be that low uncertainty avoidance is associated with "walking the walk").

The fifth dimension is usually, but not always, included. It was originally called Confucian dynamism and represents *long-term and short-term orientation*. This dimension describes how societies weigh the importance of links to their past with anticipation of future needs. Societies that are more short-term oriented prefer to maintain traditions and norms because they are focused on the short term (i.e., present and maybe past). They tend to believe in a universal good and evil, and prefer a command-based family structure. On the other hand, long-term orientation is practical and thrifty, retaining only minimally necessary traditions and "coldly" prioritizing relationships based on status. Long-term orientation is associated with education, perseverance, and personal responsibility. Sometimes, a sixth dimension reflecting *indulgence versus restraint* is included. The level of indulgence is determined by the extent to which society allows human nature to dictate behavior, as opposed to controlling human desires. Indulgent societies encourage enjoyment and fun, whereas societies high in restraint regulate these desires.

Empirical Testing and Psychometric Validation

Because this model is empirically derived, concerns about empirical testing constrain the validity of the overall model. That is to say, although this conceptualization is well known, the empirical evidence is weak, largely due to problems with measurement and interpretation thereof (e.g., McSweeney, 2002). For one, the "values survey module" (VSM94) was commonly used at one point to assess the cultural dimensions. However, this scale has unacceptably low reliability, such that a large cross-national study showed coefficient alphas ranged from 0.05 for uncertainty avoidance to 0.63 for long-term orientation, regardless of level (e.g., individual or national). In fact, some items correlate negatively with their proposed dimension and, as a result of psychometric limitations, the dimensions do not factor as expected (e.g., Spector, Cooper, & Sparks, 2001). Additionally, there is a large debate regarding the intended level of measurement. It seems that the VSM94 is intended to reflect country-level culture (e.g., "What are the values of your country?"), but is phrased at the individual level (e.g., "What are your values?"), leading to violations of assumptions regarding independence and the levels of analysis, as well as a *reverse ecological fallacy*, wherein an inference is made about a culture based on aggregated data from some portion of individuals within a group.

Another consideration is testing bias. Translation and back translation methodologies do not account for or remove bias, as even literal and clear translations can have different implications cross-culturally. For example, an item intended to assess leader satisfaction that includes voice (e.g., "My leader considers my suggestions when making decisions that affect me") might be interpreted as negative in a high power distance culture, wherein participative leadership might be viewed as weakness or incompetence. An item response theory approach can be used to detect bias in items or equate tests. There are similar analyses within confirmatory factor analysis (see Wang & Russell, 2005). However, the values measure does not meet the minimum assumptions for using item response theory (e.g., unidimensionality of each cultural dimension) and attempts to assess measurement invariance via confirmatory factor analysis do not inspire confidence (e.g., Spector et al., 2001). In addition to (or resulting from) measurement problems, there is little empirical evidence in support of this framework or the proposition that the cultural dimensions moderate employee appraisal.

Research and Practical Implications

Hofstede's work has had an enormous positive impact on the understanding of national culture within the workplace. For example, Triandis (2004) showed appreciation for Hofstede's work, which moved cultural psychology into the mainstream. Triandis developed and validated his own framework and measurement tool assessing culture, describing culture along two axes: individualism versus collectivism, and horizontal versus vertical (e.g., Triandis & Gelfand, 1998). In his model, *horizontal individualism* refers to independence and not relying on others, whereas *vertical individualism* has a more competitive element. *Horizontal collectivism* is best indicated by the item "If a co-worker gets a prize, I would feel proud," whereas *vertical collectivism* reflects close family systems. Triandis (2004) implies his framework, particularly the individualism-collectivism component, was at least partially inspired by Hofstede. Although imperfect, Hofstede's framework has value, as "perfect is the enemy of good" (Triandis, 2004, p. 89). Hofstede's cultural dimensions encouraged a more thorough consideration of cross-national values in psychology, and he was among the first to explicate such values, during a time when the "global village" was just beginning to develop.

Some of the most enlightening research on the intersection of culture and job stress combines quantitative and qualitative data. One such study compared the United States and China and found that American employees reported a higher quantitative level of job autonomy, but only American employees qualitatively reported lack of autonomy as a job stressor (e.g., Liu et al., 2007). Furthermore, quantitative data indicated no difference in interpersonal conflict, but qualitative results show that Chinese employees reported more indirect conflicts, whereas American employees reported more direct conflicts. The authors suggest that the cultural values of collectivism and long-term orientation encourage harmony and "saving face," which may inhibit direct (but not indirect) conflict within Chinese employees. In contrast, American employees are less inhibited against direct conflict than Chinese employees, and the subculture of their American participants may even encourage direct conflict. Specifically, the participants were sampled from the southeastern

United States, which is characterized by a culture of honor. Honor is defined as a drive to publicly defend personal reputation, often by aggressively responding to insults or threats (e.g., Vandello, Cohen, & Ransom, 2008). This is an example in which cross-*national* comparisons may be limited, relative to cross-*cultural* comparisons.

In this study, strains also showed interesting patterns across samples (Liu et al., 2007). Some symptoms (i.e., anger, anxiety, and feeling tired) were reported in both countries. However, qualitative investigation shows that only American employees reported frustration, feeling overwhelmed, and stomach problems, and only Chinese employees reported helplessness, hopelessness, sleep problems, and feeling hot. That said, expected job stressor–strain relationships were replicated in both Chinese and American employees, providing some evidence that the stressor-strain process is generalizable across cultures.

ECOLOGICAL SYSTEMS THEORY

Another sociocultural perspective is the ecological systems model of human development (Bronfenbrenner, 1994), which visualizes the social systems that influence a person as a series of fully nested concentric circles. At the center is the focal person, and most directly and immediately around them is the microsystem. The circles move outwardly to reflect system influences that are increasingly broad and abstract (e.g., macrosystem, chronosystem). Although the model is typically applied to children, it has implications in retirement, vocational interests, accepting a job offer, workplace prejudice and discrimination, and other multisystems effects that develop over time.

Within this model, the first level is the *microsystem*, which includes the direct, reciprocal relationships that employees have with people in their immediate environment, such as coworkers, clients, and family members. This is the most proximal system, and therefore the most influential. The *mesosystem* encompasses the interactions between the person's microsystems, such as the interactions between supervisors and coworkers, or family and friends. The third layer is the *exosystem*, which incorporates other formal and informal social structures that indirectly influence the person through effects on their microsystems (e.g., the neighborhood, spouse's workplaces, mass media). In other words, these environments are external to the person's experience, but affect them nonetheless. For example, an employee's child who has a bad day at school might get into trouble, which could affect the employee's microsystems (e.g., family time at home might afford less recovery) and mesosystems (e.g., the parent's work–family conflict). The *macrosystem* (fourth layer) focuses on how cultural factors, such as socioeconomic status and ethnicity, influence members' beliefs and perceptions about events that transpire in life. Social policies, for example, reflect these values and influences that comprise the macrosystem. Sometimes, a fifth dimension (the *chronosystem*) is considered. This consists of all of the major environmental changes that occur during the developmental span, such as marriage or historical events (e.g., the September 11 attacks in the United States).

Research and Practical Implications

Although this theory has not received much attention within job stress literature, it is applicable to a variety of workplace situations. The ecological systems theory is unique in that it overtly specifies the role of systemic cultural contexts (e.g., public policy) on individuals and their direct environment, thus providing a unique perspective from which to view stressors and strain (e.g., maternity leave, stigma). In other words, this theory describes the human experience (including stressors and strains) as nested within systems and subsystems. This theory provides implications for supporting employees and mitigating systemic disparities. One such application described *vicarious trauma* (i.e., seeing or hearing another person's trauma, resulting in the observer's own trauma) in social workers (Pack, 2013). The response to vicarious traumatization was said to depend upon four levels: the level of the individual counselor's stress responses (e.g., coping, strain); the client–therapist level (e.g., resources available to the therapist to support the client); the organizational level (e.g., resources and support available); and the societal level (e.g., stigma regarding sexual violence, societal beliefs about counseling overall). Consistent with ecological systems theory, the authors state that vicarious traumatization requires intervention within each system (e.g., individual reappraisal, organizational training, public policy) to foster healthy workplaces for social workers (Pack, 2013).

MINORITY STRESS MODEL

The minority stress model describes how minority status and stigma affect people and their circumstances in a sociocultural perspective. Minority status can arise from any social identifier, such as national origin, body shape (e.g., height, weight), dis/ability, age, ethnicity, gender/identity, race, religion, sexual orientation, and socioeconomic status. This model holds that, on top of typical stressors, minority group members incur additional stressors resulting from stigma, including marginalization, prejudice, and discrimination (Meyer, 2007). *Stigma* refers to a feature that distinguishes someone as "other" and causes them to be treated poorly due to stereotypes and negative attributions. This model is different from most job stress theories that can be applied to the stress that minority group members face, as minority status is not typically a central variable. For example, person-environment fit theory can be used to explain how minority group members feel that they don't fit the environment, which may cause them to withdraw or experience other strains. Conversely, the organization may not feel that the minority group employee fits the organizational culture, limiting the employee's opportunities for advancement. Conservation of resources theory may describe racial privilege as a resource that can facilitate resource gain through investment, or minimize the effects of resource loss. However, few theories address the unique aspects of minority stress.

Minority stress can occur via *stereotypes*, which describe an overgeneralized belief about a group of people. Stereotypes can affect how employees are regarded, such that individuals' unique attributes are overlooked and instead their characteristics are ascribed in accordance with their group membership. The role of stereotypes was discussed in an application of ecological systems theory (Leong & Tang, 2016). This study explains how Asian Americans (particularly men) are stereotyped as possessing a robotic quality, devoid of emotion or pain. More generally, the model minority myth suggests that Asian people are able to overcome almost any challenge with hard work, personal sacrifice, and long hours, which they are happy to do. By ignoring the harsh truth of Asian American hardship, this stereotype brings comfort to those who believe it.

The related stereotype that Chinese immigrant workers are naturally good at science, technology, engineering, and mathematics fosters both internal (e.g., vocational identity) and external (e.g., prejudice, expectations) career barriers. In one such example, Chinese immigrants were found to be segregated to the technical ranks of a company as scientists and engineers (Leong & Tang, 2016). During a career workshop, many of these employees expressed interest in management positions. However, the company told these employees that their excellent performance as scientists and engineers demonstrated that they should stay in these positions to be most valuable to the company. Unsurprisingly, these workers reported frustration and resentment resulting from this unfair treatment. In this way, macrosystem influences (e.g., stereotypes) caused microsystem effects (e.g., discrimination).

Theoretical Integration: Visibility and Tokenism

Visibility is defined as the extent to which a person receives full consideration from others (Simpson & Lewis, 2005). Being visible is often seen as something desirable, particularly if people can control their visibility by highlighting achievements or hiding mistakes. In contrast to visibility, *invisibility* refers to a state or condition in which a person is not fully recognized and valued (Simpson & Lewis, 2005). Consequently, invisibility places marginalized people at a disadvantage by overlooking their contributions and dismissing their voices, leading to further marginalization (Simpson & Lewis, 2005). Alternatively, *hypervisibility* reflects the state of being overly visible, which can be beneficial when voluntary. *Intersectionality* describes the presence of multiple marginalized roles, such that the meaning of one identity is considered in the context of other identities that may have varying degrees of social status and influence. For example, being a single mother may be viewed differently depending on the mother's age or race. Depending on which identity is salient in a particular situation, such individuals may be visible, invisible, or hypervisible.

Members of marginalized social groups are stigmatized, and stigma manifests in hypervisibility and scrutiny (Settles, Buchanan, & Dotson, 2019). Due to this scrutiny, normal everyday human errors are inflated and exculpatory evidence is minimized or dismissed. For example, the fundamental attribution error may guide appraisal, such that any good things the stigmatized employee has done will be attributed to external characteristics (e.g., luck), and not the employee's effort or skill. Invisibility and hypervisibility limit a person's ability to be their authentic self, which is believed to induce strain through role stress or thwarting the basic need for belonging. Furthermore, invisibility and hypervisibility may interfere with job performance via social undermining, low autonomy (i.e., monitoring), reduced access to mentoring, or other disparate treatment. Consequently, members of marginalized groups are compelled to regulate their visibility to assuage potential harm, adding demands to their work role expectations (see Settles et al., 2019).

Tokenism describes minimally effortful attempts to fulfill an expectation. Typically, this is applied to perfunctory or symbolic efforts to represent people from diverse social groups to give the appearance of inclusion. Tokenism theory posits that numerical under-representation is a primary cause of negative work experiences for minority group members (Yoder, 1991). A study on tokenism shows that the climate of gender inequality relates to job stress, as expected ($r = 0.17, p < 0.05$), and the correlations with affective commitment and turnover intentions were even stronger ($r = -0.42$ and $0.39, p < 0.01$, respectively; King, Hebl, George, & Matusik, 2010). However, there is little other research as tokenism is difficult to study due to confounding variables (e.g., social status of the token group members, overall organizational demographic composition; Yoder, 1991). A notable exception studied women who comprise less than 15 percent of their workgroup and found that there are three negative processes of tokenism (Kanter, 1977). The first is invisibility and hypervisibility, which lead to excessive pressures to perform. Next, *contrast* refers to exaggerated differences between the token employee and the majority group members, which may result in social isolation. Finally, *role encapsulation* occurs when minority group members are limited by stereotyped roles that are incompatible with work-defined roles. For example, a woman might be treated as a mother, daughter, sister, or "pet" (Kanter, 1977). These three processes have been replicated across a variety of token groups representing a broad range of occupations (e.g., Yoder, 1991).

A study potentially relevant to tokenism uses the group lens model to describe detection of racial discrimination (Kern & Grandey, 2009). Within this model, salient group identity is proposed to act as a filter for ambiguous information. In other words, when social identity is salient (as may be the case from tokenism or past experience with hypervisibility), people are likely to view ambiguous instances of discrimination as prejudiced. This phenomenon did occur, and minority group members with a more salient identity were more likely to attribute incivility to racism than were minority group members with less salient identities. However, customer incivility was more likely to be appraised as harmful and intentional by White employees than by members of racial minority groups (Kern & Grandey, 2009). Researchers inferred that this process reflected negative adaptation, such that racial minority group members were more used to unfair treatment, thus less reactive. The finding that White people were more sensitive to mistreatment is consistent with a study that showed that White participants believed that anti-White racism has increased and was now a bigger problem than anti-Black racism (Norton & Sommers, 2011).

Research within employment, financial, criminal, and health literatures all document continued, serious racial (and other group identity) disparities in treatment and outcomes for minority group members. However, most instances of discrimination are ambiguous, which coupled with prejudice of observers, results in the perpetuation of systematic discrimination. For example, there is strong evidence that women are interrupted more than men, and their ideas are frequently credited to men in the workplace (e.g., Jacobi & Schweers, 2017). However, because of prejudice, in addition to the fact that it is simply impossible to know the extent to which a single event is caused by prejudice in many cases, some people are likely to dismiss gender-based interruptions or other microaggressions. Instead, the victim may be accused of "bringing gender into everything," playing the "woman" card, or reading too much into a one-time event. In other words, being a member of a minority group is stigmatized, but acknowledging such stigma is associated with further denigration.

LATENT DEPRIVATION MODEL

In discussing job stress from the sociocultural perspective, it is also important to consider the stigma and strain that result from unemployment. A conceptual link between unemployment and psychological distress can be found in Jahoda's (1981) latent deprivation model. According to Jahoda, employment serves many other functions besides providing for a financial income. When a person becomes unemployed, they are deprived of the latent benefits of work (in addition to manifest benefits like a salary), which in turn causes distress, as only regular employment can provide a sufficient amount of latent benefits. In comparison, people such as homemakers, volunteers, retirees, or employees on leave (e.g., medical, maternity) are out of the labor force, a state that may provide some, but not enough, of the latent benefits of work.

According to Jahoda, people in Western cultures are conditioned from a young age to regiment and fill their schedules with activities. This time structure is disrupted by unemployment, which leaves people with fewer opportunities for regular activities and social interaction. Moreover, unemployed people often report meaninglessness and a loss of valuable social roles. Jahoda distilled observations such as these into the categories of time structure, activity, status and identity, collective purpose, and social contact. The theory has since been clarified and tested in methodologically rigorous investigations. In particular, meta-analytic evidence has been found for the indirect effect of unemployment on reduced wellbeing via financial benefits (a manifest, not latent, benefit), time structure, and social status (Aitken, Cannon, Kaplan, & Kim, 2021). However, other individuals out of the labor force do not exhibit the loss of latent benefits (particularly social status) to nearly the same degree as those who are unemployed, indicating that the stigma unique to unemployment may mediate the relationship between unemployment and negative outcomes (Paul & Batinic, 2010).

CONCLUDING REMARKS

In closing, national culture and organizational culture have generated a large amount of interest and empirical research. In an increasingly global society, differences between cultures are getting smaller. Nonetheless, new observations about cross-national differences would be valuable. Research using Hofstede's dimensions, on the other hand, likely has little value to add at this point. His approach is *etic* (i.e., viewing a culture from the outside), as it applies the same set of criteria to all cultures. New *emic* observations that focus on the unique behavior patterns or perspectives from within a particular culture may not be generalizable and consequently may not fit in the applied sciences. However, Hofstede might have "put the cart before the horse" (reversed the order of a sequence of events), as best practice for measuring cross-cultural differences involves three stages: (1) developing the research question; (2) aligning research contexts; and (3) validating research instruments (Schaffer & Riordan, 2003). Instead, Hofstede distributed a values survey cross-nationally and expected that these values would reflect the culture and not the (a priori) items. Further emic research could be applicable to our understanding of stress.

In an analogy, researchers are unable to predict when a volcano will erupt. Variables like air temperature, amount of water, and atmospheric changes may make a difference, but there is only a narrow range of variation on Earth. Consequently, study of volcanoes on Venus, which has very different surface temperature and atmospheric conditions, and does not even have plate tectonics, contributed to marked shifts in the understanding of volcanic activity. Perhaps the study of psychology across disparate cultures can also lead to new insight. That said, it is important to avoid an *ecological fallacy* and create differences between people. For instance, the idea that men are from Mars and women are from Venus is outdated, gender binary, and overlooks the overwhelming similarities among the genders. Research has not supported large mean differences between cultures, genders, or races. For example, meta-analytic methods have detected no significant zero-order correlations between gender and leadership effectiveness (Eagly, Karau, & Makhijani, 1995), organizational commitment (Aven, Parker, & McEvoy, 1993), work–family conflict (Shockley, Shen, DeNunzio, Arvan, & Knudsen, 2017), counterproductive work behavior (Berry, Carpenter, & Barratt, 2012), role stressors (Shirom, Shechter Gilboa, Fried, & Cooper, 2008), or many other important workplace variables.

Nonetheless, there are sizable and harmful differences in the ways that women are evaluated relative to men. For example, most measures of organizational citizenship behavior demonstrate measurement nonequivalence between genders, particularly for items with motivational content when rated by managers (e.g., the employee "goes out of their way," "shows genuine concern," or "willingly assists others"; Jang et al., 2022). Furthermore, men are rated as performing more organizational citizenship behavior than women who do the same amount and type of behaviors in experimental vignettes (Allen, 2006). Role expectations and stigma affect many aspects of work beyond performance appraisals. For example, potential mentors who do not believe that a Chinese employee needs support in order to develop (i.e., model minority stereotypes) will be less motivated to mentor this person.

To explicate, some discrimination is well intentioned. It is not necessarily a hiring manager passing over a Black person for selection because they don't think a Black person can do the job or they don't want to work with a Black person. Instead, discrimination can be benevolent, such as telling a Black woman she is eloquent because, unconsciously, the expectations for her performance were low (sometimes referred to as the *talking platypus* effect). Or denying a promotion to a pregnant person to avoid giving them stress. Modern racism also includes condemning cultural values or qualities like manner of dress or speech. In the United States, it is legal in many states to discriminate on the basis of natural Black hair/hairstyles (e.g., braids, locs, twists, cornrows, knots, Afros, or more generally certain lengths of hair). Covert racism is also evidenced as "color-blindness," which disregards a long and lurid history of policies, attitudes, violence, and disparities (e.g., medical, financial, educational) that contribute to ongoing stereotypes, prejudice, and inequalities. Other subtle (and unsubtle) racism exists in the workplace, but little research has studied these processes from a job stress perspective. However, emic observations suggest that they are occurring, as people embedded within the culture are raising awareness about their own observations of discrimination. For example, *mansplaining* or *hepeating* describe ways in which women's competence and ideas are undermined at work.

Another example of an emic observation parallels qualitative etic research showing that people of different cultures have different levels of comfort with "straight talk" (Liu et al., 2007). Specifically, this etic study found that people from individualistic cultures preferred straight talk and were more comfortable with overtly verbalizing their needs, whereas people from collectivistic cultures preferred implicit and indirect verbal interaction to maintain harmony in a conflict. This difference is rarely discussed in research but is perhaps better known among popular culture. Initially attributed to Andrea Donderi (e.g., Eichler, 2010), the idea has since been labeled on Reddit as "ask versus guess culture."[1] This observation describes how some people from the *ask culture* are comfortable with "no," and consequently ask others directly for favors (e.g., "Can you please watch my dog for me?"). They may come across as arrogant and pushy. People from *guess cultures* incur stress from saying and hearing "no," and assume others do as well. They might indirectly ask for favors ("I'd love to go see my mom this weekend, but I can't bring my dog and the kennel is booked") and be seen as timid or passive-aggressive. "Ask" culture is similar to straight talk, and this is an example of how observations that arise from within a culture may translate into the applied sciences. That is to say, while anecdotes are expressly nonscientific, observations (even unscientific layperson musings on Reddit) can be followed by testing consistent with the scientific method, and may further our understanding of the workplace in new, relevant, and insightful ways.

NOTE

1. Although this describes a comparison across ostensible cultures, this is probably not an etic approach. The term *culture* used in this example is colloquial and does not truly reflect culture in terms of the collective programming of the mind across time and people. That said, it does describe a pattern of behavior, attitudes, and beliefs, albeit in a narrow way.

REFERENCES

Aitken, J. A., Cannon, J. A., Kaplan, S. A., & Kim, H. J. (2021). *On the benefits of work: A meta-analysis of Jahoda's latent deprivation theory.* Unpublished manuscript, Department of Psychology, George Mason University.

Allen, T. D. (2006). Rewarding good citizens: The relationship between citizenship behavior, gender, and organizational rewards. *Journal of Applied Social Psychology, 36*(1), 120–143.

Aven, F. F., Parker, B., & McEvoy, G. M. (1993). Gender and attitudinal commitment to organizations: A meta-analysis. *Journal of Business Research, 26*, 3–15.

Berry, C. M., Carpenter, N. C., & Barratt, C. L. (2012). Do other-reports of counterproductive work behavior provide an incremental contribution over self-reports? A meta-analytic comparison. *Journal of Applied Psychology, 97*(3), 613–636.

Bronfenbrenner, U. (1994). Ecological models of human development. *Readings on the Development of Children, 2*(1), 37–43.

Eagly, A. H., Karau, S. J., & Makhijani, M. G. (1995). Gender and the effectiveness of leaders: A meta-analysis. *Psychological Bulletin, 117*(1), 125–145.

Eichler, A. (2010). Askers versus guessers. www.theatlantic.com/national/archive/2010/05/askers-vs-guessers/340891/

Hofstede, G. (1980). Motivation, leadership, and organization: Do American theories apply abroad? *Organizational Dynamics, 9*(1), 42–63.

Jacobi, T., & Schweers, D. (2017, April 11). Female Supreme Court justices are interrupted more by male justices and advocates. *Harvard Business Review.*

Jahoda, M. (1981). Work, employment, and unemployment: Values, theories, and approaches in social research. *American Psychologist, 36*(2), 184–191.

Jang, S., Allen, T. D., Kim, E., O'Brien, K. E., Cho, I., & Ceylan, S. (2022). Measurement invariance of organizational citizenship behavior across gender. *Applied Psychology: An International Review.*

Kanter, R. M. (1977). *Men and women of the corporation.* Basic Books.

Kern, J. H., & Grandey, A. A. (2009). Customer incivility as a social stressor: The role of race and racial identity for service employees. *Journal of Occupational Health Psychology, 14*(1), 46–57.

King, E. B., Hebl, M. R., George, J. M., & Matusik, S. F. (2010). Understanding tokenism: Antecedents and consequences of a psychological climate of gender inequity. *Journal of Management, 36*(2), 482–510.

Leong, F. T., & Tang, M. (2016). Career barriers for Chinese immigrants in the United States. *Career Development Quarterly, 64*(3), 259–271.

Liu, C., Spector, P. E., & Shi, L. (2007). Cross-national job stress: A quantitative and qualitative study. *Journal of Organizational Behavior, 28*(2), 209–239.

McSweeney, B. (2002). Hofstede's model of national cultural differences and their consequences: A triumph of faith – a failure of analysis. *Human Relations, 55*(1), 89–118.

Meyer, I. H. (2007). Prejudice and discrimination as social stressors. In I. H. Meyer & M. E. Northridge (Eds), *The health of sexual minorities: Public health perspectives on lesbian, gay, bisexual, and transgender populations* (pp. 242–267). Springer Science + Business Media.

Norton, M. I., & Sommers, S. R. (2011). Whites see racism as a zero-sum game that they are now losing. *Perspectives on Psychological Science, 6*(3), 215–218.

Pack, M. (2013). Vicarious traumatisation and resilience: An ecological systems approach to sexual abuse counsellors' trauma and stress. *Sexual Abuse in Australia and New Zealand*, *5*(2), 69–76.

Paul, K. I., & Batinic, B. (2010). The need for work: Jahoda's latent functions of employment in a representative sample of the German population. *Journal of Organizational Behavior*, *31*(1), 45–64.

Schaffer, B. S., & Riordan, C. M. (2003). A review of cross-cultural methodologies for organizational research: A best-practices approach. *Organizational Research Methods*, *6*(2), 169–215.

Settles, I. H., Buchanan, N. T., & Dotson, K. (2019). Scrutinized but not recognized: (In)visibility and hypervisibility experiences of faculty of color. *Journal of Vocational Behavior*, *113*, 62–74.

Shirom, A., Shechter Gilboa, S., Fried, Y., & Cooper, C. L. (2008). Gender, age and tenure as moderators of work-related stressors' relationships with job performance: A meta-analysis. *Human Relations*, *61*(10), 1371–1398.

Shockley, K. M., Shen, W., DeNunzio, M. M., Arvan, M. L., & Knudsen, E. A. (2017). Disentangling the relationship between gender and work–family conflict: An integration of theoretical perspectives using meta-analytic methods. *Journal of Applied Psychology*, *102*(12), 1601–1635.

Simpson, R., & Lewis, P. (2005). An investigation of silence and a scrutiny of transparency: Re-examining gender in organization literature through the concepts of voice and visibility. *Human Relations*, *58*(10), 1253–1275.

Spector, P. E., Cooper, C. L., & Sparks, K. (2001). An international study of the psychometric properties of the Hofstede Values Survey Module 1994: A comparison of individual and country/province level results. *Applied Psychology*, *50*(2), 269–281.

Triandis, H. C. (2004). The many dimensions of culture. *Academy of Management Executive*, *18*(1), 88–93.

Triandis, H. C., & Gelfand, M. J. (1998). Converging measurement of horizontal and vertical individualism and collectivism. *Journal of Personality and Social Psychology*, *74*(1), 118–128.

Vandello, J. A., Cohen, D., & Ransom, S. (2008). US Southern and Northern differences in perceptions of norms about aggression: Mechanisms for the perpetuation of a culture of honor. *Journal of Cross-Cultural Psychology*, *39*(2), 162–177.

Wang, M., & Russell, S. S. (2005). Measurement equivalence of the job descriptive index across Chinese and American workers: Results from confirmatory factor analysis and item response theory. *Educational and Psychological Measurement*, *65*(4), 709–732.

Yoder, J. D. (1991). Rethinking tokenism: Looking beyond numbers. *Gender and Society*, *5*(2), 178–192.

13. Theories of motivation and self-regulation

Motivation is an inherent and pervasive question within psychology. Ultimately, the question "why do people do this" is one of motivation. In organizational psychology, motivation is assumed to have at least three components: direction, intensity, and persistence. *Direction* reflects the choice of a behavior. A person who laments "I have no motivation today" may have a great deal of motivation, but in a direction inconsistent with their goals (e.g., to catch up on reading or have a nap). *Persistence* reflects the temporal length of motivation, and *intensity* describes the effortfulness of the motivation. Consequently, motivation is typically measured via performance outcomes.[1]

Stress and motivation are closely tied, and researchers have been discussing a motivation–stress relationship throughout the history of psychological stress. For example, Triplett described stress as an excess of arousal, whereas motivation is optimized at a moderate level of arousal. Additionally, Bandura states that stress impedes self-regulation and depletes resources that could be used for goal-directed behavior. In another example, Lazarus (2006, p. 70) claims that "without a goal at stake, there is no potential for stress or emotion." Furthermore, burnout is indicated by low motivation, such that decreased personal accomplishment is indeed one of three factors that comprise burnout. Similarly, challenge stressors increase motivation whereas hindrance stressors decrease motivation. To summarize, excessive motivation induces strain, and excessive stress (both stressors and strains) decreases motivation. In fact, physiological stress is distracting, increases arousal, depletes resources for self-regulation (e.g., negative effects on memory; Schaufeli, Bakker, Hoogduin, Schaap, & Kladler, 2001), and interferes with decision making. When work is demanding, self-regulation is even more valuable (e.g., "work smarter, not harder"). Despite the relevance, motivation theories and job stress theories are largely separate, but theoretical integrations appear very promising (e.g., self-regulation and the job demands-resources model; Bakker & de Vries, 2021).

SELF-REGULATION THEORY

Bandura (1991) stated that *self-regulation* is the control of behavior through a variety of cognitive processes, nested within the categories of self-observation (e.g., monitoring), judgment processes (e.g., personal standards), and self-reaction (e.g., rewards and punishment). In his version of self-regulation, motivation and action are proactive, not reactive, such that people consider their options before engaging in behavior. Cognitive self-regulation is evidenced by performance of intended behaviors. Without self-reflection (i.e., an individual's insight into their desires and status towards achieving those desires), behavior would be unstable and vary based on external factors. That said, self-directed behavior is governed to some extent by external conditions because our personal desires and standards are at least partially determined by social learning.

When explicating the system of self-regulation of emotion and action, Bandura (1991) emphasized the mediating role of internal standards and self-reactive influences. First, *self-observation* takes place, wherein a person monitors their activity along several dimensions, including quality, sociability, and deviance. The quality of this monitoring matters, as accurate, relevant, recent, and detailed information leads to better self-evaluation in the next step. Specifically, during *self-evaluation*, the current level of performance is compared against *personal standards* that may vary in terms of proximity, explicitness, and generality (perhaps akin to the timely, measurable, and specificity qualities of effective goals). Activity might be compared against various referents, including social references (e.g., a coworker or sibling), self-comparisons (e.g., personal record), or an external metric (e.g., quota). The activity is also judged in terms of valence to be valued, neutral, or devalued. In the final *self-reactive* step, people determine if their activity is positive or negative, and may reward or punish themselves (e.g., emotional reactions of guilt are punishing, pride would be rewarding).

There is some overlap between Bandura's self-regulation and Freudian principles (e.g., internal and external drives that must be balanced), perhaps encouraging the use of the term *ego depletion* within the self-regulation perspective. This term reflects the idea that attempts to control oneself (i.e., ego) expend resources (i.e., depletion) that inhibit future attempts at self-control. In other words, self-control is finite and can be exhausted (Baumeister, Bratslavsky, Muraven, & Tice, 1998). Later research suggested that self-control was more like a muscle that grew stronger with continued use (i.e., Muraven & Baumeister, 2000). These two propositions seem incompatible, as self-control is proposed to lead to less (i.e., depleted) self-control or more (i.e., strengthened) self-control in the future. However, empirical evidence in favor of either explanation, or the dynamic unfolding of the two processes, is largely flawed. Specifically, measurement and study design often confound self-regulation with other relevant variables (e.g., self-efficacy, negative emotion). Overall, though, the postulates of ego depletion have not been well supported in methodologically rigorous meta-analyses (e.g., Hagger et al., 2016), and there are researchers who wish to retire the term "ego depletion" altogether, in favor of self-regulation or self-control (see Inzlicht & Friese, 2019 for a critical review).

Theoretical Extension: Episodic Process Model of Affect and Performance

Other self-regulatory models have been proposed. This episodic process model emphasizes short-term, discrete, proximal job performance. This is intended to address the gap in our understanding of effects of transient emotions and traditional concepts of (stable) job performance. According to Beal, Weiss, Barros, and MacDermid (2005), self-regulation is influenced by three types of forces: *regulatory resources* (e.g., self-efficacy), *task attentional pull* (the degree to which the task is inherently rewarding or punishing), and *off-task attentional demands* (the degree to which alternative behaviors are rewarding or punishing). These factors influence how difficult (e.g., depleting) it is to stay on task. This theory has not received as much attention as Bandura's, but empirical research is supportive.

Research and Practical Implications

Self-regulation and stress are inherently linked. Although the direction of the relationship is unknown (and likely unstable, reciprocal, and/or simultaneous), a variety of relationships have been proposed. For one, self-regulatory mechanisms (e.g., cognitive self-evaluation) might precede both performance and wellbeing in a self-regulation-as-a-common-source model, or wellbeing might increase the ability to self-regulate and thus improve performance in a mediated model (Sonnentag, 2002). Furthermore, stress can disrupt the self-regulation process if stressors or strain distract people from observing the information needed for self-evaluation. Stress may also cause, or result from, irrational internal standards in the self-judgment step of self-regulation (e.g., overcommitment; Siegrist, 1996; or false internalization; Kuhl & Kazén, 1994). Finally, stress resulting from self-judgment may serve as a punishment, such that people feel the activity is not valuable, thus improving future self-regulation.

The episodic process model provides some clear implications for practice. For example, interested organizations can design jobs consistent with principles of this theory by maximizing task attentional pull (e.g., task significance via job redesign; e.g., Zhou et al., 2017) or minimizing distractions and intrusions. Individuals who hope to increase their self-regulation can likewise try to modify their pull by, for example, using challenging and specific goals to increase task pull. Distractions can be decreased, for example, by turning off notifications on the phone or computer, scheduling meetings in a way as to minimize disruption, maintaining boundaries with other people (e.g., establishing "office hours"), or addressing physiological needs.

In fact, previous empirical evidence indicates that physiological conditions clearly impact self-regulation ability. One study found that judges are up to five times more likely to grant parole at the beginning of a session (e.g., at the beginning of the day or after lunch) than at the end of a session (Danziger, Levav, & Avnaim-Pesso, 2011). This is attributed to desire to maintain the status quo (e.g., not grant parole) when cognitively depleted. It is unclear whether a meal during breaktime (e.g., glucose) or the break itself mediated this effect, but either way, this highlights the importance of breaks. Similarly, a study on effort and motivation in the military shows that effort can improve performance for some time, but even with caffeine, "effort alone is unable to sustain performance" (Revelle & Anderson, 1998, p. 12). Therefore, self-regulatory models should definitely be amended to include physical comfort, as hunger, fatigue, pain, and stress are likely to redirect attention, perhaps within the conceptualization of the Beal et al. (2005) model as off-task attentional demand or self-regulatory capacity.

Similarly, some people keep a running "to-do" list in their working memory (e.g., "don't forget to return that package") or experience other cognitive intrusions (e.g., "I wonder when a new season of my favorite show is being released," "I hope my neighbor isn't mad at me"). Making it a habit to write down these thoughts prior to or during a work session (with the intention of addressing those distractions afterwards) is a good way to improve focus and maximize cognitive resources for the task at hand. This technique is used to decrease test anxiety, as some people ruminate over an internal list of worries, which can increase arousal, aggravate anxiety, distract from the task at hand, and lead to worse performance. However, it seems likely that this technique can facilitate attention and performance across a wide array of performance situations.

GOAL-SETTING THEORY

Goal setting is a type of self-regulation. Goal-setting theory is a rich theory that describes motivation and performance in terms of goal setting and goal striving. A main tenet is that specific and challenging goals (e.g., "I will study one chapter tonight") are more effective than do-your-best goals (e.g., "I will study as much as possible tonight"), as people are challenged and feel accomplished when progress is made (Locke & Latham, 2013). Effective goals are challenging, but realistic enough to engender goal commitment. The relationship between goal commitment and performance can be affected by external factors (e.g., extrinsic rewards), internal factors (e.g., self-efficacy), and interactive factors (e.g., peer participation). Goals set according to these criteria best allow people to evaluate their performance directly, adjust their strategy and effort if necessary, and persist until the goal is achieved (Locke & Latham, 2013). However, seeking feedback from others is also adaptive. Attainment of goals may increase wellbeing through the outcomes of self-efficacy, favorable life circumstances, and praise from others (Sheldon & Elliot, 1999). On the other hand, goal abandonment may also alleviate stress if the goal is overly burdensome, such that the costs exceed the value (e.g., overcommitment; Siegrist, 1996), or incurs negative self-evaluations and feelings due to repeated failures (Latham & Locke, 2007). In some cases, desire to achieve work goals can even motivate counterproductive work behavior (Penney, Hunter, & Perry, 2011). Similarly, goal disruption and goal enhancement from workplace events affect fatigue and emotional reactions (Zohar, Tzischinski, & Epstein, 2003).

Research and Practical Implications

Beyond these proposed relationships with stress, goal setting can decrease role stress by clarifying role expectations, as people who have clear goals have less ambiguity (Quick, 1979). However, the amount of research in job stress generated by goal-setting theory is surprisingly small. Goal setting is one of the most carefully developed, widely applicable, and empirically supported theories of psychology in the workplace. The job stress literature would benefit from understanding the role of stress in goal setting, goal striving, goal-directed performance, and goal abandonment (and vice versa). For example, long-term, challenging goals are likely to have costs due to sustained effort, which is the definition of demands in the job demands-resources model. Thus, it seems that goal striving might be a demand. Furthermore, arousal associated with stress (or goal striving) might pre-empt *goal redirection*, which occurs when a person has an action tendency activated (i.e., emotion-based drive) but is unable to direct it (e.g., cleaning the office instead of doing work). Overall, there is still much to learn about goals and stress.

JOB CHARACTERISTICS AND JOB DESIGN

The work environment might give rise to motivation. Herzberg (1964) performed a series of semi-structured interviews of white-collar workers using a critical incidents approach. After analyzing the reports, he identified 14 themes (e.g., recognition, salary, work itself). According to the interviews, incidents that increased job satisfaction (e.g., recognition) were associated with completely different factors than the incidents that decreased job satisfaction (e.g., supervision). Thus, work factors were categorized as *motivators* (e.g., factors that meet the need for growth, like responsibility) or *hygiene* (factors surrounding work, like supervision and salary). In the workplace, job satisfaction is said to result from motivators, but not hygiene, which were instead associated with job dissatisfaction. Thus, in the absence of motivators, hygiene could only raise satisfaction to neutral levels. However, it became apparent that there is likely no qualitative distinction between job satisfaction and dissatisfaction (although efforts to test this were hampered by the lack of a job satisfaction measure; Behling, Labovitz, & Kosmo, 1968). Instead, the interviews were likely flawed due to self-serving bias, as it seems possible that people would attribute good workplace outcomes to their own growth, and negative workplace outcomes to others (e.g., supervisors, the work itself). Thus, hygiene was largely dropped from future testing. To some extent, the transition away from interest in hygiene may have contributed to our continued neglect of the study of pay on motivation and wellbeing.

Nonetheless, Herzberg's two-factor theory inspired the development of job characteristics theory (Hackman & Oldham, 1976). Job characteristics theory delineates five job characteristics (derived from Herzberg's motivators) that contribute positively to performance, job satisfaction, and motivation: skill variety, task identity, task significance, autonomy, and feedback. These qualities result in psychological states (i.e., experienced meaningfulness, felt responsibility, knowledge of results) that are more proximally associated with motivation. *Skill variety* describes the range of activities required for the job. People tend to feel more fulfilled when they can use a variety of skills. *Task identity* refers to whether work outcomes are whole and visible, or part and anonymous. For example, an assembly-line job that involves lifting headlights from a box and placing them onto a conveyor belt has less task identity than a manufacturing job that involves building a whole car. *Task significance* reflects the degree to which the job helps other people. These three characteristics equally contribute to the psychological state of *experienced meaningfulness*. *Autonomy* is the fourth characteristic and describes the amount of independence and discretion an employee has to plan and complete their work. Autonomy leads to the state of *experienced responsibility*, which occurs when the employee feels accountable for their work. The last characteristic is *feedback*, which represents the amount of knowledge that the employee has regarding the quality of their work. Clear, detailed, and actionable feedback, delivered quickly, is the most effective. This leads to the critical psychological state of *knowledge of results*. The three states then contribute equally, in an additive algebraic formula, to the employee's *motivating potential score* (MPS; Figure 13.1).

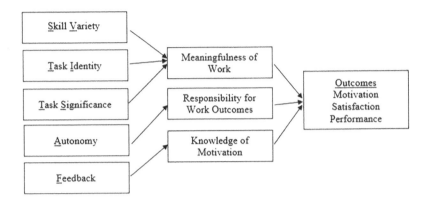

$$(SV+TI+TS)/3 + A + F = MPS$$

Formulaic representation of motivation

Figure 13.1   Job characteristics model

Theoretical Extension: Balance Theory of Job Design for Stress Reduction

The balance theory of job design is integrated from several bodies of literature regarding job design and the impact on worker wellbeing and performance (e.g., job stress, ergonomics; Smith & Sainfort, 1989). This model posits that working conditions and other environmental factors can produce a "stress load" that is affected by objective aspects of the stressor, as well as individual perceptions. Within this model, physiological and psychological loads are separate. Physiological loads produce stress when they exceed the available physical resources, such as energy resources or strength. On the other hand, psychological loads produce emotional, behavioral, and biological consequences, determined by the employee's appraisal and psychological resources, such as motivation and cognitive capacity. Resources are not stable over time, but fluctuate in response to strain and working conditions. When the load becomes too great, the person displays stress responses with physiological (e.g., epinephrine release) or psychological (e.g., negative mood) consequences. Frequent stress reactions over an extended period of time can cause health disorders. When such disorders occur, resources are depleted and unavailable for coping with the load, creating a cyclical effect unless external resources become available or the load is reduced. In an update to the model, Carayon (2007) proposed adding nonwork elements by, for example, incorporating home and social domains. Although this model is intuitive and consistent with previous empirical findings, testing of this model has been quite limited.

Research and Practical Implications

Job redesign efforts have targeted the five key job characteristics in attempts to reduce employee stressors and strain via job enrichment. For example, one study found that autonomy, skill variety, task identity, feedback from the job, and feedback from coworkers (task significance was not analyzed) correlated with mental health ($r = 0.15$ to 0.25) and emotional exhaustion (with the exception of skill variety; $r = 0.21$ to 0.29; Kelloway & Barling, 1991). Furthermore, these characteristics (again excepting skill variety) correlate with role ambiguity and role conflict ($r = 0.17$ to 0.30). Another intervention study found that autonomy, skill utilization, and feedback correlated with wellbeing ($r = 0.32$ to 0.49; Holman, Axtell, Sprigg, Totterdell, & Wall, 2010). Overall, it seems that there is sufficient evidence to suggest that job redesign can effectively reduce employee strain.

Although the job characteristics model is the most popular and well tested, there are alternative perspectives of job design. Campion and Thayer (1985) classified job design approaches as motivational (e.g., job characteristics theory), mechanistic (e.g., scientific management), biological (e.g., biomechanical approaches), and perceptual/motor (e.g., design of controls and displays). Other conceptualizations of job design emphasize knowledge (e.g., job complexity) and social (e.g., interdependence) characteristics (Carayon, 2009).

SELF-DETERMINATION THEORY

The job characteristics model describes aspects of the work that contribute to internal states that lead to motivation. Self-determination theory (SDT) somewhat parallels this model, in that SDT posits that aspects of the environment contribute to internal needs fulfillment, which then leads to autonomous motivation. Specifically, people have an innate desire for psychological growth and wellbeing to the extent that their three basic psychological needs are satisfied (Deci & Ryan, 2000). *Autonomy needs* reflect volition and self-endorsed action, *belonging needs* reflect significant relationships and interconnectedness, and *competence needs* refers to the perceived ability to influence the environment. When people's needs are fulfilled from the environment, they experience wellbeing and *autonomous motivation* – self-directed activity congruent with intrinsic goals. *Controlled motivation*, on the other hand, refers to engaging in behaviors that arise from outside the self, such as gaining rewards or avoiding punishment. When controlled, behavior is performed out of obligation or pressure, such that the behavior will stop when external pressure is removed.

SDT is a meta-theory containing six subtheories. The first is cognitive evaluation theory, which describes the importance of autonomy and competence needs fulfillment in intrinsic motivation. Causality orientations theory uses three causality orientations (i.e., autonomous, controlled, amotivated) to describe people's tendencies to regulate behavior in particular ways. Basic psychological needs theory explicates how autonomy, belonging, and competence are psychological needs (e.g., pan-cultural). The remaining theories similarly explicate particular parts of the overall SDT model, particularly regarding the need for belonging and the intrinsic versus extrinsic nature of behaviors and goals.

Research and Practical Implications

Autonomous regulation is associated with a variety of positive individual and organizational outcomes, including wellbeing, effective coping, happiness, energy, reduced turnover intentions, and fewer absences (see Manganelli, Thibault-Landry, Forest, & Carpentier, 2018 for a review). Furthermore, enhanced job performance, role fulfillment, proactive behavior, innovative behavior, and productivity also arise, perhaps mediated by better persistence, attention, effort, and engagement. This theory has been integrated with other models, such as the three-component model of organizational commitment (see Meyer & Maltin, 2010) and the job characteristics model (see Trépanier, Forest, Fernet, & Austin, 2015). However, some methodological weaknesses have been consistent in the testing of SDT. For one, much empirical research does not use basic needs fulfillment in a cohesive way. Instead, only certain needs (e.g., competence) might be chosen without adequate explanation, perhaps due to *HARKing* – hypothesizing after results are known. Because the theory emphasizes autonomous motivation, it is important to measure need fulfillment cohesively, and null findings with other needs should be mentioned for accuracy. If only one or two needs are relevant, the justification for choosing them should be carefully explicated, perhaps in line with the relevant subtheories (e.g., cognitive evaluation theory). In fact, more observations about the individual needs could be illuminating and lead to refinement of the theory, particularly regarding basic psychological needs theory and attempts to clarify whether autonomy, belonging, and competence meet the criteria to be considered basic needs.

Despite methodological inconsistencies, the theory is well supported and provides clear, actionable suggestions for improving job stress. Specifically, organizations should fulfill basic psychological needs in order to facilitate autonomous regulation. For example, autonomy can be modified through job design. Belonging can be supported through mentoring or by increasing work–life balance, or improving the social climate of the organization. Finally, competence can be improved through challenging assignments, better compensation, recognition, or job design (e.g., skill variety, task identity). See Manganelli et al. (2018) for more suggestions.

ACTION-STATE ORIENTATION

In contrast to the previous theories, action-state orientation may explain why two employees with equivocal goals, competence, and desires might not attain the same level of goal-directed behavior. Specifically, *action-state orientation* describes individual differences in the ability to initiate and maintain intentional activities and goal striving, which requires the ability to attend to goal-related signals but ignore signals from irrelevant cognitions and emotions (Kuhl & Kazén, 1994). *Goal striving* is closely related to self-regulation and refers to the process of implementing a goal by identifying and addressing discrepancies between ideal and actual performance.

Action orientation is associated with efficient performance, as individuals with an *action orientation* can focus their cognitive resources on the goal-directed behavior and flexibly redirect their attention when needed (e.g., to recover from setbacks). Alternatively, *state orientation* is associated with persistent and interfering thoughts and feelings, often about other goals, which reduces the cognitive resources available for goal striving. This inhibits goal initiation and maintenance, especially during difficult or unfamiliar tasks. Action orientation has three subdimensions. The *preoccupation–disengagement* continuum describes the extent to which people consciously process information related to a past, present, or future state. People who are more action-oriented are closer to the pole marked by *disengagement*, which reflects the ability to detach from thoughts about alternative goals or unwanted outcomes (e.g., failure). *Hesitation-initiation* is the degree to which people have difficulty with starting goal-directed behaviors. Action orientation, in this case, is associated with *initiation*, whereas state orientation is associated with *hesitation*. To compare, initiation is behavioral, whereas disengagement is cognitive in nature. Once goal-directed activity begins, there are differences in *volatility-persistence*, which describes the capability to maintain an action-oriented mode and avoid distraction. In this case, action orientation is manifested as *persistence*, or the effective maintenance of attention and intention until the goal-directed behavior is finished. People with more state orientations may have excessive activity in the action initiation system, thus inappropriately initiating new tasks. On the other hand, preoccupation and hesitation are associated with low activation of the action initiation system.

Theoretical Extension: Personality Systems Interaction Theory

Action-state orientation evolved from personality systems interaction theory and describes how emotions and personality affect cognition and behavior. Specifically, being able to down-regulate negative emotion allows for adaptive shifting between four cognitive systems (i.e., extension memory, object recognition, intention memory, and intuitive behavioral control; Kuhl, 2000). This theory originated from Freud's hypothesis that the displacement of energy between fixation (e.g., intrusive thoughts and irrational adherence to unfulfilled wishes) and flexibility (e.g., the ability to disengage from maladaptive goals) underlies psychological disorder. In healthy adults, controlled self-regulating processes should initiate when automatic responses are disrupted or unsuccessful, or the cost of failure is judged to be too high. There is evidence for a self-regulatory action initiation system at the neurological level. Specifically, patients with lesions of the frontal lobe show deficits in the ability to plan, initiate, and maintain certain activities without external influence (Stuss & Benson, 1984). For example, they might state "I would like to go for a walk" but will not initiate the behavior until someone else asks them to go for a walk.

Research and Practical Implications

In one test of action-state orientation, executive functioning was measured with nine cognitive ability measures (e.g., the Stroop test), which correlated negatively with self-control failures in an experience sampling methodology study (Plessow, Fischer, Kirschbaum, & Goschke, 2011). This negative correlation was stronger for those who are state-oriented (Wolff et al., 2016). Furthermore, a marginally significant effect showed that state-oriented people attend to irrelevant stimuli less than action-oriented people, although both groups showed evidence of this goal shielding and cognitive inflexibility. This process takes time, though, and the amount of time required is approximately the same amount of time that it takes for the HPA axis (i.e., chronic stress response) to fully activate. It is known that stress hormones bind to the prefrontal cortex, and this is believed to contribute in some (currently unknown) way to the goal-shielding effect.

In research on personality systems interaction theory, police officers' ability to shoot a gun was investigated under high- and low-pressure situations (Landman, Nieuwenhuys, & Oudejans, 2016). Officers reported higher levels of anxiety, had higher heart rates, shot faster, and shot less accurately in the high-pressure condition compared to the low-pressure condition. In a high-pressure situation, decision-related action orientation significantly predicted shot accuracy, but not perceived anxiety and heart rate.

Another study of personality systems integration theory tests the postulate that uncompleted tasks have a privileged status in working memory, especially for state-oriented participants (Birk, Mandryk, & Baumann, 2020). In other words, it is hard for people (and state-oriented people in particular) to recover from interrupted tasks. To test this, participants simply had to click a button to continue playing a fun game after receiving a message stating "Connection lost, wait 60 seconds, or click here to continue." The tendency to continue with an interrupted goal-related activity is stronger for action- than for state-oriented individuals (who were less likely to redirect attention and click the button) under stress. That is to say, state-oriented individuals were not less motivated but instead less able to initiate action. Consequently, rewards or incentives typically used to increase motivation cannot compensate for self-regulatory deficits. Instead, interventions must modify the environment to facilitate self-regulation (e.g., job design) or train self-regulatory tactics.

CONCLUDING REMARKS

Self-regulation, goal setting, and motivation are central topics within psychology and strongly related to job stress. For example, goal striving and coping both require self-regulatory processes, and good self-regulation can prevent behavioral strains (e.g., stress eating). Furthermore, stress is believed to impair self-regulation directly through fatigue or indirectly through decrements to the self-regulatory subfunctions (e.g., comparing current performance to standards). Conversely, studies investigating the job demands-resources model show the significant role of job and personal resources in sustaining work motivation, particularly when job demands are high (e.g., Zohar et al., 2003). That said, job stress theories only recognize the importance of goals in an abstract way, as they typically do not specifically mention goals or specify which goals are particularly important (Semmer et al., 2019). Instead, "goals represent the ground rather than the figure in the stress and coping literature" (Elliot, Thrash, & Murayama, 2011, p. 644). Nonetheless, a great deal of theoretical work has already been done, and specific research propositions already delineated (see Kanfer, Chen, & Pritchard, 2008), which might hopefully expedite future research in this area. It is important to note that self-regulation occurs within-person over time, and tests of self-regulation may be inconvenient to conduct.

For people looking to improve their own motivation, self-regulation theory provides actionable suggestions. The first is to establish a conducive environment that minimizes distractions and facilitates self-monitoring and feedback. For example, text messaging or checking phone notifications can be inherently rewarding, and care should be taken to prevent the self-regulatory systems from learning (i.e., being conditioned) to check for notifications due to this reward. Perhaps this can be thought of as rewarding the brain to seek distractions. Self-regulation is also tied to smart-phone use via media multitasking, such that people who have more media demands (e.g., using a book and screen at the same time) report more difficulty regulating smart-phone use and staying focused. Another method shown to effectively leverage self-regulation is goal setting (see Latham & Locke, 1991). Specific, measurable, timely goals are empirically shown to improve performance, consistent with both goal-setting theory and self-regulation theory.

NOTE

1.   People are sometimes disappointed to learn that there is no self-report measure of amount of motivation in the colloquial sense. In these cases, interested researchers might prefer to study components of specific motivation theories (e.g., basic psychological needs fulfillment, expectancies), goal setting (e.g., planning quality, goal attainment scaling), trait-level indicators of self-regulation (e.g., Protestant work ethic, conscientiousness, need for achievement, self-efficacy, action-state orientation), energy (e.g., engagement, vigor), or demotivation (e.g., fatigue, burnout, hopelessness).

REFERENCES

Bakker, A. B., & de Vries, J. D. (2021). Job demands-resources theory and self-regulation: New explanations and remedies for job burnout. *Anxiety, Stress, and Coping, 34*(1), 1–21.

Bandura, A. (1991). Social cognitive theory of self-regulation. *Organizational Behavior and Human Decision Processes, 50*(2), 248–287.

Baumeister, R. F., Bratslavsky, E., Muraven, M., & Tice, D. M. (1998). Ego depletion: Is the active self a limited resource? *Journal of Personality and Social Psychology, 74*(5), 1252–1265.

Beal, D. J., Weiss, H. M., Barros, E., & MacDermid, S. M. (2005). An episodic process model of affective influences on performance. *Journal of Applied Psychology, 90*(6), 1054–1068.

Behling, O., Labovitz, G., & Kosmo, R. (1968). The Herzberg controversy: A critical reappraisal. *Academy of Management Journal, 11*(1), 99–108.

Birk, M. V., Mandryk, R. L., & Baumann N. (2020). Just a click away: Action–state orientation moderates the impact of task interruptions on initiative. *Journal of Personality, 88*(2), 373–390.

Campion, M. A., & Thayer, P. W. (1985). Development and field evaluation of an interdisciplinary measure of job design. *Journal of Applied Psychology, 70*(1), 29–43.

Carayon, P. (2007). Healthy and efficient work with computers and information and communication technology – are there limits? *Scandinavian Journal of Work, Environment and Health, Supplement, 33*, 10–16.

Carayon, P. (2009). The balance theory and the work system model ... Twenty years later. *International Journal of Human–Computer Interaction, 25*(5), 313–327.

Danziger, S., Levav, J., & Avnaim-Pesso, L. (2011). Extraneous factors in judicial decisions. *Proceedings of the National Academy of Sciences, 108*(17), 6889–6892.

Deci, E. L., & Ryan, R. M. (2000). The "what" and "why" of goal pursuits: Human needs and the self-determination of behavior. *Psychological Inquiry, 11*(4), 227–268.

Elliot, A. J., Thrash, T. M., & Murayama, K. (2011). A longitudinal analysis of self-regulation and well-being: Avoidance personal goals, avoidance coping, stress generation, and subjective well-being. *Journal of Personality, 79*(3), 643–674.

Hackman, J. R., & Oldham, G. R. (1976). Motivation through the design of work: Test of a theory. *Organizational Behavior and Human Performance, 16*(2), 250–279.

Hagger, M. S., Chatzisarantis, N. L., Alberts, H., Anggono, C. O., Batailler, C., Birt, A. R. ... Zwienenberg, M. (2016). A multilab preregistered replication of the ego-depletion effect. *Perspectives on Psychological Science, 11*(4), 546–573.

Herzberg, F. (1964). The motivation-hygiene concept and problems of manpower. *Personnel Administration, 27*(1), 3–7.

Holman, D. J., Axtell, C. M., Sprigg, C. A., Totterdell, P., & Wall, T. D. (2010). The mediating role of job characteristics in job redesign interventions: A serendipitous quasi-experiment. *Journal of Organizational Behavior, 31*(1), 84–105.

Inzlicht, M., & Friese, M. (2019). The past, present, and future of ego depletion. *Social Psychology, 50*(5–6), 370–378.

Kanfer, R., Chen, G., & Pritchard, R. D. (2008). *Work motivation: Past, present, and future.* Routledge.

Kelloway, E. K., & Barling, J. (1991). Job characteristics, role stress and mental health. *Journal of Occupational Psychology, 64*(4), 291–304.

Kuhl, J. (2000). A functional-design approach to motivation and self-regulation: The dynamics of personality systems interactions. In M. Boekaerts, P. Pintrich, & M. Zeidner (Eds), *Handbook of self-regulation* (pp. 111–169). Academic Press.

Kuhl, J., & Kazén, M. (1994). Self-discrimination and memory: State orientation and false self-ascription of assigned activities. *Journal of Personality and Social Psychology, 66*(6), 1103–1115.

Landman, A., Nieuwenhuys, A., & Oudejans, R. R. (2016). Decision-related action orientation predicts police officers' shooting performance under pressure. *Anxiety, Stress, and Coping, 29*(5), 570–579.

Latham, G. P., & Locke, E. A. (1991). Self-regulation through goal setting. *Organizational Behavior and Human Decision Processes, 50*(2), 212–247.

Latham, G. P., & Locke, E. A. (2007). New developments in and directions for goal-setting research. *European Psychologist, 12*(4), 290–300.

Lazarus, R. S. (2006). *Stress and emotion: A new synthesis.* Springer Publishing Company.

Locke, E. A., & Latham, G. P. (2013). Goal setting theory, 1990. In E. A. Locke & G. P. Latham (Eds), *New developments in goal setting and task performance* (pp. 3–15). Routledge.

Manganelli, L., Thibault-Landry, A., Forest, J., & Carpentier, J. (2018). Self-determination theory can help you generate performance and well-being in the workplace: A review of the literature. *Advances in Developing Human Resources, 20*(2), 227–240.

Meyer, J. P., & Maltin, E. R. (2010). Employee commitment and well-being: A critical review, theoretical framework and research agenda. *Journal of Vocational Behavior*, *77*(2), 323–337.

Muraven, M., & Baumeister, R. F. (2000). Self-regulation and depletion of limited resources: Does self-control resemble a muscle? *Psychological Bulletin*, *126*(2), 247–259.

Penney, L. M., Hunter, E. M., & Perry, S. J. (2011). Personality and counterproductive work behaviour: Using conservation of resources theory to narrow the profile of deviant employees. *Journal of Occupational and Organizational Psychology*, *84*(1), 58–77.

Plessow, F., Fischer, R., Kirschbaum, C., & Goschke, T. (2011). Inflexibly focused under stress: Acute psychosocial stress increases shielding of action goals at the expense of reduced cognitive flexibility with increasing time lag to the stressor. *Journal of Cognitive Neuroscience*, *23*(11), 3218–3227.

Quick, J. C. (1979). Dyadic goal setting and role stress: A field study. *Academy of Management Journal*, *22*(2), 241.

Revelle, W., & Anderson, K. J. (1998). *Personality, motivation and cognitive performance: Final report to the army research institute on contract MDA 903-93-K-0008.* Technical Report, Northwestern University.

Schaufeli, W. B., Bakker, A. B., Hoogduin, K., Schaap, C., & Kladler, A. (2001). On the clinical validity of the Maslach Burnout Inventory and the Burnout Measure. *Psychology and Health*, *16*(5), 565–582.

Semmer, N. K., Tschan, F., Jacobshagen, N., Beehr, T. A., Elfering, A., Kälin, W., & Meier, L. L. (2019). Stress as offense to self: A promising approach comes of age. *Occupational Health Science*, *3*(3), 205–238.

Sheldon, K. M., & Elliot, A. J. (1999). Goal striving, need satisfaction, and longitudinal well-being: The self-concordance model. *Journal of Personality and Social Psychology*, *76*(3), 482–497.

Siegrist, J. (1996). Adverse health effects of high-effort/low-reward conditions. *Journal of Occupational Health Psychology*, *1*(1), 27–41.

Smith, M. J., & Sainfort, P. C. (1989). A balance theory of job design for stress reduction. *International Journal of Industrial Ergonomics*, *4*(1), 67–79.

Sonnentag, S. (2002). Performance, well-being and self-regulation. In S. Sonnentag (Ed.), *Psychological management of individual performance* (pp. 405–423). Wiley.

Stuss, D. T., & Benson, D. F. (1984). Neuropsychological studies of the frontal lobes. *Psychological Bulletin*, *95*(1), 3–28.

Trépanier, S. G., Forest, J., Fernet, C., & Austin, S. (2015). On the psychological and motivational processes linking job characteristics to employee functioning: Insights from self-determination theory. *Work and Stress*, *29*(3), 286–305.

Wolff, M., Krönke, K.-M., Venz, J., Kräplin, A., Bühringer, G., Smolka, M. N., & Goschke, T. (2016). Action versus state orientation moderates the impact of executive functioning on real-life self-control. *Journal of Experimental Psychology: General*, *145*(12), 1635–1653.

Zhou, L., Wang, M., Chang, C. H., Liu, S., Zhan, Y., & Shi, J. (2017). Commuting stress process and self-regulation at work: Moderating roles of daily task significance, family interference with work, and commuting means efficacy. *Personnel Psychology*, *70*(4), 891–922.

Zohar, D., Tzischinski, O., & Epstein, R. (2003). Effects of energy availability on immediate and delayed emotional reactions to work events. *Journal of Applied Psychology*, *88*(6), 1082–1093.

14. Leadership and organizational support

Leadership theories applied to job stress describe how leaders impact followers stress or how stress impacts leaders. Although the term "leader" is used informally to represent any person at a higher hierarchical level, within organizational psychology, a *leader* is a person who is formally or informally selected to regulate and coordinate work within a group. To be a leader, this person must have influence over followers. Influence is described within the bases of power (e.g., legitimate, reward, coercive, and referent). Coercive power (e.g., influencing via threats of punishment) and abusive supervision are both stressors. Some types of leadership, though, improve employee strain (particularly transformational leadership behaviors and high-quality leader–member exchange). Perceived organizational support and preventative stress management also confer protections to the employees through leaders.

In particular, leadership is expected to influence organizational culture, which represents a pattern of behaviors and beliefs developed by a group of people and conferred to new members, in order to cope with its demands. Culture and leadership represent "two sides of the same coin," such that "neither can really be understood by itself" (Schein, 1990). The *strength* of culture is specifically theorized to reduce ambiguity by providing clear expectations, but little research has empirically investigated this phenomenon (an exception is Dickson, Resick, & Hanges, 2006).

FRENCH AND RAVEN'S (1959) BASES OF POWER

Power is the ability to influence others and can be based within the position (e.g., organizational rank) or person (e.g., personality). *Position* power includes legitimate power, reward power, and coercive power. *Legitimate* power is based on the rights and responsibilities associated with particular positions within an organization (e.g., a manager has the right to expect compliance from employees). *Reward* power is associated with the ability to confer tangible benefits such as promotions or better schedules, or status symbols like a larger office or special parking space. *Coercive* power derives from the potential to punish, sanction, and withhold rewards. Compared to position power, *personal* power originates from a person's individual characteristics and is therefore inherent to the person, such that these leaders would retain their power even if leaving the organization. A personal base of power is *expert* power, which reflects competence in performance and problem solving. *Referent* power describes a person's ability to influence others (mostly through imitation) as a result of personal liking, charisma, and reputation. More recently, other power bases like *informational* or *prestige power* (i.e., status with people outside of their group or organization) have been proposed, and clarifications made to the original bases (e.g., positive and negative expert and referent power).

Research and Practical Implications

Some research has specifically investigated the relationships between power and subordinate stress (Erkutlu & Chafra, 2006). Position powers (legitimate, reward, and coercive) were related to increased subordinate stress ($r = 0.51$, 0.29, and 0.72, respectively), whereas expert and referent were associated with decreased subordinate stress ($r = -0.60$ and -0.78, respectively). Some of these correlations are so strong as to approximate acceptable internal reliabilities, thus raising concerns about the possibility of measurement overlap. The scale used for coercive power is best indicated by the items "My superior can fire me if my performance is consistently below standards" and "My superior can fire me if I neglect my duties" (Rahim, 1988). Meanwhile, referent leadership is best indicated by "I like the personal qualities of my superior." The job stress subscale used in this study includes 30 indicators of job pressure (e.g., insufficient personal time, frequent interruptions, competition for advancement, lack of participation). Because the qualities of the items seem distinct, the overlap may be conceptual, rather than related to the measurement. That is to say, coercive power may be better conceptualized as stressor or strain than predictor of stressors (i.e., low personal control), and referent power may directly represent resources or wellbeing. Future research is needed to disentangle (or integrate) these constructs (e.g., confirmatory factor analysis, multitrait multimethod matrix).

Theoretical Extension: Abusive Supervision

Not all supervisors are leaders, but all supervisors have position power (e.g., legitimate, coercive, and/or reward). *Abusive supervision* refers to employee perceptions about the extent to which their supervisors enact sustained hostile behaviors (Tepper, 2000). There are various reasons why this might occur. For example, social interaction theory states that aggression is instrumental and intended to either effect compliance in others, to be consistent with a person's self-identity, or to maintain the ideal of a just world (Tedeschi & Felson, 1994). Therefore, supervisors may act aggressively to gain compliance or conformity, to act as they believe a supervisor should, or to restore justice, among other reasons. However, this theory has been extended to account for employee provocation of abusive supervision (Lian, Ferris, Morrison, & Brown, 2014). This is to say, employees might act aggressively and violate norms, either in their own attempts to maintain identity (e.g., saving face), even a score, or gain compliance from others (e.g., provoke a supervisor to act aggressively; Lian et al., 2014). This may explain three causal relationships in which abusive supervision causes, results from, or mutually amplifies employee deviance. In fact, abusive supervision is meta-analytically related to deviance towards supervisor ($r = 0.54$) and deviance towards the organization ($r = 0.44$; Park et al., 2019).

Another factor underlying abusive supervision is the supervisor's inability to inhibit behavioral impulses due to resource loss or ego depletion. In an experimental study, participants imagined they were leading a group of subordinates within a company's marketing team, and that one of these subordinates had a task that they performed (depending on random assignment) either successfully or unsuccessfully (Lam, Walter, & Huang, 2017). Participants then reported their likelihood of engaging abusive behaviors toward the subordinate. Results indicate that the likelihood of abusive supervision was related to perceived subordinate performance ($F = 33.67$, $p < 0.01$), but not emotional exhaustion, self-monitoring, or the interaction among any of those (although the three-way interaction was marginally significant; $F = 0.504$, $p < 0.10$). In another study, subordinate-rated abusive was correlated with supervisor reports of their own role overload and frustration ($r = 0.44$, 0.45, respectively), indicating that supervisor levels of stress relate to abusive supervision enacted (Eissa & Lester, 2017). Overall, meta-analytic evidence shows that higher levels of stress and burnout are associated with lower levels of transformational leadership and higher levels of abusive supervision (Harms, Credé, Tynan, Leon, & Jeung, 2017).

However, there seems to be little consensus about personality traits related to supervision. For example, one study shows correlations between subordinate-rated abusive supervision with supervisor ratings of their own levels of conscientiousness, agreeableness, and neuroticism ($r = -0.27$, -0.35, and 0.51, respectively; Eissa & Lester, 2017). This is inconsistent with another study using similar methods, which showed relationships between subordinate-rated abusive supervision and self-reported supervisor personality, including honesty-humility ($r = -0.45$), agreeableness ($r = -0.42$), conscientiousness ($r = -0.28$), and openness ($r = -0.31$; Breevaart & de Vries, 2017).

An interesting update to the model has investigated how supervisors react to their own abuse enacted. A study using experience sampling methodology showed that daily abusive supervisor behavior led to guilt, which in turn led to reparative actions in the form of consideration and initiating structure, but only for morally attentive and courageous leaders (Liao, Yam, Johnson, Liu, & Song, 2018). Altogether, this study suggests that when supervisors impulsively aggress against their subordinates, they should attempt to repair relationships proactively through consideration and initiating support in order to alleviate guilt and prevent negative emotion from causing further self-regulatory failure.

OHIO STATE LEADERSHIP STUDIES

Early research on leadership unsuccessfully attempted to identify traits of effective leaders. In fact, even definitions of leadership were lacking at the time. To improve upon these weaknesses, a group of Ohio State researchers attempted to study the observable behaviors of leaders. These investigations led to the discovery of behaviors reflecting consideration and initiating structure, and the Leader Behavior Description Questionnaire was developed to measure the behaviors (Schriesheim & Kerr, 1974). *Consideration* describes the degree to which a leader exhibits concern for the wellbeing of followers, as evidenced by mutual trust, fair treatment, and friendship. Conversely, *initiating structure* is task-oriented and describes the degree to which a leader initiates actions, defines how tasks are to be accomplished by the group, and explicates leader and group member roles. This is measured with items referring to maintaining standards of performance, scheduling the work to be done, and emphasizing deadlines.

Research and Practical Implications

This theory is well supported overall, although empirical tests of the model slowed down in favor of research on contingency theories and transformational leadership theory. However, meta-analytic evidence from over 159 samples shows that leadership outcomes (e.g., effectiveness, cognition, attitude, and behavior) are correlated with both consideration ($r = 0.48$) and initiating structure ($r = 0.29$; Judge, Colbert, & Ilies, 2004). Furthermore, consideration is more strongly related to follower attitudes and motivation, as well as leader effectiveness, than initiating structure. On the other hand, initiating structure was associated more strongly with leader job performance and group-organization performance than was consideration. Within job stress, consideration received was correlated with trust in the supervisor ($r = 0.73$), job satisfaction ($r = 0.44$), and affective commitment ($r = 0.51$), whereas initiating structure was correlated with these, but in slightly lower magnitude ($r = 0.32–0.54$; Lambert, Tepper, Carr, Holt, & Barelka, 2012). This makes sense because consideration specifically reflects concern for employee wellbeing, whereas initiating structure does not. Perhaps consideration has a direct relationship, and initiating structure an indirect relationship, with strain. Findings also suggest that outcomes are more favorable when actual–preferred fit (i.e., leadership needed versus leadership received) is higher, rather than lower. That said, another study found that subordinates report less burnout when their supervisors provide more consideration and *less* structure (Seltzer & Numerof, 1988). However, in this study, initiating structure was indicated by lack of autonomy.

FIEDLER'S CONTINGENCY THEORY

In the 1960s, researchers shifted their focus from leadership behaviors to the interaction, or contingency, between the leader and the environment. Fiedler's (1978) contingency theory is among the most well known. This is a prescriptive theory that makes suggestions about what type of leader would be best in a particular situation. Leadership style is usually measured with the least preferred coworkers (LPC) scale, which asks leaders to rate whether they would prefer to (generally speaking) work with interpersonally warm versus task-oriented coworkers. Once the leader's LPC is determined, the situation should be assessed in terms of the leader's amount of power, structure of the project, and interpersonal relationship between the leader and group. When leader–member relations are either low or high, a task-oriented leader is believed to be most appropriate, but when leader–member relations are moderate, a relationship-oriented leader is most appropriate. Generally speaking, it was believed that task-oriented leaders are better in difficult or high-stakes situations because a decisive leader is needed.

Research and Practical Implications

This theory and its components have been tested within job stress. In a field application, data from 51 university administrators showed that when leadership style and level of situational control were matched, administrators reported less job stress, fewer health problems, and fewer work absences (Chemers, Hays, Rhodewalt, & Wysocki, 1985). That said, field data have largely not supported the predictions laid out in the theory. The use of the LPC measure is also criticized due to a lack of correlation with other measures of leadership and general lack of clarity about the LPC measures. Regardless, LPC does have implications for job stress. For example, low LPC (i.e., task-oriented) leaders were more likely to experience depersonalization as a result of stress than high LPC leaders (Cummins, 1990). Furthermore, social support only buffered the effects of job stress on job satisfaction for high LPC leaders.

Theoretical Extension: Cognitive Resource Theory

Cognitive resource theory was refined from Fiedler's contingency theory and describes the influence of the leader's intelligence and experience on their reaction to stress (Fiedler & Garcia, 1987). Specifically, the principal tenet is that stress reduces the ability for the leader to think logically and can result in negative outcomes unless the leader has the experience to offset these decrements. In other words, intelligence predicts good outcomes in low-stress situations, but experience is more important than intelligence in high-stress situations, when cognitive resources are diverted from planning and problem solving to self-regulation (e.g., self-observation, self-evaluation, self-reaction). A leader who lacks the resources to diagnose problems and build strategies must therefore rely on previous experiences.

Overall, this theory is meta-analytically supported, as intelligence had a positive nonzero correlation with leadership when the leader's stress level was low but not when the leader's stress level was high (Judge et al., 2004). This theory and empirical observations thereof have contributed to Kuhl's (2000) personality systems interaction theory (see Chapter 13, this volume). Furthermore, empirical support allows organizational implications. Specifically, leaders should receive stress management training so that organizations can best capitalize on their intelligence.

LEADER-MEMBER EXCHANGE THEORY

Leader-member exchange (LMX) theory states that the nature of the leader's behavior is contingent upon the follower with whom they are interacting. Each leader–member dyad has a different relationship, and these can be categorized as high- (i.e., supportive) or low-quality exchanges (Dienesch & Linden, 1986). This is to say, leaders form strong relationships based on liking and respect with some members of a group (i.e., the ingroup or cadre), but not others (i.e., the outgroup or hired hands), leading to disparate treatment that, in turn, leads to subordinate work-related attitudes and behaviors.

As expected, employees with high-quality relationships perceive better competence and autonomy, access more organizational and job-related information, experience more job direction, and receive higher objective performance ratings (Sonnentag & Pundt, 2016). Meanwhile, they also report less role conflict, role ambiguity, perceived organizational politics, and better competence, autonomy, vitality, work engagement, and positive emotion (Sonnentag & Pundt, 2016). Furthermore, research indicates that high-quality LMX correlated negatively with leader-reported role stress, turnover intentions, and perceived organizational support (Kim & Mor Barak, 2015). Given the one-on-one leader interactions with followers inherent with high-quality

LMX, it makes sense that depleted leaders were associated with lower-quality relations.

TRANSFORMATIONAL LEADERSHIP

Like LMX, transformational leadership highlights the importance of leader–follower relationships (e.g., Avolio & Bass, 1995). Transformational leadership is a well-known typology of leadership style, and serves as a counterpart to transactional leadership. *Transactional leadership* is short-term oriented and influence attempts are made through appeals to employee self-interests via rewards and punishments (often conceptualized as exchanges). On the other hand, *transformational leadership* is focused on long-term influence by appealing to the employee's contributions to an organizational goal via motivating and engaging relationships with followers. Transformational leadership contains four dimensions. First, *idealized influence* reflects being perceived as a charismatic and ethical role model. *Inspirational motivation* refers to energizing followers, strengthening confidence, and instilling a sense of purpose, often achieved by communicating a clear vision. *Intellectual stimulation* describes being open to creative thinking and problem solving, and encouraging creativity in followers. Finally, *individual consideration* includes treating subordinates as individuals, spending time developing followers, and generally demonstrating care for each follower.

Research and Practical Implications

Transformational leadership, and transactional leadership to a slightly lesser extent, are very well studied in regards to leader effectiveness and have been applied to employee wellbeing with some frequency (see Skakon, Nielsen, Borg, & Guzman, 2010). These studies are fairly standardized due, in part, to a well-validated and widely used measure of full-range leadership entitled the Multifactor Leadership Questionnaire (Avolio & Bass, 1995), which is available for purchase through MindGarden.

Several studies show that transformational leader behaviors are associated with reduced burnout for followers. One such study on mental health teams showed that idealized influence, inspirational motivation, and individual consideration dimensions of transformational leadership were negatively associated with emotional exhaustion (Corrigan, Diwan, Campion, & Rashid, 2002). Another study compared concept-based inspirational motivation (i.e., behaviors communicating standards and expectations) with image-based inspirational motivation (i.e., behaviors creating vivid ideas and a shared vision) and found that these were negatively related to emotional exhaustion or depersonalization, respectively (Densten, 2005). Other studies, however, show differential relationships with specific facets of transformational leadership. For example, articulating a vision and high-performance expectations were associated with follower ambiguity and higher stress levels, whereas leader behaviors of acting as an appropriate model, providing individualized support, fostering the acceptance of group goals, and intellectual stimulation were associated with role clarification and lower levels of follower stress (Diebig, Bormann, & Rowold, 2016).

Altogether, transformational leadership has generally positive effects, but transactional leadership has mixed outcomes, with some studies showing positive effects or no effects of transactional leadership on stress and wellbeing (Skakon et al., 2010). To illustrate, one study showed that passive-avoidant transactional leadership was associated with follower burnout (Hetland, Sandal, & Johnsen, 2007). Future research should investigate dynamic or curvilinear effects of transformational leadership on employee burnout, anxiety, and role ambiguity. For example, some evidence indicates that people become weary of transforming and being inspired after some time. In general, it would be helpful to clarify the extent to which leadership affects follower strain in generally good working conditions, self-efficacy, or other characteristics.

ORGANIZATIONAL CULTURE

"Leaders first create cultures when they create groups and organizations. Once cultures exist they determine the criteria for leadership and thus determine who will or will not be a leader" (Schein, 1990, p. 22). There are many theories of organizational culture, and the most commonly discussed comes from Schein's (1990) book about organizational culture and leadership (see Cooke's 1987 model of constructive, passive, and aggressive cultures for an alternative). Schein (1990) defines *organizational culture* as a set of fundamental beliefs that have been developed and maintained by a given group. Behavior and patterns of behavior are said to derive from culture, not comprise culture. Specifically, there are three nested, hierarchical levels to organizational culture, which is sometimes visualized as an onion. The outermost, most visible layer includes employee patterns of behavior and other artifacts (e.g., mission statement or dress code). *Artifacts* are overt or visible characteristics of the organization. The second level includes *espoused beliefs and values*, wherein the individual values of each employee contribute towards overall organizational values. The third level includes *underlying assumptions*. These assumptions are not inherent to an individual, but reflect contexts of the organization. For example, an organization consisting of mostly men may have a different culture than one consisting of mostly women. Ultimately, those automatic and shared patterns of affect, behavior, and cognitions inherent to culture provide meaning and predictability in an ambiguous situation (Schein,

1990). In other words, a strong culture is believed to buffer or prevent strain arising from uncertainty.

Research and Practical Implications

Despite the regular reference to uncertainty, culture and cultural strength are infrequently applied to the study of role ambiguity (see Dickson et al., 2006 for a notable exception). Instead, many researchers who invoke Schein's model focus on specific *organizational climates*, which are manifestations of culture that reflect an overall impression based on characteristics of the workplace as well as social interactions within and outside of the organization. For example, one study of withdrawal in nurses includes work pressure, supervisor support, peer cohesion, and autonomy as separate indicators of organizational climate (Hemingway & Smith, 1999).

Organizational culture is sometimes investigated qualitatively. In one such study, members of an organization were asked how they identify and deal with stress (Länsisalmi, Peiró, & Kivimäki, 2000). Interviews showed that collective stressors were evident in Division C, the manufacturing division of the organization. This division was located in a dark, isolated basement and received the reputation of the "penal colony." A collective stressor resulting from the group bonus system was resolved through peer monitoring and influence (e.g., giving remarks to the "lazy ones"). In terms of coping, when minor behavioral deviations occurred, workers engaged in a hierarchy of rules (e.g., contacting the foreman) to immediately squelch the unwanted behavior. This is a very different response to stressors than in Division B of the organization, which had no manufacturing activities. Instead, Division B was marked by a highly competitive and unpredictable work environment. They had the reputation of being very successful and had been spared from previous lay-offs. In this division, stressors were mostly eliminated through coworker instrumental support and effective information sharing. This collective commitment was viewed as "workaholism" and personal sacrifice. Altogether, aspects of the organizational culture (i.e., hectic, money-focused) were found to moderate the appraisal of stressors and guide collective coping responses.

Theoretical Extension: Supportive Organizational Climates

The way in which employees are treated contributes to perceptions of a supportive organizational culture or climate. According to organizational support theory, employees develop overall beliefs about the extent to which the organization supports them, which in turn relates to positive outcomes for the organization. *Perceived organizational support* can be defined as an employee's perception that the organization values their work contributions and cares about their wellbeing. To explain its positive impact on employee and organizational outcomes, several potential processes have been proposed (e.g., needs fulfillment). Most commonly, though, the norm of reciprocity is used to explain that employees who are treated well by their organizations are motivated to repay their debts and reciprocate favorable treatment.

There is good evidence that perceived organizational support relates positively to employee resources (e.g., self-efficacy) and negatively to employee strains (e.g., perceived stress, work–family conflict, burnout; Rhoades & Eisenberger, 2002). Theoretically, perceived organizational support may result in positive expectancies regarding workplace treatment and outcomes, which might in turn reduce threat appraisals inherent to the stressor-strain processes (Lazarus & Folkman, 1984). This is supported by meta-analytical research that found that perceived organizational support was negatively associated with job stress, emotional exhaustion, burnout, and work–family conflict (Kurtessis et al., 2015).

THEORY OF PREVENTATIVE STRESS MANAGEMENT

The theory of preventative stress management holds that the objectives of preventive stress management exist at every organizational level and require committed leadership. This theory integrates public health into the job stress context. Specifically, *preventive stress management* is defined as "an organizational philosophy and set of principles that employs specific methods for promoting individual and organizational health while preventing individual and organizational distress" (Quick, Quick, Nelson, & Hurrell, 1997, p. 149). So, a distinguishing feature of this model is that it intentionally targets organizational health.

The model is an extension of a stressor-strain model, in which stressors (i.e., demands) cause an acute stress response (i.e., fight or flight) that might be positive (e.g., eustress) or negative (e.g., distress). Buffer variables (e.g., genetics, social support) guide the experience of eustress versus distress within the stress response. Eustress and distress, in turn, lead to positive and negative outcomes (e.g., vigor, disease). Failure to maintain organizational health via individual wellbeing can result in direct (e.g., poor job performance, accidents) and indirect consequences (e.g., poor communication, lost opportunities). This model then overlays three levels of intervention onto this stressor-strain model (see Hargrove, Quick, Nelson, & Quick, 2011). *Primary intervention* is intended to reduce stressors or people's perceptions of them, *secondary intervention* is designed to mitigate the stress response through enhanced coping with stressors once they occur, and *tertiary intervention* is meant to reduce harm after strain has resulted.

Research and Practical Implications

This theory is specifically developed to provide organizations with suggestions for preventing stress. In order to do so, the effects of stress should be measured at both the individual and organizational levels in keeping with this model. The authors state that preventive stress management should be developed in conjunction with representative data, collected from validated measures and adjusted for organizational culture (see Simpson, O'Brien, & Beehr, 2017 for an overview of individual-level stress diagnosis).

In terms of practical applications, primary intervention is intended to prevent stressors to the amount reasonable, acknowledging that elimination of all stressors is impractical (e.g., difficult conversations, time pressure) or impossible (e.g., bad weather). Instead, interventions might build psychological capital, promote positive coping, and facilitate eustress. This might include either short-term (e.g., every few hours) or long-term (e.g., sabbatical) rest periods or social support (e.g., instrumental help and cognitive reframing). Mentoring might be valuable in managing work stress, but more information is needed on this topic (O'Brien, Roach, & Mann, 2018). The theory also suggests that coaching, peer support, and journal writing may target leader stress and lead to improvements for more organizational members (Cooper & Quick, 2017).

Secondary prevention is intended to help employees meet the demands inherent to work by building resilience and facilitating productive coping. This might include relaxation, mindfulness, or breathing techniques. Another approach includes encouraging light exercise through "default options" (e.g., reserving close parking spots for customers to encourage employee walking), "cues to action" (e.g., a sign near the elevator indicating where the stairs are), and encouraging breaks for walks, which are shown to be effective for reducing job stress (O'Brien & Beehr, forthcoming).

Tertiary prevention occurs after stressors have resulted in strain and are intended to heal strain to employees, observers, or the organization in general. Strain can have behavioral (e.g., smoking, violence), psychological (e.g., mood, cognitive errors), and physiological (e.g., reduced immune response) symptoms. Employee assistance programs are offered at this tertiary level, or specific behavioral consequences (e.g., smoking) can be targeted (e.g., smoking cessation programs). Tertiary intervention is often handled by trained external professionals (e.g., clinical psychologists, nutritionists), but managers can support their employees (e.g., incentives, coaching) to facilitate their recovery.

Altogether, the strength of this theory is the incorporation of other valuable stress theories (e.g., translating problem-focused coping to primary prevention and emotion-focused coping to secondary prevention; Lazarus & Folkman,

1984), which has led to model refinement and better validity. For example, the model now accounts for the proposition that stressors are neither positive nor negative until a person evaluates and appraises the stressor. Despite the relevance and ready applicability of these guidelines to the workplace, though, there are some concerns about these suggestions. For one, some of the recommendations (e.g., breaks for religious reflection, hypnosis, group social support to minimize the effects of bullying) seem legally risky and require the oversight of a trained clinical psychologist or (less optimistically) an employment lawyer.

CONCLUDING REMARKS

It is not surprising that leaders can influence follower stress, and that leader stress can impact leadership behaviors, as the very nature of leadership is defined by the ability to influence others. Beyond the leadership styles already reviewed, ethical leadership is likely to reduce stress. For example, *ethical leadership* (i.e., modeling and encouraging normatively appropriate behaviors) is related to lower levels of ethical ambiguity and job stress (Wu, Kwan, Yim, Chiu, & He, 2015). Other leadership behaviors associated with stress reduction include support, integrity, empowerment, and (negatively) hostility, and the leader's own stress and poor wellbeing negatively impact employee stress and wellbeing (Skakon et al., 2010). A study on athletic coaches, however, found that coach emotional exhaustion was associated with more participative decision making, and consequently less athlete burnout (Price & Weiss, 2000). However, emotionally exhausted coaches also provided less training, instructions, and social support. In some cases, this was associated with more athlete anxiety and burnout, and reduced enjoyment and competence.

An area that warrants further research is in reference to the cultural context of leader behaviors. For example, employee reports of abusive supervision meta-analytically relate to supervisor justice, organizational justice, deviance towards supervisor, and deviance towards the organization (Park et al., 2019). However, these correlations were larger in low power distance cultures (using country as a proxy) than high power distance cultures, indicating that the effect of leader behavior on job stress may vary depending on power distance.

REFERENCES

Avolio, B. J., & Bass, B. M. (1995). Individual consideration viewed at multiple levels of analysis: A multi-level framework for examining the diffusion of transformational leadership. *The Leadership Quarterly, 6*(2), 199–218.

Breevaart, K., & de Vries, R. E. (2017). Supervisor's HEXACO personality traits and subordinate perceptions of abusive supervision. *The Leadership Quarterly, 28*(5), 691–700.

Chemers, M. M., Hays, R. B., Rhodewalt, F., & Wysocki, J. (1985). A person–environment analysis of job stress: A contingency model explanation. *Journal of Personality and Social Psychology, 49*(3), 628–635.

Cooke, R. A. (1987). *The organizational culture inventory.* Human Synergistics.

Cooper, C. L., & Quick, J. C. (Eds). (2017). *The handbook of stress and health: A guide to research and practice.* John Wiley & Sons.

Corrigan, P. W., Diwan, S., Campion, J., & Rashid, F. (2002). Transformational leadership and the mental health team. *Administration and Policy in Mental Health and Mental Health Services Research, 30*(2), 97–108.

Cummins, R. (1990). Job stress and buffering effects of supervisory support. *Group and Organizational Studies, 15*(1), 92–104.

Densten, I. L. (2005). The relationship between visioning behaviours of leaders and follower burnout. *British Journal of Management, 16*(2), 105–118.

Dickson, M. W., Resick, C. J., & Hanges, P. J. (2006). When organizational climate is unambiguous, it is also strong. *Journal of Applied Psychology, 91*(2), 351–364.

Diebig, M., Bormann, K. C., & Rowold, J. (2016). A double-edged sword: Relationship between full-range leadership behaviors and followers' hair cortisol level. *The Leadership Quarterly, 27*(4), 684–696.

Dienesch, R. M., & Linden, R. C. (1986). Leader–member exchange model of leadership: A critique and further development. *Academy of Management Review, 11*(3), 618–634.

Eissa, G., & Lester, S. W. (2017). Supervisor role overload and frustration as antecedents of abusive supervision: The moderating role of supervisor personality. *Journal of Organizational Behavior, 38*(3), 307–326.

Erkutlu, H. V., & Chafra, J. (2006). Relationship between leadership power bases and job stress of subordinates: Example from boutique hotels. *Management Research News, 29*(5), 285–297.

Fiedler, F. E. (1978). The contingency model and the dynamics of the leadership process. In L. Berkowitz (Ed.), *Advances in experimental social psychology* (Vol. 11, pp. 59–112). Academic Press.

Fiedler, F. E., & Garcia, J. E. (1987). *New approaches to effective leadership: Cognitive resources and organizational performance.* John Wiley & Sons.

French, J., & Raven, B. H. (1959). The bases of social power. In D. Cartwright (Ed.), *Studies in social power* (pp. 150–167). Institute for Social Research.

Hargrove, M. B., Quick, J. C., Nelson, D. L., & Quick, J. D. (2011). The theory of preventive stress management: A 33-year review and evaluation. *Stress and Health, 27*(3), 182–193.

Harms, P. D., Credé, M., Tynan, M., Leon, M., & Jeung, W. (2017). Leadership and stress: A meta-analytic review. *The Leadership Quarterly, 28*(1), 178–194.

Hemingway, M. A., & Smith, C. S. (1999). Organizational climate and occupational stressors as predictors of withdrawal behaviours and injuries in nurses. *Journal of Occupational and Organizational Psychology, 72*(3), 285–299.

Hetland, H., Sandal, G. M., & Johnsen, T. B. (2007). Burnout in the information technology sector: Does leadership matter? *European Journal of Work and Organizational Psychology, 16*(1), 58–75.

Judge, T. A., Colbert, A. E., & Ilies, R. (2004). A meta-analysis of the relationship between intelligence and leadership. *Journal of Applied Psychology, 89*(3), 542–552.

Kim, A., & Mor Barak, M. E. (2015). The mediating roles of leader–member exchange and perceived organizational support in the role stress–turnover intention relationship among child welfare workers: A longitudinal analysis. *Children and Youth Services Review, 52*, 135–143.

Kuhl, J. (2000). The volitional basis of personality systems interaction theory: Applications in learning and treatment contexts. *International Journal of Educational Research, 33*(7–8), 665–703.

Kurtessis, J. N., Eisenberger, R., Ford, M. T., Buffardi, L. C., Stewart, K. A., & Adis, C. S. (2015). Perceived organizational support: A meta-analytic evaluation of organizational support theory. *Journal of Management, 43*(6), 1854–1884.

Lam, C. K., Walter, F., & Huang, X. (2017). Supervisors' emotional exhaustion and abusive supervision: The moderating roles of perceived subordinate performance and supervisor self-monitoring. *Journal of Organizational Behavior, 38*(8), 1151–1166.

Lambert, L. S., Tepper, B. J., Carr, J. C., Holt, D. T., & Barelka, A. J. (2012). Forgotten but not gone: An examination of fit between leader consideration and initiating structure needed and received. *Journal of Applied Psychology, 97*(5), 913.

Länsisalmi, H., Peiró, J. M., & Kivimäki, M. (2000). Collective stress and coping in the context of organizational culture. *European Journal of Work and Organizational Psychology, 9*(4), 527–559.

Lazarus, R. S., & Folkman, S. (1984). *Stress, appraisal, and coping.* Springer.

Lian, H., Ferris, D. L., Morrison, R., & Brown, D. J. (2014). Blame it on the supervisor or the subordinate? Reciprocal relations between abusive supervision and organizational deviance. *Journal of Applied Psychology, 99*(4), 651.

Liao, Z., Yam, K. C., Johnson, R. E., Liu, W., & Song, Z. (2018). Cleansing my abuse: A reparative response model of perpetrating abusive supervisor behavior. *Journal of Applied Psychology, 103*(9), 1039.

O'Brien, K. E., & Beehr, T. A. (forthcoming). Workplace interventions involving employees. In L. Lapierre & C. L. Cooper (Eds), *Cambridge companion to organisational stress and wellbeing.* Cambridge.

O'Brien, K. E., Roach, K. N., & Mann, K. J. (2018). Mentoring: Resource for lowering job stress or just another headache? *Journal of Applied Biobehavioral Research, 23*(4), 1–16.

Park, H., Hoobler, J. M., Wu, J., Liden, R. C., Hu, J., & Wilson, M. S. (2019). Abusive supervision and employee deviance: A multifoci justice perspective. *Journal of Business Ethics, 158*(4), 1113–1131.

Price, M. S., & Weiss, M. R. (2000). Relationships among coach burnout, coach behaviors, and athletes' psychological responses. *The Sport Psychologist, 14*(4), 391–409.

Quick, J. C., Quick, J. D., Nelson, D. L., & Hurrell, J. J. (1997). *Preventive stress management in organizations.* American Psychological Association.

Rahim, M. A. (1988). The development of a leader power inventory. *Multivariate Behavioral Research, 23*(4), 491–503.

Rhoades, L., & Eisenberger, R. (2002). Perceived organizational support: A review of the literature. *Journal of Applied Psychology, 87*(4), 698–714.

Schein, E. H. (1990). *Organizational culture.* American Psychological Association.

Schriesheim, C., & Kerr, S. (1974). Psychometric properties of the Ohio State leadership scales. *Psychological Bulletin, 81*(11), 756–765.

Seltzer, J., & Numerof, R. E. (1988). Supervisory leadership and subordinate burnout. *Academy of Management Journal, 31*(2), 439–446.

Simpson, D. A., O'Brien, K. E., & Beehr, T. A. (2017). Diagnosing the problem. In A. M. Rossi, J. A. Meurs, & P. L. Perrewé (Eds), *Stress and quality of working life: Conceptualizing and assessing stress.* Information Age Publishing.

Skakon, J., Nielsen, K., Borg, V., & Guzman, J. (2010). Are leaders' well-being, behaviours and style associated with the affective well-being of their employees? A systematic review of three decades of research. *Work and Stress, 24*(2), 107–139.

Sonnentag, S., & Pundt, A. (2016). Organisational health behavior climate: Organisations can encourage healthy eating and physical exercise. *Applied Psychology, 65*, 259–286.

Tedeschi, J. T., & Felson, R. B. (1994). *Violence, aggression, and coercive actions.* American Psychological Association.

Tepper, B. J. (2000). Consequences of abusive supervision. *Academy of Management Journal, 43*(2), 178–190.

Wu, L. Z., Kwan, H. K., Yim, F. H. K., Chiu, R. K., & He, X. (2015). CEO ethical leadership and corporate social responsibility: A moderated mediation model. *Journal of Business Ethics, 130*, 819–831.

15. Perspectives on job stress

In 1978, the first edited book on job stress was published, including chapters on coronary heart disease, person–environment fit, managerial stress, and *epistemology* (the study of how we know what we know; Cooper & Payne, 1978), as well as the first integrated job stress theory (facet theory; Beehr & Newman, 1978). Since then, over 100 theories, models, and hypotheses have been applied to job stress. These decades of observation, theoretical refinement, and empirical scrutiny have afforded psychologists with iteratively better theory and understanding of job stress. Specifically, researchers have proposed transtheoretical models, which are attempts to assemble observations from a variety of perspectives into a single (or at least broader) unified theory. *Transtheoretical models* are thoughtful integrations of various theories, like the multidimensional model of burnout and facet theory, among others covered elsewhere in this volume (e.g., effort–reward imbalance, balance theory; Chapters 6 and 13, respectively).

These transtheoretical models are helpful, but future theoretical development should also be guided by critical evaluation of job stress research. For one, *philosophical meta-theories* describe theory from an epistemic perspective or delineate the ideal qualities of theories (e.g., grounded theory; Locke, 1996). Some philosophical meta-theories include the chrysalis effect and relational cultural theory (RCT). Furthermore, expert insight regarding the state of job stress theory can help to encourage future research and guide practitioners in the application of existing theory. To this end, we include commentary from notable researchers (Terry Beehr, Alicia Grandey, and Paul Spector; see endnotes) about the past, present, and future of job stress theory.

THE MULTIDIMENSIONAL THEORY OF BURNOUT

The multidimensional theory of burnout is transtheoretical. Burnout itself is a meta-theory (a principle that can be applied across a variety of other theories) because it is nearly synonymous with strain and the anticipated endpoint of a variety of job stress theories. Specifically, *job burnout* is defined as a prolonged response to chronic *interpersonal* stressors on the job. The multidimensional theory conceptualizes burnout in terms of its three core components: emotional exhaustion, depersonalization, and reduced personal accomplishment (Maslach, 1998). *Emotional exhaustion* is an individual strain that occurs when emotionally overextended and depleted, usually from work overload and interpersonal conflict. *Depersonalization* refers to a negative, cynical, or detached response to other people in response to emotional exhaustion. This is an interpersonal dimension of burnout and has self-protective effects that can develop into dehumanization. *Reduced personal accomplishment* refers to self-evaluative strain indicated by a decline in feelings of competence and productivity at work. This is linked to a lack of social support and professional development opportunities. The outcomes can include depression and reduced coping.

The theory posits that job burnout arises from chronic mismatches (e.g., Leiter & Maslach, 1999). *Lack of control* occurs when people have little influence over the work they do (e.g., rigid policies, monitoring, unpredictable situations), which precludes the ability to solve problems, make choices, and manipulate their situations or consequences. *Insufficient reward* involves a lack of appropriate rewards (e.g., salary, benefits, pride) that devalues the employee and their work. *Work overload* occurs when job demands (quantitative or qualitative) exceed human limits. *Absence of fairness* reflects the lack of procedures or norms that maintain mutual respect in the workplace (e.g., unfair workload or pay, organizational politics). *Breakdown of community* occurs when people lose a sense of positive connection with others in the workplace due to isolation or impersonal connections, which leads to feelings of frustration, hostility, and distrust. *Values conflict* describes a mismatch between the requirements of the job and the employees' values, such that these employees may feel compelled to engage in activities that they feel are unethical or hypocritical.

The study of burnout originated from Maslach's involvement in the Zimbardo Stanford Prison Experiment (see Maslach, 2000). The prison had caused incredible changes in the prisoners and guards, certainly, but also in Zimbardo, to whom Maslach was engaged and later married. Because of their closeness, she observed that, once a "gentle and compassionate" person, he was now delighting in the guards' aggression and the prisoners' conformity. Consequently, she emphasizes the context of the organizational environment, rather than the person, particularly in caretaking roles. She writes that she learned about dehumanization from her experience, "how basically good people can … treat others who rely on their help or good will as less than human, as animals, inferior, unworthy of respect or equality" and how burnout can "lead initially dedicated and caring individuals to dehumanize and mistreat the very people they are supposed to serve" (Maslach, 2000, p. 21).

Maslach's model is the leading model in the field of burnout research and has inspired some other areas of study. *Engagement* is in many ways the opposite of burnout. However, the absence of burnout is not engagement. Instead, engagement consists of a state of high *energy* (rather than exhaustion), strong *involvement* (rather than cynicism), and a sense of *efficacy* (rather than a reduced sense of accomplishment). There are, nonetheless, concerns about job burnout. Most importantly, a great deal of research shows that burnout may not be distinct from depression. These studies, though, likely neglect the conceptual distinction wherein burnout is job-related and situation-specific. That said, chronic exhaustion can lead people to distance themselves from work, which may manifest as depersonalization (Maslach, 1998).

FACET THEORY

Another transtheoretical model is facet theory. Specifically, Beehr and Newman (1978) proposed an extensive and complex model of stress that placed over 150 variables into seven facets or categories. This review was *Personnel Psychology*'s most cited article of the entire 1970s (see Beehr & Newman, 1998). In this theory, personal (e.g., personality, ability) and environmental (e.g., stressor) facets lead to a process facet, which in turn leads to human consequences (i.e., strain) facet and organizational consequences (e.g., absenteeism, turnover) facet. These facets lead to an adaptive responses facet. The response then affects the various facets in a cyclical pattern over time (i.e., time facet) until long-term consequences and adaptations occur. The time facet is relatively unique to this model, but there is strong evidence that time is important to strain and adaptation (e.g., habituation; McGrath & Beehr, 1990).

This theory has been refined (Beehr, 1998). It is now more specific in terms of moderator effects and conceptualization of the facets (e.g., the organizational facet can be differentiated into stressors and context). An extension of this theory is entitled the uncertainty theory of occupational stress. This proposes that strain is a multiplicative function of uncertainty, importance, and duration (Beehr & Bhagat, 1985). That is to say, because people in the workplace are motivated to perform certain behaviors, expectancies are relevant to their stress. However, this model does not rely upon the expectancies within Vroom's valence, instrumentality, expectancy theory, but instead states that stress is based on the certainty with which the employee can estimate expectancies. For example, if the employee is not certain that their best efforts have a 10, 50, or 90 percent probability of resulting in good performance, they don't know how much effort to expend. This lack of clarity leads to stress.

APPRAISAL, ATTRIBUTION, AND ADAPTATION MODEL

In the appraisal, attribution, and adaptation (AAA) model, Mackey and Perrewé (2014) describe cognitive processes used by employees when experiencing organizational demands. Challenge and hindrance stressors lead to primary appraisal (i.e., benign positive, irrelevant, or threatening), which in turn leads to attributions. Attributions of causality and locus can then result in positive or negative emotion, which inform secondary appraisal. Secondary appraisal pertains to the employee's beliefs about whether or not they can cope with the stressor. Action tendencies then arise from secondary appraisal and should result in coping behavior. This coping process, though, is dependent upon self-regulation. These coping behaviors lead to health and strain, which then cyclically affect primary appraisal.

In creating this model, the authors integrated research from numerous job stress perspectives to develop a cohesive theoretical model that includes appraisals, attributions, emotions, self-regulation, resources, and adaptation. The theory incorporates eustress a bit better than others. This theory has some commonalities with facet theory, although all integrated models will likely share many features. That said, AAA is more sophisticated, which is not necessarily a good or bad quality. Facet theory does not explicate the mechanisms, so AAA is more of a theory and facet theory is more of a model. A combination of the two models might collapse the elaborations of the cognitive processes and result in a more applicable and testable model (see Figure 15.1). Nonetheless, the cognitive processes elaborated in AAA are well supported and very likely accurate. These processes, while valid, are simply unnecessary in many situations, in which the more parsimonious facet theory is appropriate.

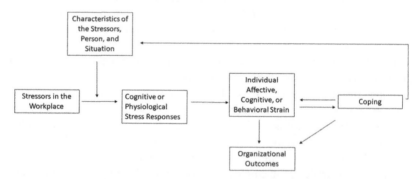

Note: The revised facet model (Beehr, 1998) is integrated with the AAA model of job stress (Mackey & Perrewé, 2014).

Figure 15.1   Integrated model of occupational stress

MOVING FORWARD: PHILOSOPHY OF THEORY

Philosophical meta-theories are theories about theories. That is to say, they either describe or prescribe what theories should be. Locke (1996) presents a helpful framework for programmatic research to build grounded theory, for example. Mostly, he describes ways to avoid confirmation bias, and states that the best empirical evidence comes from challenging existing theory and attempting to find when it is no longer true. Beyond this, the article departs into a critical evaluation of how researchers are applying theory. There are other papers that make similar points – we know what theory is and should be, but we are not holding ourselves to these high standards. For example, Hambrick (2007) published the aptly named "The field of management's devotion to theory: Too much of a good thing?" and Healy (2017) more succinctly writes "F... Nuance" (he did not use ellipses). Despite well-argued and insightful cautions, we continue to see deviations from good theoretical testing published in our journals. One description of the suboptimal testing and use of theory is described in the chrysalis effect.

The Chrysalis Effect

Theory is meant to guide empirical testing. That is to say, researchers should begin with a theory (written into an introduction section of a manuscript) and then scrutinize it (written into a results section) to allow better confidence in the theory's veracity. That is, however, not what is typically done. This is because when the introduction does not match the results, the manuscript is generally unpublishable. However, researchers depend upon publication for their careers, and research needs to be disseminated as part of the scientific process. Thus, when an a priori theory is not supported (assuming there is one), researchers embark on a thought experiment in order to identify the best-fitting, least irrelevant, most publishable theory (Cortina, 2016). However, this post hoc theory likely won't fit the data perfectly either, which is typically handled atheoretically by using proxy variables (e.g., gender to represent risk taking), or contaminated/deficient definitions of the focal constructs (e.g., generalized self-efficacy instead of task self-efficacy, need for autonomy instead of basic psychological needs fulfillment). Superfluous pathways may be added, or omitted components ignored, even when absolutely imperative to the model (i.e., invoking transactional theory without measuring appraisal, or identity theory without measuring job involvement or similar). Finally, unjustified theoretical control variables may be included, which generally muddy interpretation and are rarely appropriate in nonlaboratory research (see Bernerth & Aguinis, 2016, among many others).

This "modification of putatively a priori hypotheses" in order to survive the review process is referred to as the *chrysalis effect* (O'Boyle, Banks, & Gonzalez-Mulé, 2017). Evidence for this can be found in the ratio of statistically supported to unsupported hypotheses in rigorous unpublished manuscripts (e.g., dissertations) versus published work. Rarely in research do we so clearly build hypotheses from a theory as within a dissertation. The proposal must be approved before data are collected, so this is likely a good indicator of rigorous theory testing. However, the ratio of significant to nonsignificant findings in published studies is twice that found within dissertations (O'Boyle et al., 2017), indicating that there is some culling of hypotheses prior to publication. This process includes, but goes beyond, *HARKing* (hypothesizing after results are known) and cherry picking (e.g., publishing only select hypotheses, variables, portions of a sample). In other disciplines, theories are constantly trimmed into the more specific and accurate. Instead, we tend to add pathways. Thus, moving forward, our theories might suggest a range of possible values around a parameter (e.g., the correlation between attitudes and behaviors is in the 0.30s) instead of stating only a direction (Cortina, 2016).

Stone Center Relational Cultural Theory

Stone Center RCT has qualities of a philosophical meta-theory because it describes theory and offers suggestions for improving theory testing. RCT posits that most existing psychology theories are gendered and reflect the values and strengths of dominant social groups (e.g., Miller, 2008). To elaborate, most psychological theories view independence and achievement as the focal constructs and ignore the realities of an interdependent world. Even person–environment fit, which acknowledges mutually influential relationships between the person and the environment, does not elaborate on the process by which this happens, or evaluate the quality of this influence. Motivation theories generally predict goal-directed behavior, and not interpersonal growth and support. Subjective outcomes (e.g., satisfaction) are less "valuable" than objective outcomes (e.g., an assessment that relates to job satisfaction but not performance may be seen as weak). Human nature (e.g., human error, goal abandonment) is rarely celebrated. In light of observations such as these, RCT explicitly includes relational attributes (e.g., empathy, warmth) as strengths that should be developed, rather than as weakness, neediness, or insufficiency.

RCT may not be a philosophical theory because it proposes its own unique tenets. These define the self-in-relation (rather than as an independent unit), mutually growth-fostering interactions, and outcomes of ideal social interactions. The fourth tenet describes systematic power. Miller argues that the "myth of individual achievement" is an irrational belief that independence is a state to be achieved, but ignores the reality that success requires interdependence. An entrepreneur cannot earn a fortune without people to provide support and infrastructure. Consequently, the myth reflects a tautology that maintains systemic power, such that some people (typically of marginalized groups) are expected to quietly support majority group members. These supporters are required to develop relational skills in order to anticipate the needs, desires, and implicit requests of more powerful people, and these relational skills consequently become associated with powerlessness (Miller, 2008). Therefore, future theorizing should work towards inclusion of social performance and stop viewing the default or prototypical worker as a white-collar office worker. This could extend theories to include outcomes like helping (e.g., altruism, organizational citizenship behavior) or measuring collaboration or support provided, in addition to performance (e.g., within leadership, self-regulation).

Commentaries on the Past, Present, and Future of Job Stress Theory

Beyond these philosophical meta-theories, further guidance for rigorous theory testing can come from reading the literature (hopefully this volume provides a helpful starting point), as well as expert insight. To this point, we interviewed three experts in the field for their insights regarding the current state and future of job stress theory. These experts are (in alphabetical order by last name) Drs. Terry Beehr,[1] Alicia Grandey,[2] and Paul Spector,[3] all of whom are well represented within this volume. These were informal, largely unstructured interviews in which we posed a few broad questions (e.g., what are the criteria for a good theory?) but did not direct researcher responses. Their responses are sorted into categories, reported below. Some examples or context are ours, but attempts were made to maintain the integrity of their statements.

Suggestions for theory development

Each expert gave *criteria for a good theory* and a few commonalities emerged. For one, each expert emphasized a balance between narrow and overly broad theories. To illustrate, a benefit of the job demands-resources model is that it is broader than the excessively narrow job demands-control model. However, conservation of resources theory (COR) is so diffuse that it allows for any resource in any application but does not clearly define what is and – importantly – what is not a resource, making it hard to falsify the ideas (Grandey). Also relevant to this point, all respondents indicated that good theories should be testable. Some models are tautological, or at least not amenable to testing, due to reciprocal effects and regulatory loops (Grandey).

The experts also spoke to the *practical value* of a theory. For example, although the job demands-control model is too narrow, the job demands-resources model is not readily applied within an organizational intervention because it is too broad (although control and social support are almost universally helpful; Beehr). Instead, organizations would have to diagnose strain and identify sources of stress before applying the theory (Beehr) or choose/modify a theory based on context or a moderator (Grandey). Similarly, experts agree that we already know how to apply these theories but often do not. For example, we know that email load is a major cause of stress, but workplace interventions are not addressing this (Grandey). Likewise, the job characteristics model suggests low-cost modifications that may simultaneously improve performance and wellbeing. However, during job design, strain is not a criterion ("It's not that health takes a backseat; it doesn't even have a seat," Beehr). From an academic perspective, more information on interventions will help us inform organizations about the best ways to address job stress without harming productivity.

Finally, every expert suggested *integrating theories*. For example, COR and job demands-resources model have enough commonalities to warrant integration. Additionally, the matching hypothesis within the job demands-resources model is likely no different from traditional person–environment fit (i.e., competencies must fit the job). However, experts were mixed on the value of an overarching theory. While the emphasis on a single overarching framework can discourage integration (Beehr), researchers attempting to apply multiple theories often do so in a piecemeal, superficial way (Grandey, Spector). Spector elaborates that hypotheses cannot be supported by the simple presence of a citation (e.g., "because of equity theory, agreeableness should relate to strain; Adams, 1965"). Instead, researchers must overtly state how the theory makes the argument. Thus, tests of competing hypotheses might be a good way to integrate and trim theories (Spector). All three experts also mentioned testing for boundary conditions and generalizability.

Suggestions for theory testing
In terms of theory testing, each expert emphasized the importance of using *appropriate methods*. For example, lack of power precludes the ability to test for moderators (i.e., moderators would work with samples larger than 800–1000 people; Spector). Another theme was a desire for more research using physiological measures (Beehr), particularly if our interest is in understanding employee health as a valued outcome in itself (Grandey). A related comment reflects the need for objective measurement despite low power. Specifically, due to failure to reach statistical significance, these measures are difficult to publish. Nonetheless, verifiable measures, or at least peer reports, are appropriate because many job stress theories assume objective stressors (Grandey). In fact, COR sets itself apart from appraisal theory by focusing on objective events and changes (Grandey). Instead, we mostly measure appraisals, but this is insufficient when studying interpersonal conflict, in particular. When an employee is experiencing racist microaggressions, for example, the

solution is not that they change their appraisal or take a wellness day. The environment must change, and objective measures are necessary in order to identify how to do so (Grandey).

A few specific *critical suggestions* were given for researchers. Beehr emphasizes the need to carefully evaluate measures chosen for a study. Sometimes, measures do not reflect what researchers describe in the hypothesis development (e.g., leader-member exchange theory to study coworker support, emotional exhaustion to measure general burnout). Grandey encourages researchers to thoroughly investigate their theory of choice before implementing it. Too often, researchers choose a theory based on early research but do not adequately incorporate updates and modifications to the theory when applying it. For example, the original COR theory has recent extensions that now more clearly define resources and outline specific predictions that need to be empirically tested (see Hobfoll, Halbesleben, Neveu, & Westman, 2018). Spector has published a plethora of suggestions, all readily available from the respective publishers, regarding (among others) common method variance, reverse-coded items, measurement validation in cross-cultural research, time delays in longitudinal measurement, and unjustified control variables (including negative affectivity). When asked about the application of testing to theory, he suggests choosing the most appropriate method, which is not necessarily the hardest (e.g., structural equation modeling, longitudinal designs with five-year time lags). Instead, the most appropriate design should be carefully considered and justified within the manuscript.

When asked about what they want to see more of in the future, each expert raised different points. There were no common themes (beyond those already described), but Beehr and Spector both voiced a desire for more *inductive research*, in which observations are made, then tested, and only after that contribute to theory. Both also mentioned that a valuable alternative is to have theory first and then test observations of that theory in a replicative manner. *Replication*, perhaps via meta-analysis, has benefits in terms of demonstrating generalizability, defining bounds of theories, and trimming unnecessary paths. In fact, other fields (e.g., physics) test their models for hundreds of years (Spector). In our current literature, many of our theories are tested once or not at all, and are instead taken at face value with just one study. If future tests don't find the same results, it is assumed the replication is incorrect, not the original theory. These are not published, so it is unclear if the original study is the fluke.

Some experts called for *new observations* through exploratory research (Beehr, Spector). To illustrate, Spector commented "I want to see something I haven't seen before," such as a new phenomenon or relationship. However, he does not feel there is a need for new theory. Ultimately, the goal should be "fewer theories, more tests of theory," including use of different methodologies or samples. Similarly, Beehr called for more intervention research. Currently, our knowledge about effective components of interventions is weak, and more research should be done to investigate long-term effects of interventions, or strain in general. Grandey did not call for new observations, but she did emphasize a need for *new insight*. Grandey is interested in new or better explanations for things we already know, perhaps incorporating well-supported theories from other literature (e.g., applying the biopsycho-social model to violence). New insight would also benefit our understanding of established relationships that are taken for granted. For example, Grandey states "we have to accept that sometimes people work for money," because salary and pay are often neglected from research on job stress. To this point, two researchers called for more research on behaviorism (Grandey, Spector). Grandey also emphasized the importance of the study of stress resulting from membership in minority groups. Stress from minority status is often included in theory as just more stress, but it is potentially qualitatively different.

Other perspectives
Stress researchers from other fields also provided their perspectives. One such researcher, Wiline Pangle,[4] is a behavioral ecologist. She studies behavioral decisions in mammals (mostly hyenas and chipmunks) under stress, which is relevant to the research on job stress. When asked about the causes of stress in these mammals, she states that it is mainly lack of food, presence of predators, and social stressors (somewhat less relevant to job stress, but corollaries certainly apply). Regarding humans, though, she points out that we are the only species that lies awake at night, worried about our retirement, even as young adults (e.g., Sapolsky, 2004). No other animal has any such concern. Cognitive mediation is uniquely human, but also dangerous in that we have a stress response to things that haven't happened and might not even occur. This stress response can be amplified via rumination or other cognitive processes. Most importantly, stress can have transgenerational effects (e.g., via DNA methylation) on behavior and health. Mother hyenas who were stressed during pregnancy had cubs who were more aggressive, for example. Her take-away point is that "stress affects our health in a real way even if we don't know we are stressed." Thus, we should take active steps to reduce stress.

Clinical psychologist James Gerhart and cognitive psychologist Emily Bloesch (both of Central Michigan University) also provided perspective. Interestingly, and quite reflective of their backgrounds, each had a very different point of view. Gerhart spoke about the kindling effect and how a large portion of his time with clients is spent helping them to modify distorted schemas regarding work stress (particularly from the manager). On the other hand, Bloesch emphasized the importance of habituation and how stress is an everyday occurrence. It would not be advantageous for humans to amplify the harmful aspects of stress. Thus, stress will likely go away on its own via habituation. The difference in perspective likely reflects disparities between intense stress and daily stressors, as well as between stress as a clinical disorder versus typical cognitive processing.

CONCLUDING REMARKS

In order to advance our understanding of job stress, we must learn from our colleagues. Our neighbors in neuroscience, medicine, biology, and human resource management may all have valuable information that can progress the job stress literature. In particular, organizational psychologists are skilled with studying long-term strain in the field, and we could perhaps lean into this with better intervention research. However, an alternative is to research short-term (i.e., acute) strain within self-regulation. That said, dynamic processes are unclear, as habituation and kindling are opposite but likely outcomes of stressors. Although fleeting and capricious stress seems less meaningful than stable or chronic spirals, most people don't want to be stressed even for short periods of time. It may behoove organizational researchers to better reflect the human experience. That is to say, when employees experience job stress, they are feeling "stressed out," which is often accompanied by cognitive redirection, uncomfortable emotion, and physical symptoms. Even targeted attempts to understand what stress feels like (particularly across cultures, including both national and organizational cultures) would provide researchers with an important outcome measure. Instead, when a friend says "I'm stressed out from work. How can I fix it?," we may find we have limited suggestions.

That said, there are some clear implications for individuals experiencing job stress. From biological research, the first implication is to attend to bodily states and needs (e.g., listen to your body). Research has established that, for example, night shifts and working more than 60 hours per week leads to strain (e.g., cancer, infertility, cardiovascular disease), but only when these demands are involuntary. Similarly, emerging research shows that not sleeping enough (i.e., less than seven to nine hours per night) isn't dangerous for people who are not tired. Some people just need less sleep. But, if a person is tired and denies themself sleep, this can cause accidents and other health problems. That is to say, allostatic processes do not only fix the physiological problem in a direct manner – these processes also motivate people to change their environment or behaviors. To illustrate, if a person is cold, allostatic processes will make them shiver, but these processes will also motivate them to go inside or put on a coat. To rebuff these behavioral drives is to negate the physiological mechanisms that maintain good health, thus shifting the load from behavioral to physiological mediation. That is, a person can force themself to work through discomfort, but this does not spare them from the health consequences.

Other suggestions for individuals experiencing strain comes from different areas of psychology. Ergonomics would suggest that people alter their environments to have less stress. For example, employees can minimize their use of a personal phone during work hours, turn off email notifications, take time to set up the office in a comfortable way (when possible), and take steps to reduce distractions (e.g., only check emails during designated times). Another recommendation, from stressor detachment theory, suggests using mindfulness or recovery activities to counteract stress. Furthermore, changing appraisal, perhaps through self-help worksheets available on www.therapistaid.com, or through professional guidance, can also help people to change schemas and better cope with their challenges. Other attempts to change the environment (e.g., for better fit, or to seek role clarification) are also likely to help.

In this book, there are over 100 theories, models, and hypotheses referenced, but there are only a few pages worth of implications for employees. Part of the reason for the lack of clear applicability of job stress theories is that new theories are infrequently tested, particularly in the last ten years. In fact, many times, theories were not tested at all! Thus, the key take-away is for researchers to test theory more often, and to meet the standards established by best practices (e.g., Cortina, 2016). Clear operationalization of theory (e.g., if using equity theory, explicate which model is being used – Adams's, Homan's, Blau's, etc.) and measurement are necessary. Specifically, measures should avoid the use of proxies and have good coverage of the content without contamination or deficiency.

Furthermore, theoretical choices should be explicated and adhered to. For example, if using job demands-resources theory, be sure to test demands to avoid results that can be interpreted to support either job demands-resources theory or COR. We also challenge researchers to avoid confirmation bias by testing competing hypotheses and identifying the bounds of relevant theories (e.g., Locke, 1996). In doing so, theories should be tested with fidelity, with interactions (e.g., job demands-control) or mediators (e.g., transactional theory) tested when using those models (acknowledging that not every study must test every pathway, but the overall theme of the theory should be prioritized). Finally, note that Bliese, Edwards, and Sonnentag (2017) reported the most influential theories are relevant to white-collar and service jobs. Theory and testing should consider the breadth of employees in the world – there are employees in sweatshops, gig employment, seasonal work, farmers, etc. who deserve attention. Research on these employees may provide more variance, hopefully the variance that allows researchers to identify effects more easily. If not, research on these topics will at least contribute to a more generalizable understanding of stressors, strains, and the job stress process.

NOTES

1. Terry Beehr has been Professor Emeritus in Psychology at Central Michigan University since 2019. He arrived there in 1978 after stints at Illinois State University and the Institute for Social Research (Ann Arbor). He earned his PhD from the University of Michigan in 1974. His research interests include much of organizational psychology, including occupational stress, retirement, leadership, and careers. He is a Fellow in the Midwestern Psychological Association, the Society for Industrial and Organizational Psychology, and the Association for Psychological Science, and he is listed in Stanford University's top 2 percent 2020 World Ranking of Scientists.

2. Alicia Grandey is a Liberal Arts Professor in the industrial-organizational psychology program at the Pennsylvania State University. Her award-winning research, on how emotional labor and mistreatment in a diverse workplace (gender, racial, age, and political differences) contribute to performance and health, is published in 55 journal publications, 11 book chapters and one book, and is frequently cited by both scholars and media (e.g., *Harvard Business Review*, *The New Yorker*, Reddit, NPR, BBC). She is an associate editor for the *Journal of Applied Psychology*, and Fellow of the Association for Psychological Science and Society for Industrial and Organizational Psychology.

3. Paul Spector joined the University of South Florida (USF) Psychology Department in 1982 where he retired in 2020 as a distinguished professor. He still teaches in USF's executive DBA program and is an organizational development consultant at Tampa General Hospital. Spector is extremely influential in the field, publishing on both methodology and organizational behavior (e.g., accidents and safety, counterproductive work behavior, the control theory of job stress). The Academy of Management Research Methods Division awarded him a lifetime achievement award in 2014, and he was listed among the ten most influential scholars in business and management worldwide in a 2019 Stanford University study.

4. I used Google to find a biologist in my area who studies stress. I came across Wiline Pangle's information at the top of my search. The irony is that Dr. Pangle is my neighbor. The reality is that we are not talking to our literal and figurative neighbors about stress, even though there is so much knowledge already out there.

REFERENCES

Beehr, T. A. (1998). An organizational psychology meta-model of occupational stress. In C. L. Cooper (Ed.), *Theories of organizational stress* (pp. 6–27). Oxford University Press.

Beehr, T. A., & Bhagat, R. S. (Eds) (1985). *Human stress and cognition in organizations: An integrated perspective*. Wiley-Interscience.

Beehr, T. A., & Newman, J. E. (1978). Job stress, employee health, and organizational effectiveness: A facet analysis, model, and literature review. *Personnel Psychology, 31*(4), 665–699.

Beehr, T. A., & Newman, J. E. (1998). Research on occupational stress: An unfinished enterprise. *Personnel Psychology, 51*(4), 835–844.

Bernerth, J. B., & Aguinis, H. (2016). A critical review and best-practice recommendations for control variable usage. *Personnel Psychology*, *69*(1), 229–283.

Bliese, P. D., Edwards, J. R., & Sonnentag, S. (2017). Stress and well-being at work: A century of empirical trends reflecting theoretical and societal influences. *Journal of Applied Psychology*, *102*(3), 389.

Cooper, C. L., & Payne, R. (Eds) (1978). *Stress at work*. John Wiley & Sons.

Cortina, J. M. (2016). Defining and operationalizing theory. *Journal of Organizational Behavior*, *37*(8), 1142–1149.

Hambrick, D. C. (2007). The field of management's devotion to theory: Too much of a good thing? *Academy of Management Journal*, *50*(6), 1346–1352.

Healy, K. (2017). Fuck nuance. *Sociological Theory*, *35*(2), 118–127.

Hobfoll, S. E., Halbesleben, J., Neveu, J. P., & Westman, M. (2018). Conservation of resources in the organizational context: The reality of resources and their consequences. *Annual Review of Organizational Psychology and Organizational Behavior*, *5*, 103–128.

Leiter, M. P., & Maslach, C. (1999). Six areas of worklife: A model of the organizational context of burnout. *Journal of Health and Human Services Administration*, 472–489.

Locke, E. A. (1996). Using programmatic research to build a grounded theory. In P. J. Frost & M. S. Taylor (Eds), *Rhythms of academic life: Personal accounts of careers in academia* (pp. 99–106). Sage.

Mackey, J. D., & Perrewé, P. L. (2014). The AAA (appraisals, attributions, adaptation) model of job stress: The critical role of self-regulation. *Organizational Psychology Review*, *4*(3), 258–278.

Maslach, C. (1998). A multidimensional theory of burnout. In C. L. Cooper (Ed.), *Theories of organizational stress* (pp. 68–85). Oxford University Press.

Maslach, C. (2000). An outsider's view of the underside of the Stanford Prison Experiment. In P. Zimbardo, C. Maslach, & C. Haney (Eds), *Reflections on the Stanford Prison Experiment: Genesis, transformations, consequences* (pp. 214–20). Psychology Press.

McGrath, J. E., & Beehr, T. A. (1990). Time and the stress process: Some temporal issues in the conceptualization and measurement of stress. *Stress Medicine*, *6*(2), 93–104.

Miller, J. B. (2008). How change happens: Controlling images, mutuality, and power. *Women and Therapy*, *31*(2–4), 109–127.

O'Boyle, Jr., E. H., Banks, G. C., & Gonzalez-Mulé, E. (2017). The chrysalis effect: How ugly initial results metamorphosize into beautiful articles. *Journal of Management*, *43*(2), 376–399.

Sapolsky, R. M. (2004). *Why zebras don't get ulcers: The acclaimed guide to stress, stress-related diseases, and coping*. Holt.

Index

AAA (appraisal, attribution, and adaptation) model 199–200
abusive supervision 50, 182, 183–5, 193
action research model 3, 100
action-state orientation 176–8
action tendency 46, 48–51, 171, 200
activation theories 43–5
actor–observer bias 56
acute stress response 4, 26–8, 30, 32, 102, 191
Adams, J. S. 67–71
adaptation theory 142–3
adrenaline *see* epinephrine
AET *see* affective events theory
affect 1
    see also emotions
affective events theory (AET) 33, 40–41, 49–50
affective wellbeing model 47
    see also belonging, need for
affiliation hypothesis 86, 88
aggression
    abusive supervision 183
    ego threat and 88
    see also CWB
Ajzen, I. 18–19
Alameda County Study 6, 13
allostasis 26, 30–31
allostatic load 30–31, 101–103, 207
anecdotes 2
anxiety, definition 4
appraisal 7, 30
    attribution distinction 57
    COR and 114–16
    predictive power 117
    of resource loss 110–11
    transactional theory 54–5, 58, 114–16
appraisal, attribution, and adaptation (AAA) model 199–200
appraisal model of stress 54
appraisal theory, testing methods 204–5

Aristotle's justice theory 68
arousal-activation theory of personality 45
arousal theories 40–53, 96, 118–19, 130
ASA (attraction-selection-attrition) model 123–5
ask vs. guess cultures 164
attitudes, definition 20
attraction-selection-attrition (ASA) model 123–5
attribution theory 57–8
attributions and appraisal 200
autonomous motivation 175–6
autonomy
    appraisal and 111
    job characteristics theory 172
    job control and 111–12
    need for 174, 176
    PE fit theory 126
    PO fit theory 129
avoidance coping 56

balance theory of stress 173–4
Bakker, A. B. 63, 101
Bandura, A. 15, 81–3, 131, 167–8
bases of power 182–5
Beehr, T. A. 117, 199, 203–6, 209
behavior
    attitude relationship 18–19
    in psychology 1
    social learning theories 81–4
behavioral ecology 206
behavioral health, origins 12–25
behavioral intention 19
behavioral learning theory 15–16
    see also behaviorism
behavioral medicine 13, 15
behavioral strain, definition 3
behaviorism 15, 44, 81, 112, 115, 206
    see also conditioning
belonging, need for 88–9, 174, 176

Bernard, Claude 26–7, 29, 37–8
Bhagat, R. S. 6
big five factor model *see* personality
    theory
biopsychosocial model 23, 206
Blau, P. M. 67, 73–4, 142
border theory 147
boredom 41
boundary-spanning theory 138, 141–2
boundary theory 147
broaden and build theory 40, 48
buffering effect, definition 112
burnout
    affective wellbeing model 47
    challenge-hindrance stressors 120
    effort–reward imbalance 76
    job demands correlation 99
    kindling hypothesis 33
    leadership types and 188, 189
    multidimensional theory of 197–9

Cannon, W. B. 6, 26–7, 29, 109
Cannon–Bard theory of emotion 27, 40
Carayon, P. 174
causal attribution theory 57
Cavanaugh, M. A. 5, 109, 118–19
challenge demands 119
challenge-hindrance model 109, 117–19
challenge stressors 97, 102–3, 130,
    199–200
    see also challenge demands
chronic stress response 4, 14, 26, 29, 30,
    32, 143, 177
chrysalis effect 201–2
circumplex model 46–7
coercive power 16, 182, 183
cognitions, definition 1
cognitive ability 61–3
cognitive activation theory of stress
    44–5, 103
cognitive dissonance 85–6
cognitive distraction 59
    see also distractions
cognitive emotion model of
    organizational change 58
cognitive load 36
cognitive resource theory 187
cognitive resources
    information interpretation 35
    intelligence as 61–2

cognitive theory of emotions 45–7
cognitively mediated model 54
    see also transactional theory
collectivism 154, 156
common method variance 5, 97–8, 115,
    120, 126
competence needs 174–6
conditioned immunomodulation 16
conditioning
    attitudes and 20
    classical and operant 15–16
    drives and 42
    escape and avoidance 56, 64
    see also reinforcement
conditioning models 15
conflict theory 143
conservation of resources (COR) theory
    7, 109–22, 203
    adaptation theory and 142
    testing methods 204–5
    transactional theory and 112–17
consideration, leadership 185
contingency awareness 15
contingency theory 186–7
control theory *see* cybernetic theory
controlled motivation 175
coping
    AAA model 200
    activation theory 44
    definition 3
    measurement 64
    organizational psychology and 7
    social learning theory 83
    see also emotion regulation
coping theories 54–66
COR theory *see* conservation of
    resources theory
cortisol 4, 6, 27
counterproductive work behavior (CWB)
    50, 69–70, 88, 171
Cropanzano, R. 49, 77
crossover of resources 101
cue management 132
cultural dimensions 154–7
culture
    axes of 156
    definition 153–4
    leadership and 182
    use of term 164

CWB *see* counterproductive work
    behavior
cybernetic theory 27, 130–31

Darwin, Charles, *The Expression of
    Emotions* 40
decision latitude 7, 96
deep acting 60–61
demand–abilities fit 127
demands
    allostatic load 32
    burnout and 198
    challenge and hindrance 102–3
    COR and 110, 114
    definition 95–6
    demands–abilities fit 125
    holistic model of stress 58–9
    mindfulness and 104
    role demands 143
    transactional model 55
    see also stressors
Demerouti, E. 98, 114
depersonalization 198
detachment 101–4
diabetes 28
discrimination 163
    see also prejudice
distractions 36, 62–3, 170, 176, 179, 208
distributive justice 68, 70–71, 74
drive theories 42–3

EAP *see* employee assistance programs
    (EAPs)
ecological systems theory 157–8
Edwards, J. R. 126, 128–9, 131
effort-recovery model 95, 102–4, 119
effort–reward imbalance 69, 74–7
ego depletion 60, 103, 168–9, 184
ego defense 60
ego threat 60, 87–9
Ekman, P. 4, 40, 51
emic research 162, 164
emotion-focused coping 55–6
emotion regulation 54, 59–61
    see also coping
emotional exhaustion *see* burnout
emotional labor 60–61
emotions
    Cannon–Bard theory 27, 40

cognitive theory of 45–7
definition 40
discrete 47, 58
positive 48, 51
propositional 46
as social information 87
stress contrast 3–4
    see also affect
employee assistance programs (EAPs)
    56, 192
engagement 47, 63, 99, 101, 105, 198
epinephrine 27–8
episodic process model 169
epistemology 197
equity theories 67–80
ergonomic theories 26
ergonomics 34–7, 208
escape coping 56
ethical leadership 193
etic research 162, 164
eustress 3, 30, 99
    definition 58
    distress versus 51, 58, 99, 191
exchange theories 67–80
executive health 6
exosystems 157
expectancy 17, 44–5, 82–3, 130, 191
expectancy theory 117, 199
expressive suppression 59
extraversion 45, 133
    see also introversion
eye tracking 63
Eysenck, P. 45

facet theory 199–200
fairness heuristic theory 72
fairness theory 71–2
Festinger, L. 85–6, 131
Fiedler, F. E. 186–7
field theory 123–4
fight or flight response 6, 27–8, 29, 32
flow 63
Folkman, S. 7
framework–theory comparison 2
Framingham Heart Study 6, 13
Fredrickson, B. L. 48, 58, 64, 104
Freudian perspectives 60, 87, 168, 177
    see also psychodynamic tradition
Frijda, N. H. 87
frustration-aggression hypothesis 50

Gardner, D. G. 43, 51
gender discrimination 161
general adaptation syndrome 29–30, 143
general mental ability *see* cognitive
    ability
glucose 6, 31, 170
goal abandonment 171, 202
goal-setting theory 2, 131, 170–71
goal striving 171, 176
gossip 85
Grandey, A. A. 61, 203–6, 209
gratitude 48
guess cultures *see* ask vs. guess cultures

habituation 33–4, 43, 143, 206–7
HARKing 175, 202
health behaviors 12–13, 15, 17, 19, 21
health belief model 12, 16–18
helplessness 44
Herzberg, F. 48, 171–2
hindrance stressors 71–2, 97, 102–3, 109,
    117–19, 199–200
Hobfoll, S. E. 7, 111, 112–17, 133
Hofstede, G. 154–7, 162
holistic model of stress 58–9
Homans, G. C. 67–8
homeostasis
    allostasis maintaining 30–31
    definition of stress 9
    negative feedback loop 26–7
homostasis 27
hopelessness 45
human error 34–5, 202
human factors *see* ergonomics
hygiene *see* two-factor theory, Herzberg
hypothalamus-pituitary-adrenal (HPA)
    axis 4, 27
    see also chronic stress response
hyperarousal 41–2

identity theory 89–92, 138
immunomodulation 15–16
impact, activation and 43
individual differences 116
    personality 129
individualism–collectivism 154, 156
inductive research 205
inferential processes 87
information processing 36

initiating structure, leadership 185–6
inspirational motivation 188
integrated behavioral model 19
interleukins 31–2
interpersonal deviance 85
    see also CWB
    see also abusive supervision
intelligence 61–2, 187
    see also cognitive ability
interactional justice 70
interruptions 62–3, 115, 161
introversion 45, 116, 131, 133

Jahoda, M. 161–2
James–Lange theory 40
jangle fallacy 67, 68, 143
jingle fallacy 67, 87, 143, 153
job characteristics 7, 44, 134, 144–5,
    171–4, 204
job control 90, 95–8, 111–12, 203
job demands-control model 95–8, 203
job demands-control-support model 90,
    96–7
job demands-resources model 95–108,
    114, 171, 203–4
job design theories 126–7, 171–4, 204
job enrichment 174
job resources, definition 98
job satisfaction 46–7, 172
job scope 134
job stress theory
    foundations of 1–11
    historical perspective 5–8
    past, present, and future of 203
    perspectives on 5–8, 197–210
just world beliefs 73, 183
justice
    global 70–71
    interactional 70
justice judgment model 68–9
justice norms 68–9

Kahn, R. L. 138, 141
Karasek, R. A. 7, 95–6
kindling hypothesis 26, 33–4, 206
Kuhl, J. 176–7, 187

Laird, D. A. 6
latent deprivation model 161–2

Lazarus, R. S. 7, 54, 57–8, 64, 112–17, 133, 167
leader, definition 182
leader-member exchange (LMX) theory 86, 186, 187–8
learning *see* behaviorism
least preferred coworkers (LPC) scale 186
Lewin, Kurt 3, 85, 100, 123–5
LMX theory *see* leader-member exchange theory
Locke, E. A. 171, 201
locus of control 82
loneliness 89
LPC (least preferred coworkers) scale 186

McEwen, B.S. 30, 37
McGrath, J. E. 125, 131
Mackey, J. D. 199
macrosystems 157–8
Maslach, C. 133, 197–9
Maslow's hierarchy of needs 42
media interruptions 62–3
mentor–protégé matching 129
mesosystems 157
meta-cognitive states 104
meta-theories 131, 175, 197, 201–7
Meurs, J. A. 3
microaggressions 115
microsystems 157
milieu intérieur 26–7
Miller, J. B. 141, 202–3
mindfulness 103–5, 192
mindfulness-to-meaning theory 103–4
minority stress model 153, 158–61, 206
monetary incentives 70
motivation
    definition 167
    measurement 179
motivational incongruence 57
multidimensional theory of burnout 197–9
multiple resource theory 35
multitasking 62–3

narcissism 88
needs–supply fit 127
needs theories 126, 175

negative affectivity 47–8
negative feedback 90
negative feedback loop 26–7, 125, 130, 143
negotiation 73
neuroticism 45, 116
    see also negative affectivity

objective environment 5, 7
objective measurement 5, 111, 114–15, 128
OCB (organizational citizenship behavior) 73–4
occupational health psychology 1
Ohio State leadership 185–6
optimistic bias 17
Organ, D. W. 74
organizational change theories 58
organizational citizenship behavior (OCB) 73–4
organizational climate 190
organizational culture 133–4, 159, 182, 189–91
organizational justice model 69
organizational support 182–6
ostracism 34
overcommitment 75–6, 128
overpayment 70

parasympathetic nervous system 102, 105
PE fit *see* person–environment fit
perceived barriers, health belief model 17–18
perceived behavioral control 19–20
perceived organizational support 190–91
perception
    measurement of 5
    sensation and 35
Perrewé, P. L. 3, 58, 199
person–environment (PE) fit 113, 123–37, 158–9, 202
    measurement 126–8
person–job (PJ) fit 61, 96–7, 129, 134
person–organization (PO) fit 127–9
person–person fit 124
person–situation debate 112, 116, 126, 132–3
person–team fit 129

personality systems interaction theory 177
personality theory 45, 116, 132, 184
philosophical meta-theories 197, 201–7
physiological strain, definition 3
PJ fit *see* person–job fit
planned behavior, theory of 12, 18–20
PO fit *see* person–organization fit
post-traumatic stress disorder (PTSD) 33
power, bases of 182–5
prejudice 34, 72, 153, 157–9, 161, 164
preventative stress management theory 191–3
primacy of loss hypothesis 110, 142
primary appraisal 54–5, 57–8, 200
primary intervention 192
problem-focused coping 55–6
procedural justice 69, 70–71
Prochaska's transtheoretical model 21–2
psychoanalysis *see* psychodynamic tradition
psychodynamic tradition 59–60
psychological loads, balance theory 173
psychological science 1–5
psychological theories, focus of 202
psychology
    defining 1
    history of 6
psychoneuroimmunology 12, 14
PTSD (post-traumatic stress disorder) 33
punishment 15–16, 115, 141, 169, 182
    see also conditioning

racism 34, 161, 206
RCT *see* relational-cultural theory
reappraisal 55, 57–60, 104
reasoned action, theory of 18–20
reciprocal determinism 83
reciprocity 73–5, 78, 191
recovery experiences 102, 119
red tape 5
reinforcement 15–16, 115, 141, 169, 182
    see also conditioning; punishment
relational-cultural theory (RCT) 141, 202–3
resource loss 101, 110–11, 116–17, 184
resource theory 74
resources
    appraisal 7

COR 7, 109–22, 142, 159, 203–5
    crossover of 101
    definitions 109–10
    ergonomics and 35
    job demands-resources model 95–108, 113
    self-esteem as 90
    transactional theory 113–14
    see also cognitive resources
rest break intervention 12
reticular activation system 43
role ambiguity 139–41
role analysis intervention 141
role conflict 139–40, 143
role overload 140
role stressors 138, 140, 171
role theory 138–52
Rotter, J. B., *Social Learning* 82
Rousseau, D. M. 134

savoring 58, 104
Schachter, S. 86
Schaufeli, W. B. 99–100
Schein, E. H. 189–90
Schneider, B. 123, 135
scientist-practitioner model 2–3
    see also action research model
SDT (self-determination theory) 174–6
secondary appraisal 55, 58, 113, 200
secondary intervention 192
segmentation 147, 149
self-determination theory (SDT) 174–6
self-efficacy 21, 63, 75, 82–4, 99, 102, 115, 171
self-esteem 75–6, 86, 87–8, 90, 101
self-expansion theory 101
self-regulation 75, 87, 131, 167–81
Selye, H. 6, 27, 29–30, 143
Semmer, N. K. 89–90
sensation 35
sensitization 33–4
sensory overload 36
Shirom, A. 101
Siegrist, J. 74–6
similarity–attraction paradigm 124
situationists 116, 133
sleep 1, 13–14, 207
social cognitive theories 81, 83–4
social comparison theory 85–7, 131

social exchange theory 67–8, 73–4
social facilitation theory 42
social-functional approach to motivation 87
social information 81–94
social information processing theory 84–7
social inhibition 42
social interaction theory 183
social learning theories 81–4
social media 83
social network analysis 91
social referencing 84
social support 89, 90–92, 96
    measurement 91
    negative effect of 91
    theory 90
sociocultural systems perspective 153–66
SOS (stress as offense to self) 89–92
Spector, P. E. 47, 50, 88, 111, 155–6, 203–6, 209
spillover 144
stability through change 30
stage theories 21–3
Stanford Prison Experiment 198
state orientation 176–8
STEM (science, technology, engineering, and mathematics) 1
step models 23
stereotypes 159
stigmatization 153, 158, 160, 162
strain
    definition 3
    general adaptation syndrome 29
    stressor-strain model 32
strain hypothesis 96
stress
    definition 3–7, 9, 54
    etymology 6
    physiological response to 4
    physiological measurement 31
stress as offense to self (SOS) 89–92
stress-diathesis model 12, 14
stressor-detachment theory 95, 101, 103, 208
stressor-emotion model of CWB 50
stressor-strain model 26, 32–3, 47
    buffering effect 112
    eustress 58
    job demands 100

preventative management 191
    TMGT effect 130
stressors, definition 3
subjective measurement 114
    see also objective measurement
subjective norms, behavior 19–20
subjective occupational success 100
success-resource model 100
supportive organizational climates 190–91
surface acting 60–61
survey feedback intervention 20
sympathetic adrenomedullary axis (SAM) 4, 29
    see also acute stress response
sympathetic nervous system 27

tend and befriend response 28
tertiary intervention 192
    see also EAPs
Theorell, T. 96
theory
    criteria for 203
    definition 2–3
    development of 203–4
    model–theory comparison 2
    practical value of 203–4
    testing methods 204–6
Theory X and Theory Y 43
Thoits, P. A. 89
threatened egotism, theory of 88, 92
TMGT (too-much-of-a-good-thing) effect 129–30
tokenism 159–61
too-much-of-a-good-thing (TMGT) effect 129–30
trait activation theory 131–2
transactional leadership 188, 189
transactional theory 54–8, 112–17, 125
transformational leadership 188–9
transtheoretical models 12, 21–2, 197, 199
    definition 197
    Prochaska's 21–2
    in stress 199
Triandis, H. C. 156
Triplett, N. 40, 42, 167
two-factor theory, Herzberg 48, 172
two-factor theory of emotion 86

ulcers 3, 14
uncertainty avoidance 154
unemployment 161–2
"user-determined" change 37

values survey module (VSM) 155
vicarious traumatization 158
victim blaming 84, 114–15, 145
vigor 102–3
    see also engagement
vigorous organization 101
visibility 126, 131, 159–61
vitamin model 130
vivisection 37–8, 40
VSM (values survey module) 155

Warr, P. 47, 130
Weiner, B. 27, 57
Weiss, H. M. 49
workaholism 47
work-life-cycle models 8
work–family border theory 146–7
work–family conflict 91, 101, 138,
    143–6
work–nonwork enrichment 44
work–nonwork interface 144–6

Yerkes Dodson Law *see* arousal theories

Zajonc, R. B. 42
Zellars, K. L. 58

.